Reflections on Anti-Semitism

Reflections on Anti-Semitism

ALAIN BADIOU, ERIC HAZAN
AND IVAN SEGRÉ

TRANSLATED BY
DAVID FERNBACH

VERSO
London • New York

INSTITUT
FRANÇAIS

This book is supported by the Institut français as part of the
Burgess programme (www.frenchbooknews.com)

This English-language edition published by Verso 2013
Translation © David Fernbach 2013
' "Anti-Semitism Everywhere" in France Today' first published as
L'antisémitisme partout – Aujourd'hui en France
© La Fabrique 2011
'The Philo-Semitic Reaction: The Treason of the Intellectuals'
first published as *La Réaction philosémite ou la trahison des clercs*
© Nouvelles Editions Lignes 2009

1 3 5 7 9 10 8 6 4 2

Verso
UK: 6 Meard Street, London W1F 0EG
US: 20 Jay Street, Suite 1010, Brooklyn, NY 11201
www.versobooks.com

Verso is the imprint of New Left Books

ISBN-13: 978-1-84467-877-8 (PBK)
ISBN-13: 978-1-78168-115-2 (HBK)

British Library Cataloguing in Publication Data
A catalogue record for this book is available from the British Library

Library of Congress Cataloging-in-Publication Data
Badiou, Alain.
[Antisémitisme partout. English]
Reflections on anti-semitism / Alain Badiou, Eric
Hazan, Ivan Segre ; Translated by David Fernbach.
pages cm
ISBN 978-1-78168-115-2 (hardback) –
ISBN 978-1-84467-877-8 (pbk) – ISBN 978-1-78168-226-5 (ebk)
1. Antisemitism–France–History–21st century.
I. Hazan, Éric. II. Segré, Ivan. III. Title.
B2430.B273A5813 2013
305.892'4044–dc23
2013015615

Typeset in Bembo by MJ & N Gavan, Truro, Cornwall
Printed in the US by Maple Press

Contents

'Anti-Semitism Everywhere' in France Today

Alain Badiou and Eric Hazan

1

A Year of Excitement

In 2002 war was declared against the forces of evil in the Middle East. In Afghanistan, the US army had invaded six weeks after 11 September 2001 and was continuing its project of liberation. A further liberation was also taking shape, that of Iraq: generals and diplomats were openly preparing to invade the country to establish democracy. In Palestine, where the Second Intifada was under way, the Israeli army reoccupied the whole of the West Bank and Operation Rampart swept away what remained of the autonomy granted at Oslo. In April, the seizure of the Jenin refugee camp and its destruction by bulldozers caused the death of several dozen civilians.

In France, meanwhile, the first round of the presidential election was marked by the success of the Front National. Roger Cukiermann, president of the CRIF,* wrote in *Haaretz* (23 April 2002) that then FN leader Jean-Marie Le Pen's success 'will serve to reduce Islamic anti-Semitism and anti-Israeli behaviour, as his vote sends a message to Muslims to behave peacefully'.

It was in this context that a campaign developed denouncing a 'wave of anti-Semitism' in France:

---

* Conseil Représentatif des Institutions Juives en France, the official representative body of Jewish organizations. [All footnotes are the translator's. The authors' notes have numerical cues in the text and appear at the back of the book.]

Synagogues are burned, rabbis molested, cemeteries profaned, community institutions and universities forced to clean walls scrawled with filthy messages in the night. It takes courage to wear a kippa in those wild places known as 'sensitive estates', or on the Paris metro.[1]

Why this campaign? It was important to create a diversion, as public opinion and even the media were shocked by the brutal way in which the Israeli army repressed the Second Intifada. Denouncing the 'wave of anti-Semitism' was a good way to distract attention from the bloody Operation Rampart, or still better, to present this as a defensive measure in the context of a 'general upsurge of anti-Semitism'.

The terrain was propitious for this kind of operation: in the wake of 11 September, hatred against Arabs and Muslims was on the rise throughout the Western world. They were – of course – the propagating agents of this anti-Semitic wave:

> The revival of both verbal and physical anti-Semitic attacks in France and Europe, since the outbreak of the 'Second Intifada' in autumn 2002, has undoubtedly brought to the fore new agents of anti-Jewish hatred, in particular aggressors hailing from the *banlieues* or from immigration, victims of racism and discrimination who embark on behaviour towards Jews of a kind they are entitled to be protected from.[2]

This notion of a 'wave of anti-Semitism' was not entirely without foundation. It is undeniable that the years from 2002 to 2004 saw insults against Jews, hostile graffiti, wooden crates burned outside synagogues, and fights among youths. Even if those acts that attracted the most media coverage, triggered the strongest words among politicians and the greatest indignation from Jewish organizations were the act of a fantasist (the 'aggression' of Marie Leblanc on an RER train in July 2004),* or of a poor simpleton,

---

* On 9 July 2004, the young woman Marie Leblanc reported what she described as an anti-Semitic assault on her by several black or North African

himself Jewish (the arson at a Jewish social centre on rue Popincourt in August that year),* the reality of hostile acts against Jews in this period is not open to doubt, and we do not take any acts of this kind lightly. Yet nothing happened that a reasonable person could see as particularly serious, nothing irreparable, and even Simone Veil sharply criticized Alain Finkielkraut for calling 2002 a 'year of crystal'.[3]

For the initiators and activists of this campaign, however, the real scope of the so-called wave mattered little: the impulse had been given. In tandem with the police-style listing of 'acts of an anti-Semitic character' in the press, designed to demonstrate their proliferation, we had the publication in October 2004 of the Rufin report, commissioned by the minister of the interior, which denounced 'an imported anti-Semitism, particularly rife among young people whose families come from countries where anti-Semitism is culturally commonplace'. Rufin equated 'anti-Zionism' with 'surrogate anti-Semitism', and proposed legislation that would criminalize criticism of the state of Israel.

This was also the time of the first prosecutions for 'incitement to racial hatred' brought by a group calling itself Avocats Sans Frontières (Lawyers Without Borders) – against the journalist Daniel Mermet, against the publisher La Fabrique, then against philosopher Edgar Morin, political scientist Sami Naïr and novelist Danielle Sallenave.[4] We also saw the appearance of a series of publications denouncing the anti-Semitism of 'Maghrebians'. In *Les Territoires perdus de la République*, a collective work edited by Emmanuel Brenner and focusing on the question of schools, the general theme was that

---

men in the suburban train RER D. The event created a mediatic and political storm but Leblanc admitted four days later that she had invented the story. See *Le Monde*, 25 July 2004.

   * In August 2004, a Jewish social centre on the rue Popincourt was the object of an arson attack. The culprit turned out to be a middle-aged Jewish man, possibly with the motive of creating an ostensible 'anti-Semitic outrage'.

the anti-Semitism that finds free rein in the educational establishments of certain quarters, the fear of the adults in charge in the
face of unacceptable utterances and behaviour, the intellectual
retreat in the face of the Islamist offensive, are all symptoms of the
abyss that divides France more than ever between the common
people and the elites.[5]

Nicolas Weill, in *La République et les antisémites*, took it as an
'accepted fact' that there was 'a particularly virulent Arabo-Muslim
anti-Semitism, tolerated when convenient by a certain far left that
is often passive – if not fascinated – in the face of this extremism'.[6]

We might note in passing the new emphasis placed on the word
'Republic', already wielded to support the ban on the 'Islamic
headscarf' in schools: as if, by a singular paradox, a word generally
seen as indicating a certain political universalism, even oriented
to the defence of the right of 'those below', now serves as a
token of hostility towards the Arabic and Muslim workers of the
housing estates.

The bulky tome *Prêcheurs de haine*, by Pierre-André Taguieff, is
a 968-page denunciation of this alleged phenomenon, proscribing
a whole list of 'archeo-Trotskyists and anti-globalist new leftists,
extravagantly Palestinophile ... despite the increasing Islamization
of the Palestinian cause'.[7]

This denunciation of an 'upsurge of anti-Semitism' was relayed
and amplified by almost the whole of the media and what is known
as the 'world of politics'. On the left, its most vocal proponents
were the habitual enemies of French 'Arabo-Muslims': secularist
zealots and misguided feminists. (We should note in passing that
the composite 'Arabo-Muslim', along with 'Islamo-leftist' of the
same coinage, originates with the police, just like other couples
of the same ilk: 'Judeo-Bolshevik', 'Hitlero-Trotskyite', or more
recently '*anarcho-autonome*' [anarcho-autonomist].)

On the right, the government side, there was unanimity in
the 'solid determination' to struggle against the revival of anti-
Semitism. It might seem strange to see Jews so well 'defended'

by an ideological current – the right – that has traditionally been hostile to them. This phenomenon inevitably recalls a Jewish joke: 'What is a philo-Semite? An anti-Semite who loves Jews.' During the years 2002–2003, the number of these philo-Semites and their activity seemed to increase considerably.

2

Anti-Semitism Real and Imagined

The forms anti–Semitism takes today in France are very varied, and often have little or nothing in common. Since the Second World War, anti–Semitism has no longer been supported in France by a certain abject consensus (which in the 1930s was even shared by many celebrated writers, such as Céline). It persists in the form of disparate minorities, some publicly active, others concealed.

At the darkest end of the spectrum lurk a few people nostalgic for the Third Reich, neo–Nazis who daub swastikas on synagogues. It is very likely they were involved in the genuinely anti–Semitic acts committed in 2002: the desecration of tombs is certainly their style. They may represent a danger in certain Nordic countries or in Austria, but in France they are no more than a few dozen hotheads, whose actions should certainly be monitored and banned, but who cannot at this time have any political future. In France today, there are unfortunately votes to be won by denouncing the 'Islamic peril' and seeking to destroy mosques, whereas desecrating synagogues happily arouses almost unanimous repulsion.

Another tiny group is that of the Holocaust deniers. Some of them clearly stand on the far right: often linked to the Front National, they try here and there to embed themselves in the universities, such as Assas (Paris II) and Lyon III. But presenting

this kind of commodity in an academic guise, advancing under the cover of historical research, remains a fragile and challenged attempt. Their strength, of course, has been to force people to discuss them; they have managed to arouse debate, and some historians have made the effort to refute their assertions with scholarly fairness. But these anti-Semitic ideologists are anything but fair, and what inspires them is certainly not the critical spirit of science. Historical and academic refutation amounts to falling into their trap: proving that the gas chambers really did exist only maintains round the negationists precisely what they desire, i.e. to spread the idea that this is a 'real problem'. They can always say that, if people write whole books to demonstrate the existence of the Nazi gas chambers, this shows it is questionable even today. Sowing doubt about an indubitable historic fact is the only thing that interests them, and in this sense, in a familiar fascist tradition, the negationists are intellectual provocateurs. But they are only a handful, with no real influence. We should note also the exist-ence of 'left-wing' negationists, in the lineage of La Vieille Taupe.*
These people refuse to call themselves anti-Semites, but they are so all the same. Sometimes the mask slips, and the hatred hidden behind the Third Worldist positions of these camouflaged ideolo-gists becomes visible. None of these groups, whether far right or 'left', represents very much, but it is important to recognize their existence, not to give them free passage or be taken in by their clever ruses, as happened for example to Chomsky.† The fact they managed to entrap someone like Chomsky proves they have more than one trick up their sleeve. In the same way, we should pay

---

   * From being a far-left book shop and publisher in the late 1960s, this 'old mole' was re-launched in 1980 as a negationist publishing house.

   † Noam Chomsky's text 'Some Elementary Comments on the Rights of Freedom of Expression' made the distinction between defending the right to free expression and sharing the views of that person. Chomsky gave per-mission for this text to be used as a preface to Faurisson's book *Mémoire en défense. Contre ceux qui m'accusent de falsifier l'histoire. La question des chambres à gaz* (Paris: La Vieille Taupe, 1980), without of course in any way endorsing its contents.

attention to people like Dieudonné* and those who support him, and say clearly that this is real anti-Semitism, no matter what the starting-point of their position.

Very different from these small groups of hotheads, more dignified and still more hypocritical in their way of presenting themselves, is the old anti-Semitic bedrock of what one of us has called the 'Pétainist transcendental'.† This remains somewhat of a phantom, as it does not present itself on the political stage with anti-Semitic declarations or manifestoes. But among these people, some – such as Renaud Camus,‡ for example – are prepared to declare publicly what others think privately, or admit only at family gatherings, when you are 'among your own people', i.e. that in many sectors of activity 'there are too many Jews'.

It goes without saying that neither in its numbers, its strength nor its influence does this tendency have anything in common with the situation before the Second World War, when it was practically dominant. At that time, in all the 'democratic' countries, there was an anti-Semitic current of public opinion that was able to express itself in certain newspapers and could even count on the voices of recognized intellectuals. This anti-Semitism was part of a broader ideological constellation, a complex-free chauvinist and racial worldview, in which the figure of the *'métèque'*,§ the outsider, could be freely used – and indeed, even a 'racist' view in the strictly biological sense of the word. In the 1932 edition of the Larousse dictionary, black people were still presented and

---

* M'bala M'bala Dieudonné, a comedian originally associated with anti-racist causes but who has in recent years has been associated with prominent figures of the Front National and Holocaust deniers.

† See Alain Badiou, *The Meaning of Sarkozy*, trans. David Fernbach, London: Verso, 2009.

‡ Renaud Camus: French writer, born in 1946, who attracted controversy by publishing certain comments widely regarded as anti-Semitic in his diary *La Campagne de France. Journal*, Paris: Fayard, 2000.

§ Despite its Greek derivation, this term – very current in France until the 1940s – has more the insulting sense of 'wop'.

drawn as midway between ape and man. And in such racial arguments, anti-Semitism played a major role.

Today there is nothing of this kind in France, and for good reason. Before the War, the majority of Jews were foreigners who had arrived from Poland, Lithuania or Romania, who spoke Yiddish and belonged to the poorest section of the working class: they were the Arabs and Africans of their day. Nowadays, Jews are pretty well 'integrated', and this kind of anti-Semitism and racism finds other targets.

This anti-Semitism of the 1930s was, in fact, a component of the same anti-popular sentiment that still stigmatizes the most recent arrivals in France. In the nineteenth century, it was the Auvergnats, Bretons, Italians and Savoyards; after the 1914–18 War, the Poles, the Jews from the east, the Spanish; after the Second World War, the Portuguese and, with a strong additional racist component which was exacerbated by the colonial wars, the Algerians and Moroccans – today the Malians and Congolese. Without grasping this continuity it is impossible to understand either pre-WWII anti-Semitism or the present situation. This is an element which is still able to resurge, even at the state level, with a view to stoking up resentment against a poor section of the population: a very classic manoeuvre of anti-popular division, which struck a large section of Jews before the Second World War and is practised today against those people called 'immigrants', to whom Gypsies have recently been added – the 'Roma' who do not seem to have benefited morally from their mass extermination by the Nazis. The operation was conducted in a typical fashion: following a murder committed by the police, an entire group was collectively spotlighted – a group who are mainly of French nationality (like the rest of those terrible 'youth from the *banlieues*'), but whose origin and anomic way of life are such that the state finds it tempting to arouse against them the supposedly latent hostility of a section of the population.

We might say traditional anti-Semitism has waned because its target – the Jew of the caricatures in *Der Stürmer*, the Jew of

Gringoire and *Je suis partout* – has disappeared. It continues to exist as a ghostly residue only among the most backward and nostalgic part of the French bourgeoisie, which combines in its memory each successive wave of '*métèques*'.

The sentiment that a large section of black and Arab French youth feel towards the Jews is something quite different, having nothing in common with historic anti-Semitism. Even Taguieff accepts this is something different – simply that he coined the mistaken term of 'Judeophobia' to refer to it. The hostility of these young people towards Jews is fundamentally bound up with what is happening in Palestine. They know that, over there, Jewish Israelis are oppressing the Palestinians, whom they consider, for obvious historical reasons, as their brothers. And the people here who are visibly Jews are above all those organizations that claim to be 'representative' of the 'Jewish community', meaning that they speak in place of others and cut off their speech, especially that of Jews who disagree with them. The support of these organizations for everything done by the state of Israeli is practically absolute. There are also, sometimes, Jews in their locality who present themselves as unconditional supporters of Israel. The young people we are referring to then make an amalgam between the Israeli state's anti-Palestinian repression and this distorted image of French Jews, which can lead them to believe all the Jews in the world, here and elsewhere, are their enemies.

Words have their importance in this business. Israel defines itself as the Jewish state, producing a kind of fusion between the word 'Jew' and Israeli government practice. It was less confusing when the term used in France was the 'Hebrew state'. The fusion between the name adopted by a historical diaspora present in dozens of countries, and the name of a state in the Middle East, is important in symbolic terms. These young people understand that the Jewish state is responsible for what is happening over there. And, between a Jewish state and a state of Jews, there is at least an ambiguity, maintained by the fact that the Israeli state proclaims itself the state of the Jews of the whole world. A certain grasp of the nuances of the actual situation is needed to understand that a very large number of Jews do not in any way consider this state as *their* state. For a young French person, Arab or black, son or daughter of a Maghrebian or African peasant who came to France in the last few decades as a worker and living on a blighted housing estate, it is not so easy to disassociate the persecutory practice of Israel as a state from the Jewish label that is granted it by almost universal agreement. An attentive and politicized eye is needed to seek out the exceptions to this consensus. It is not obvious that a large number of French Jews have no other opinion on Palestine than that of other French people who know only the official position repeated by the mass media. As for those French Jews opposed to Israeli policy, they are carefully kept invisible, just like the radical opposition within Israel itself – a minority, of course, but no more than opposition to the Algerian War was in France around 1956.

What these young people feel is not anti-Semitism, but rather a hostility, 'political but not well politicized', to what is perceived as the position of the Jews in France. Added to which are the more or less conscious reminiscences from the colonial era in Algeria, when France managed to divide Jews from Arabs by giving the former French nationality – the *Loi Crémieux* of 1870 – while classifying the latter, right to the end, as 'indigenous' under one appellation or another.

Choosing the term 'anti-Semitic' as a description for the political mood of these young people, and claiming an 'upsurge' of this anti-Semitism, is not the description of an actual situation, but an *operation of stigmatization*. A wrong term is deliberately chosen. Besides, many other ills are attributed to them as well: for Alain Finkielkraut, for example, not only are they anti-Semitic, but it is their fault that republican education is in tatters, that a kind of savagery has established itself on the margins of our big cities, etc. In this series, the word 'anti-Semitic' is not only the most violent choice, but also the one with least bearing on the present reality.

This is a double-barrelled operation: it not only targets black and Arab youth, but also those who support them – and who are almost all hostile to the policy of successive Israeli governments. It is essential to prevent these people from interfering, as they sometimes write books and may at times make their voices heard. To try and reduce them to silence, they are also accused of anti-Semitism; no matter that this accusation is totally absurd.

Sowing distrust and hostility towards young people from the lower classes is of course a very traditional class practice. Today, however, one particular aim is to establish a kind of frontier dividing them from the white, educated petty bourgeoisie, to create a trench between the barbarism of the *banlieues* and our own dear school and university students – which is why the theme of education is so recurrent in these debates. The point is to establish a social segregation, and the accusation of anti-Semitism is again very useful for this.

This whole operation amounts to yet another of those entwinements, so frequent in French history, in which domestic questions about class relations are tackled by using external figures of the colonial or imperial type. Under the Third Republic, for instance, right up to the Second World War, the exaltation of great colonial figures, especially the generals who conducted successive 'pacifications', went hand in hand with detestation of '*métèques*'. After the liquidation of the Paris Commune, there was an interaction between the colonial situation and domestic confrontations – with a great deal of ambiguity, and indeed a stubborn complicity from forces of the 'left'. We are currently experiencing a somewhat twilight example of this kind of propagandistic combination. The aim is to convince people there is an underlying unity between the support given to the struggle of the Israelis against Arab 'fundamentalist' barbarism, and the struggle at home against the young barbarians of the *banlieues* – whose 'barbarian' description is well attested to by the double fact that they are not only Arab or Muslim, but also criticize Israeli government policy – which, the propaganda says, amounts to supporting global Islamist barbarism in its struggle against the reasonable and democratic state of Israel.

The muddiest aspect of this whole business is that, to make this combination effective, another history has to be brought in which has nothing to do with the other two scenes (the Middle East and our own 'banlieues') and that this propaganda attempts to unify. This ingredient, whose instrumentalization is particularly shameful, especially towards the dead, is that of the extermination of European Jews by the Nazis. The propaganda makes use of this as a kind of fog to cast over its own three entirely fallacious axioms, i.e. 'Jewish = Israeli', 'Palestinian = Islamic fundamentalist', 'young people from the banlieues = Islamic fundamentalist'. The accusation of anti-Semitism, and thus of ideological complicity with the Nazis, is built up by using the emotional reaction to genocide to cloud these three non sequiturs, despite the Nazi genocide being entirely foreign to anything at issue here.

This accusation made against Arab and black youth is constructed from false axioms and the addition of an event that has no real historical relationship with the actual policy of Israeli governments or with the state of abandonment and segregation in which these young people are left, and yet this event is the ultimate argument – the destruction of the Jews of Europe.

3

A Strange Rhetoric

A number of different facets can be identified in contemporary reactionary rhetoric: the violent and vulgar form of regular fascism, the ironic and rather shrill form of the civilized right, and then – very different – the discourse of the professional assailers of what they call anti-Semitism. The agents of this third facet are intellectuals, often sophisticated, whose argument has one common feature: their object, by way of stages and connections that are quite particular, is to link together things that, as we have just seen, actually have no connection at all. Let us look more closely at the rhetorical details that make this supposed connection.

One of its links, deployed very frequently, runs as follows: the kernel of anti-capitalism is anti-Americanism, the focus of anti-Americanism is anti-democracy, and at the pivot of anti-democracy – their final leap – lies anti-Semitism. A good example of this linkage is offered by Bernard-Henri Lévy:

French anti-Americanism, that political passion whose appearance, it is worth constant reminder, dates from the *French fascist current* of the 1930s, that ideological delirium which poorly conceals such dubious sentiments as the hatred of American democracy à la Tocqueville ... the fantasy of a *cosmopolitan country living under the law of the Jewish lobby* – French anti-Americanism, then, attracts the worst, and its seductions will be all the more dangerous if a symbolic restraining blow from above does not very quickly oppose it.[8]

Another variant of this amalgam is no less interesting. It is clear anti-imperialism today is anti-Americanism. Anti-Americanism is evidently anti-capitalism. And anti-capitalism, via the classic fantasy figure of the 'Jewish financier', is anti-Semitism. Ergo, anti-imperialism is anti-Semitism. The advantage of this variant is that those who support the Palestinians often do so on the grounds of anti-imperialism: there can thus be no doubt as to their anti-Semitism!

A further example, this time drawn from the realm of metaphor. One of us (A.B.) compared those people who abandoned the left after its defeat in the last presidential election with rats leaving a sinking ship.[9] In his blog, the literary columnist Pierre Assouline commented: 'The last time in this country that men were compared with rats was in 1942, I believe, in a propaganda documentary on the Jewish peril.'[10] To talk about rats is thus tantamount to stigmatizing Jews. Bernard-Henri Lévy latched onto this quarrel, writing in *Le Monde* (22 July 2008):

> Alain Badiou uses his just struggle against what he finds 'disgusting' to reintroduce into the political lexicon those zoological metaphors ('rats', 'the Rat Man') which Sartre unequivocally showed, in his preface to [Fanon's] *The Wretched of the Earth*, always bear the mark of fascism.[11]

As often with this author, not only is the accusation about the 'zoological metaphor' inconsistent (A.B.'s use of the word 'rat' was never anything more than the use of a classic proverb about people who change sides in order to save their skins), but the reference is also false: there is absolutely nothing in the text of Sartre's to which Bernard-Henri Lévy refers that has any kind of relationship with what he has Sartre say. We might add that if anyone did use animal metaphors to express political positions, it was Sartre himself. 'Every anti-Communist is a dog' is a famous example, and one could cite many others.* The linkage leading from Badiou's rat via Sartre to fascist anti-Semitism is a complete fabrication.

Another peculiar linkage is the syllogism dreamed up by Nicholas Weill of *Le Monde*. Any criticism of the media is an attack on journalists (unchallengeable premise). Now there are many Jewish journalists (a strange convergence here between Nicholas Weill and the anti-Semite Renaud Camus). Ergo, those who criticize the media are anti-democratic and anti-Semitic. And just as, if all men are mortal and Socrates is a man then Socrates is mortal, so also, if all criticism of the media is anti-Semitic then any particular criticism of the media is anti-Semitic. In fact, Nicolas Weill himself has three particular cases in mind: 'The majority of these attacks [on the media], whether arising from a rebel journalist such as Serge Halimi (*Les Nouveaux Chiens de garde*), Pierre Bourdieu (*On Television*) or Jacques Bouveresse (*Schmock ou le triomphe du journalisme*), have in common an unavowed tendency to anti-democratism' – whose close link with anti-Semitism we have seen. Nicolas Weill, comforted by a combination of Aristotelian logic and striking examples (the philosopher Jacques Bouveresse as anti-Semite, indeed …) reaches the following general conclusion: 'Criticism of journalism in the nineteenth and early twentieth century was closely linked with a different phenomenon, that of anti-Semitism, since certain people viewed journalism as a Jewish profession par excellence' (*Le Monde*, 2 April 2004).

Criticizing the United States, talking about animals, attacking the media – all of these, according to our polemicists, are convoluted procedures that our anti-Semites resort to. There is also one more, just as scandalous, and that is comparison. It has been a while now since Claude Lanzmann argued that the destruction of European Jews was a unique and ineffable fact that defied explanation, still less comparison with anything else. Anyone who argued against this was accused of anti-Semitism or even Holocaust denial. By extension, any reference to the Second World War and

---

* Attributed to Sartre in the early 1950s, at the time he wrote 'The Communists and Peace'.

the Occupation in discussing the present is something criminal. This was again the response to one of the present authors (E.H.) after he wrote:

> When an armed group destroys a fortified Israeli position at Rafah, to term that act a 'terrorist attack' (France 2) or an 'outrage' (France 3) is to echo the words used against the Resistance by the late-lamented Philippe Henriot, secretary of state for information under the Vichy government, who was killed by a Resistance commando in April 1944.[12]

Nicolas Weill, always on the alert, immediately responded: 'One wonders who plays the role of Nazi occupier in his mental universe' (*Le Monde*, 15 April 2006). By one of those mortal leaps that are par for the course with these modern inquisitors, explaining that one person's terrorist is very often the other's freedom fighter amounts to equating the Israeli army with the Wehrmacht, and thus clearly indicates anti-Semitism.

All these procedures, however far-fetched they might be, end up constituting a rhetoric of intimidation whose sole purpose is to pin on its opponents the 'anti-Semite' label, with the idea that once applied, it will be no more possible to remove it than Captain Haddock's celebrated sticking plaster.

4

The New Inquisitors

However different they are in terms of generation, intellectual formation or professional career, those who have made the hunt for 'anti-Semitism' their stock in trade have one feature in common: they come from the left. Claude Lanzmann was in the Resistance, and behaved courageously during the Algerian war; André Glucksmann is a former Maoist, and likewise Jean-Claude Milner; Pierre-André Taguieff was close to the Situationists at Nanterre; Jean Birnbaum, the vigilant censor at *Le Monde des livres*, belonged to the Trotskyist organization Lutte Ouvrière; Alexandre Adler was a member of the PCF for more than ten years, a teacher at the party's central school and joint editor of *La Pensée*.

These origins show once more how intellectual legitimacy in France derives from the left. And for the most infamous tasks such antecedents are absolutely necessary: in the hunt for new protocols aimed at disqualifying representatives of progressive and revolutionary thought, people only have a genuine authority if they can say, 'I was one of them!' This reference to lived experience and vivid memory has two advantages. The first is that one can say 'I know these people, I saw them close up' – with the implication – 'and I could tell you a thing or two, I've got documents …' The second lies in wielding a pseudo-ethics of guilt: 'I got involved in that, and I understood "never again"!' A double protocol, in other words, of both familiarity and judgement, making up a particular subjectivity which combines both proximity and distance. Such are the typical virtues of the renegade from the left, who has played such a major role in France for the past forty years.

This is an objective reality. In terms of effectiveness, it has been commonly acknowledged in France, ever since the eighteenth century, that an intellectual hailing from the right has little prospect of success. The few exceptions, such as Joseph de Maistre or Charles Maurras, are almost oddities, and are paid little attention in official teaching. It is no surprise, then, that those who have made a profession out of branding their political opponents as anti-Semites should come from the left, and in many cases even the far left. Despite changing sides, they have kept their little foibles. Alexandre Adler, for example, from the PCF, maintains the same arrogance, the same certainty that what he says is true because he says it, the same tranquillity when his predictions are refuted by events – a typically Stalinist attitude: when the line changed 180 degrees, it had to be supported with the same aplomb as when it was attacked the day before. This operates in a very different way from the rhetoric of the classical right, already in power and always convinced that the order it upholds is the natural one, without need of argument. Those coming from the left, on the other hand, have maintained a rhetoric that is based on the categorical opposition of two terms, needing only a reversal of meaning: for the imperialists against the occupied and mistreated peoples, for the police against the popular youth in revolt, for the Israeli government against the Palestinians, for the checking and expulsion of undocumented workers – in short, for the established order and against whatever seems incompatible with it.

Equally homogeneous to the rhetoric of former communist or Maoist groups, particularly the Gauche Prolétarienne, is the taste for plots, the permanent hunt for infiltrators, the denunciation of opponents as manipulated by others still more frightful, and so on. In the case we are concerned with here, the accusations of anti-Semitism are paralleled by the idea, often expressed by the new inquisitors, that the radical left has been taken over by Islamism.

Éric Marty* told one of us (A.B.): 'Whatever you think, the only global force working in the direction you favour is radical Islam, and French intellectuals of your type are only the Western cover for Islamic terrorism.' For these people, in fact, anyone who protests against the abuses of the Israeli government in occupied Palestine or is bothered by the police persecution of young people in France, suffers from nostalgia and, without always being aware of it, has replaced the defunct proletariat with bearded terrorists. In similar terms, we might ask them in turn if they are fully aware of being, for their part, a specialist detachment of intellectuals in the service of the present forms of reactionary domination, under the protection of the US army and with the state of Israel as the advance post in the face of barbarism. Because this is indeed their role, and it is only logical that André Glucksmann should receive the Légion d'honneur from the hands of Nicolas Sarkozy.

Very talkative when it is a matter of slandering their opponents, our inquisitors are far more reticent about what they are defending at the end of the day. The West, whose end Spengler already proclaimed a century ago? The market economy? The invasion of Iraq? The construction of walls throughout the world to stop the movement of people? The living standards of the petty bourgeoisie in our countries? The set-up they construct – anti-Semitism, Islamism, terrorism – might well be a crude tool, but it is well enough adapted to the contemporary conditions of opinion formation in which all that matters is to pin labels on one's opponents. And yet it is so visibly disconnected from today's real problems, so visibly fictitious, that the question arises as to how far they believe in it themselves. The degree of cynical manipulation varies according to the individual concerned. Finkielkraut, for example, is undoubtedly convinced of what he says, which leads him to utter more naïve foolishness than the others. He is

---

* Éric Marty (b. 1955): author of numerous books on literary topics, editor of Roland Barthes' complete works and professor of comparative literature at the University of Paris VII. In 2007, Marty published *Une Querelle avec Alain Badiou, philosophe*, which was seen as accusing Badiou of anti-Semitism.

fond of exposing himself to blows, and then displaying his suffering at not having been understood – he likes to appear as a kind of Christ figure. He stands up against what he sees as misguided prevailing opinion, armed with extravagant accusations that only feed a nostalgic subjective complaint. But the majority of the others are complete cynics. For them, this hunt for an imaginary anti-Semitism is simply their bread and butter, and their way of increasing their power as good little soldiers encouraging the worst.

5

What Interests, What Aims?

Besides the hypothetical desire to defend Jews, it is possible to question the reasons that impel certain intellectuals to use the very serious accusation, 'You're an anti-Semite', as a universal stigmatizer. These reasons are diverse, but it is possible to discover a common foundation: support for the existing order, collusion with the existing government, historical anti-Communism, conviction that the American army is the ultimate bulwark of 'freedom', defence of the state of Israel – not to mention an understandable concern for personal advancement.

We should not forget that among those who were Maoists in their youth, several really did believe they were going to seize power. It was when they realized things were a bit more complicated, that it would take a good deal longer and demand harsh and unrecognized work in factories and communities, that they changed direction and organized the new reactionary ideology under the name of anti-totalitarianism. Nothing is more 'new', in certain circumstances, than a recycling of the old: the arguments of the 'new philosophers' were simply a reprise of the anti-Communist arguments of the 1950s. Our ex-Maoists came up with the idea that the main contradiction was no longer between proletariat and bourgeoisie, or between socialism and imperialism, but rather between democracy and totalitarianism – or, to keep to the vocabulary of their American masters, between 'Communist dictatorship' and the 'free world'. A neat calculation, after all: this turn brought them a good deal more than their former Maoism had done.

Today they act as the advance guard in the hunt for imaginary anti-Semitism. One of the most important figures in this movement, Jean-Claude Milner, a former member of the Gauche Prolétarienne, holds a particular place as the most original thinker among them, the one who tries to avoid commonplace repetitions and worn-out propaganda. He also tries to give a sense to the connection between the abandonment by the renegade Maoists of any popular vision of politics, on the one hand, and the sudden promotion of the 'Jewish question' as the centre of all valid thought, on the other. In this way he aims to equip the strange campaign against anti-Semitism with a historical and conceptual scaffolding, despite the meagre concrete foundation he offers.

Jean-Claude Milner maintains that the great event of the twentieth century was the obsolescence and gradual disappearance of the name 'worker', and the return in strength, as reference for everything that divides and opposes, of the name 'Jew'. This substitution is a case of what Lacan, Milner's teacher, calls the 'master-signifier', i.e. the name under which thought and action find their contemporary impulse. Just as 'worker', in the years from 1966 to 1976, drove many young students to go and work in factories with the aim of organizing political nuclei there, so, Milner explains, the name 'Jew' compels us to understand today that all universality is based on an identity. For him, 'Jew' is the exemplary name of this connection between identitarian perseverance and the desire for truth. It follows that any other interpretation of universality, which Milner refers to as 'progressive', is secretly anti-Semitic. In particular, any remaining attachment to the name 'worker' in politics, and more generally to words such as 'imperialism', 'popular politics', 'internationalism', 'emancipation', etc., means a failure to recognize the major function of the name 'Jew' and is thus an anti-Semitic archaism. This is the underlying reason why Milner was able to declare without flinching, in one of Alain

Finkielkraut's radio programmes on France Culture (13 January 2007), that Bourdieu was anti-Semitic, after already insinuating that he was a Holocaust denier.

For all those whose enthusiasm is roused by Milner's analysis, the new master-signifier has big advantages: not only does it no longer authorize opposition to the established government, as did the word 'worker' and all the others bound up with it, but on the contrary it demands collusion with this government in the name of 'democracy'. It is as if something has been found with a similarly convincing power to 'worker' or 'proletariat', but with a diametrically opposing aim.

If you take 'worker' as the master-signifier, there is no immediate reward. The injunction is one of protracted work as an activist, which is rather unpleasant (in the typical petty-bourgeois view), and with at best only a historic perspective. The new construction, on the other hand – whose subtle theorist is Milner but which is also fuelled by Lanzmann and *Les Temps Modernes*, by recent statements of Benny Lévy (who was the charismatic leader of the Gauche Prolétarienne before rallying to the figure of the 'studious Jew'), likewise by the majority of intellectuals who appear on television, and is homogeneous with the view of all the government parties without exception – this construction allows a flock of people in a hurry to frequent the corridors of power. They render this machine and its masters the eminent service of protecting them 'intellectually', while obtaining for themselves a little 'critical' freedom. Besides, being on the dominant side, they enjoy a great striking power against those who do not have the same position. It is in order to feed this power that the theme of anti-Semitism has such great importance for them.

It is important that the name 'Jew' – as against the name 'democracy', which is too abstract and compromised by too vigorous a conflict – should make possible a labelling based on something historical and irremediable. To this end, the destruction of European Jews has to be seen as the absolute crime, the event of the twentieth century that cannot be compared with anything else. Here again, Milner is the most systematic theorist of this construction, with a line of argument just as fragile as the others, but served by a subtlety of expression and a strength of language that give it a disturbing power. His effort, however sophistic it might be, leads in the eyes of a number of intellectuals to the destitution of former references − those of the Maoists, the *marxisant* intellectuals, commitment à la Sartre − and to the paradoxical transformation of the adjective 'progressive' into a kind of insult. For Milner and his followers, the progressives are those people who believe the twentieth century saw other important events besides the Judeocide. By clinging to this anachronistic nostalgia and rejecting the unique importance of the name 'Jew', they are anti-Semitic whether this is their intention or not. This point is the key: for Milner, being anti-Semitic does not necessarily involve intention. It is not an explicit ideology. Anti-Semitism is not a matter of consciousness, a project, or a decision. Certain choices that appear to be far removed from it − in which 'Jew' does not appear − are none the less anti-Semitic. Like the old Stalinists who were able to judge that certain anodyne music was 'objectively imperialist', the great victory of Milner and this whole current has been to create 'objective' anti-Semitism, leading to the interesting possibility of declaring almost anything and anyone 'anti-Semitic'.

6

The Role of Israel

Was it necessary for this name, 'Jew', whose polemical use always ultimately rests on the idea of complicity with the destruction of European Jews, to be dogmatically welded together with the state of Israel? Couldn't the same operation have been staged while leaving open the possibility of criticizing Israel, even doing so in the name of the name 'Jew'? This is indeed the position of count-less numbers of 'progressive' Jews (a word we shall continue to use, despite Milner) throughout the world, Israel included. If this did not become the dominant position, despite its logic, this derives from a particular vision of the state of Israel, in which the name 'Jew' plays only a quite subordinate role. In this vision, the state in question is identified as an advance outpost of the West. It is 'more one of us than we are ourselves', out there on the front line. If, before the Second World War, Jews were viewed as foreigners without a homeland and incapable of integration, now, on the contrary, those established in the Middle East are more European than the Europeans here, as they are defending our values against 'Islamic' barbarism, on an exposed frontier that is also our own.

At any event, for our inquisitors any referential name has to be that of a state. The old petty-bourgeois conviction that political commitment can only be towards a state, failing which one is lost and reduced to the hateful plebeian condition, is a conviction still intact among the renegades from official Communism, Maoism and Trotskyism, despite the turn taken by their dialectic. Behind the return of the name 'Jew' there has to be support for a state, a secondary nationalism for the state of Israel. And this nationalism takes the same characteristic as support for the Soviet Union or Maoist China once took: that of unconditional defence, not of a certain politics, but of a state, just as at the time when the Nazi–Soviet pact or the invasion of Hungary had to be swallowed without demur.

An additional interest that the Israeli state presents is that of assuring a merger between the Jew/Arab theme and the democracy/totalitarian theme – in which the argument that 'Israel is the only democracy in the Middle East' plays a capital role. The Israeli army is simultaneously defending both the name 'Jew' and democracy, which is all the more important in that, like the Roman legions on the Germanic borders, this army fights at the advanced outposts of civilization. If it were to be defeated, the barbarians would rush in – those hostile hordes that come from another world, but who, in the terrible form of workers and their children, have their representatives at the very gates to our cities.

We can put forward a hypothesis here. For the people we are talking about, whatever they say, what matters to them is not the 'name "Jew"' but rather the 'fate of the West'. This is the reason they identity 'Jew' with the state of Israel, and so eagerly support this state's war against the Palestinians and other Arabs. This also explains why the American far right, traditionally anti-Semitic, has organized, under Bush and his successors, an unlikely alliance between Christian ultra-conservatives and formerly 'progressive' Jews who have converted to the new world order. In France, too, we now find Marine Le Pen showing nothing but kindness towards the Jews, at the very moment when she maintains that the most dreadful problem of the country is that a few 'Arab-Moslems' say their prayers in the street. We must expect the Front National in the near future to condemn these 'youth from the banlieues' and 'progressive intellectuals' as anti-Semites – proving that novelty really does exist in the camp of reaction.

Looked at in more empirical terms, the construction of an 'upsurge of anti-Semitism in France' is a major argument directed at French Jews, to press them to make their *aliyah* and settle in Israel. The French diaspora is the second largest in the world after that of the United States, and the Israeli state, haunted by a 'demographic problem', attempts to tap all overseas sources available. As it is hard for the Israeli secret services to set fire to synagogues in France as a way of making Jews emigrate (as they did in Iraq and Morocco), a different method is needed. A number of Israeli envoys have spread among the Jewish population the simple message: 'Leave now, France is no longer a safe country for Jews.' Ariel Sharon, speaking on 18 July 2004 to a Jewish-American organization, claimed: 'We see the spread of one of the wildest anti-Semitisms in France.' The explanation of this 'wildness', according to him, was that 'nearly 10 per cent of the population are Muslim, which permits the rise of a new form of anti-Semitism based on anti-Israeli sentiments'. In conclusion: 'If I had to address our brothers in France, this is what I would tell them: "Emigrate to Israel as soon as you can."' The campaign against the 'upsurge' of anti-Semitism is one of the means of making the transition from 'Jew' to 'citizen of Israel' increasingly necessary, in a world where this is not the case for a majority of Jews.

Finally, 'anti-Semitism' is a form of defence against hard knocks. In February 2007, the investigative journalist Pierre Péan published a book on Bernard Kouchner,[13] in which he demonstrated Kouchner's activities as a consultant in the health sector to President Bongo in Gabon: two private companies, controlled by members of his family, had obtained contracts for a sum of over two million euros. The invoices were only settled when Kouchner became foreign minister. The book made tremendous waves, and Kouchner was forced to defend himself in the National Assembly. He did not take issue with the substance, but claimed the book was 'anti-Semitic', using as it did the word 'cosmopolitan': 'Doesn't the accusation of cosmopolitanism at this difficult time remind you of something? It does me.' The context, however, amply justified the author: '… a national independence flouted in the name of an Anglo-Saxon, human-rights and neoliberal cosmopolitanism'. But Pierre Péan, traumatized by the word 'anti-Semitism', only put up a weak defence and the matter was buried. A successful action.

Another example. To counter the great success in France of Shlomo Sand's book *The Invention of the Jewish People*,[14] Éric Marty published in *Le Monde* on 28 March 2009 an article accusing the author of anti-Semitism and negationism:

> It is unnecessary to play apprentice chemist in order to declare the harmlessness of Zyklon B, or act the archaeologist to make the Wailing Wall an outcrop of the Al-Asqa mosque, since, if the Jewish people is only a nineteenth-century invention under the Western paradigm of the nation-state, the question is already settled.

But Sand is not French, and is impervious to this kind of attack. His reply to Marty in the same newspaper was shattering:

> Why flinch at equating my approach with that of people who deny the gas chambers? That's direct, it's crude, and it's acceptable, and the basic thing is to mobilize a lot of people against my book. I would like to stress that in Israel, no such comparison has ever been made in all the stormy debates around my book. But Paris is not Tel Aviv. In France, nothing is easier in order to silence one's critics than to insinuate that they're anti-Semitic, or perhaps worse still, they're not sufficiently fond of Jews!

An attack that failed.

The lesson from these anecdotes is that the construction and use of the term 'anti-Semitic' is today a variant of the 'French exception', one of the forms that this 'exception' takes when it confers its singularity on a very stubborn fact in our history: the existence, ever since our great Revolution, of a powerful political and intellectual reaction.

7

Legal Actions

Until 2009, the majority of prosecutions for 'incitement to racial hatred' were initiated by the organization Avocats Sans Frontières, whose president, Maître William Goldnagel, won his spurs as the advocate for Arkadi Gaydamak, an arms trafficker who took refuge in Israel after his involvement in Angolagate, and for Oriana Falacci, the Italian journalist who wrote a whole book to prove that Muslims were subhuman. In the case against Daniel Mermet, on 31 May 2002, the witnesses for the prosecution were Alain Finkielkraut, Pierre-André Taguieff, Alexandre Adler and Roger Cukierman, then president of the CRIF. Despite this prestigious cast, Goldnagel lost the case, as he had all the others – which mattered little, since the essential thing was always to intimidate, and it is seriously intimidating to find oneself before the courts when you are not used to this.

The campaign for the boycott of Israeli products led to a major escalation of such legal actions: to date, eighty charges for 'provocation to discrimination on the grounds of national membership'. These have almost all been brought by a certain Sammy Ghozlan, retired police commissioner and member of the governing body of the CRIF, who is openly connected with the French far right and with Israeli settlers. Ghozlan was the founder of the 'Bureau national de vigilance contre l'antisémitisme' in whose name these charges were made, often in tandem with the France–Israel chamber of commerce, LICRA, and Avocats Sans Frontières. It is already unusual that Ghozlan should bring charges by the dozen, but what is far more so is that the minister of justice should take these up each time. There is not the least obligation for him to do so, and if he did not, such actions would have far less prospect of success. The courts followed without hesitation the advice of the government. It is worth noting that at the CRIF official dinner at Bordeaux on 19 February 2010, the Minister of the Interior Michèle Aliot-Marie declared: 'I find it unacceptable that certain people call for a boycott of products on the grounds that they are kosher and come from Israel.' Kosher products! It is hard to know whether to ascribe such a comment to perverse opportunism or pure and simple idiocy, though a combination of the two cannot be ruled out. It follows precisely from the prevailing logic that any action against the state of Israel should be identified with a surreptitious detestation of Jews, their religious customs and all their 'products'. Just imagine if the 'progressives' of a foreign country, at the time of the Algerian war, had tried to organize a boycott of French exports, in protest against the horrors of this colonial war. Would the minister of justice or the interior minister have declared: 'I find it unacceptable that certain people call for a boycott of products on the grounds that they are Christian cheeses and red wine and come from France'? Perhaps ... What ministers of justice and police throughout the world say is often beyond comprehension.

8

The Inquisitors' Resources and Ruses

The voices of those who have made a profession out of 'struggling against anti-Semitism' are powerful in the media. They are, as we have seen, intellectuals with old service records on the far left, which gives them a kind of legitimacy. They are not actually organized, but speak in their own names, which gives them a certain freedom and strength. In no way can they be described as a 'lobby' – nothing comparable with the situation in the US, where AIPAC and the Anti-Defamation League have premises in the best locations, permanent staff, and direct means of pressure on both press and public authorities. In France, those who see anti-Semites everywhere are not a genuine group which meets and decides collectively on actions to take. They are more like an orchestra without a conductor: each of them follows their own score, playing it when the occasion presents itself. If, for example, anyone chances to write or utter the word 'Auschwitz', Claude Lanzmann considers whether this was in a permissible context, and if he decides that the author transgressed this, he takes up his trumpet and sends *Le Monde* an article that is always published in a good position. For a book, it might be Éric Marty, and for an article or a broadcast, Bernard-Henri Lévy.

These instrumentalists all have a very strong position in the media. Alain Finkielkraut has a weekly programme on France Culture, at a peak listening time. He also has a spot on Radio de la Communauté Juive, a community radio station where he can express himself still more freely, calling one of us (E.H.), for example, the 'inventor of the kosher pogrom'. Bernard-Henri Lévy, apart from being on the supervisory board of the new-look *Le Monde*, has his column in *Le Point*, his magazine *Le Règle du jeu*, and a major position with Grasset, one of the main publishing imprints of the Hachette group. Jean Birnbaum edits the 'Essais' page in *Le Monde des livres*, which allows him to censor books that do not conform to his views, or to present if need be his own version of them. Alexandre Adler has free entry to *Le Figaro*, and it was in this paper that he explicitly called one of us (A.B.) an 'anti-Semite'. Was this simply due to uncontrolled anger? With our inquisitors, the adjective liable to prosecution is pressed on the reader, but often remains implicit. This is the case with the venerable magazine *Les Temps Modernes*, founded by Sartre but run today by Lanzmann, in which we find the high-flown prose of Milner, the rather ragged style of Marty, and the quite crazed writing of Robert Redeker.

The hostility of these influential figures reaches beyond the field of the media; they are able to compromise a career. When *Route 181: Fragments of a Journey in Palestine–Israel*, a documentary by Eyal Sivan and Michel Khleifi, was shown at the Centre Pompidou in 2003, as part of the Cinéma du Réel season, Claude Lanzmann got together a cabal to write in a collective letter signed, among others, by Bernard-Henri Lévy, Philippe Sollers, Eric Rochant and Arnaud Desplechin, calling on the state to 'assume its responsibilities'. The Minister of Culture, Jean-Jacques Aillagon, invoking the 'risk of disturbance to public order', had one of the two planned screenings cancelled – though the Centre did not completely capitulate, and kept the other screening at a late-night hour. After this, Sivan was unable for several years to carry out other projects in France, where he had been working for more than two decades. Blocked from any programming opportunities or subsidies, he was forced to move to London.

Being a Jew (and even, like Eyal Sivan, an Israeli) is no guarantee of protection against the accusation of anti-Semitism. We can even maintain that, by an interesting paradox, when the inquisitors detect a new 'anti-Semite', as happens all the time, noting that they are Jewish only functions in their eyes as an aggravating circumstance. Here are two examples.

When A.B. wrote 'The Use of the Word "Jew"',[15] he included in this short collection of texts written over twenty years an article by Cécile Winter. Considering that being Jewish is not an argument one way or another in intellectual debates, Winter did not mention her Jewish origin. When the inquisitors, led by Éric Marty, saw this book as an anti-Semitic libel, quite against common sense, they singled out Winter's contribution for attack in particularly crude terms, outing and stigmatizing her as Jewish.

When Ivan Segré, a 'studious Jew' who lives with his family in Tel Aviv, wrote this most rigorous, rational, calm and well-documented book on the logic of our inquisitors and the real wellsprings of the hunt for 'anti-Semites', the boycott of this major work was virtually complete, and if it was mentioned at all, it was in the style: 'If a Jew could write such things, and a religious one living in Israel at that, the only thing to do is neither read it nor speak of it.' In sum, this kind of Jew can be discounted completely.

Many anti-Semites, as we know, have their 'good Jews'. Those hunting for a dreamed-up anti-Semitism, for their part, have their 'bad Jews'. Of course, this is not a new procedure. Talk of the 'self-hatred' of certain Jews goes back a long way, indicating the difficulty necessarily faced, especially in the late nineteenth century, by Jews seeking to integrate fully in a major country (England, Germany, France, etc.) marked by chauvinism, colonial racism and anti-Semitism. The positions of French Jews today, when they want to freely criticize the actions of the state of Israel, have no connection with the suspect notion of 'self-hatred' that the subtle Milner has polished in order to construct the 'Jew of negation'.

If some people are taken in by such nonsense as the 'return of the name "Jew"', the calumny of 'progressivism', the baneful character of the 'Jew in denial' or the dreaded 'Islamic peril', this indicates less the strength of the opponent than our own ideological and political weakness. All this mental material, after all, serves only to defend those who rule, from our 'democratic' governments in the service of profit through to the brave American army that throttles 'Islamists' with the help of our 'Western' outpost in the Middle East. And that the extermination of the European Jews is brought in to help with this task, the magnificent 'Jew of affirmation' in the guise of the racist settler, can only add to our indignation.

As always, what matters is to hold steady and return blow for blow. Nothing is more important than to have our own idea as to what, in the dispositions and combats of the contemporary world, has universal value. If we are invulnerable on this point in terms of thought, the inquisitors will know that we feel entirely free to take their prophecies, not as a peril for us, but as a further symptom of their own unworthiness.

9

Why France?

In order to explain why the hunt for an imaginary anti-Semitism should be more developed in France than anywhere else, one reason often put forward is the latent guilt of the French for the way Jews were treated under the Occupation.

Just like the 'self-hatred' of the 'Jew in denial', so the notion of a people's historical guilt is both old and unfounded. A typical example is how the French military collapse in 1940 is very often ascribed to a defeatist mentality on the part of the people, who are blamed for not having wanted to fight and for having preferred to capitulate rather than repeat the butchery of 1914–18. All the evidence, however – all serious investigations of the actors in that drama, whether they were reserve officers or rank-and-file soldiers – shows it was the high command and the political class that were imbued with defeatism, quite simply because those in positions of power at the time, especially in the army, preferred Hitler and fascism by far to the Communists, still trembling as they were with the fear the Front Populaire had inspired in them. The French bourgeoisie replayed yet again the capitulation to the Prussians of 1871 (rather invasion than the people of Paris in revolt), and that of 1815 to the anti-Napoleonic coalition (rather foreign troops than the legacy of the Revolution). There are excellent reasons to believe that the people, had they been energetically led, would have wanted and been able to fight against the Nazi armies.

More recently, Jacques Rancière has demolished 'the assumption that sees racism as a popular passion, the fearful and irrational reaction of backward layers of the population' – a reaction opposed by the universalist logic of the rational state. This distorted vision makes it possible to give the racist policies of the state a certification of anti-racism.[16] To top it all, we are told that if we do not rapidly pass scurrilous laws against foreigners, 'populism' and the Front National will be strengthened. In sum: do what your supposed 'enemy' proposes, and it will be easier to confront him.

We must therefore view with suspicion the well-established theme of the guilt of the French people towards the Jews. First of all, anti-Jewish persecution was prepared and organized by the Pétainist state apparatus and its high-placed functionaries, particularly in the judiciary and police – all people whose anti-Semitism was well-known and long-established. It never took the form of 'populist' pogroms. Many ordinary people, especially in the countryside, hid Jews during the War. And finally, we are now at the third generation after these events. The two previous generations, encouraged after the Liberation by the tacit agreement between the PCF and the Gaullists not to make a fuss about the 'Jewish question', scarcely showed any signs of guilt. Has this suddenly struck their grandchildren, half a century later? It is more reasonable not to appeal to national psychologies and rather suspect that the phenomenon comes from above. Whatever one may think of the legitimacy of this or that decision, we have to note that injunctions about the 'duty of memory', vain 'demands for pardon' for the crimes of the Pétainist state, and initiatives such as Sarkozy's proposal that each schoolchild should sponsor a dead child from the concentration camps, all come from above, likewise the decision to put black plaques on schools in memory of deported Jewish children. Today these stand alongside banners protesting at the expulsion of children of undocumented immigrants, without this juxtaposition arousing any particular remarks 'from above'.

Far indeed from having its roots in a sense of guilt on the part of the French population, the relative success of the campaign against 'anti-Semitism' has, among its underlying reasons, that of washing the white population clean of any suspicion of racism. In one and the same movement, the government shows its attachment to the memory of murdered Jews while casting what Taguieff calls Judeophobia out to the margins of the big cities, the ruined '*banlieues*'. It is here, in populations viewed today with the same suspicious contempt that was displayed towards the Jews who arrived from central Europe before the Second World War, that the servants and propagandists of the state see all the ills as lying: machismo, homophobia, sexism, violence, religious fanaticism, *and* detestation of Jews. It is these people who are responsible for all evils, starting with anti-Semitism – not the petty-bourgeois whites who are at home in our country.

It is fundamentally very odd to see the notion of collective guilt, the basic fuel of historical anti-Semitism ('they' killed Christ, 'they' have hateful rituals, 'they' breed like rabbits, etc.) applied almost verbatim to Arabs, blacks and Muslims by intellectuals in the name of the struggle against anti-Semitism. It is amazing to hear former friends, former leftists, who are refined and subtle thinkers into the bargain, say that 'these people' (African Muslims) 'can never share our values', and that we should therefore favour the immediate expulsion en masse of these 'non-integrable' classes of people. In similar vein, neither Brasillach nor Céline were imbeciles, even though they looked forward to the complete disappearance of Jews.

It is in this context, clearly dominated by a classist propaganda, chauvinist and persecutory, that the accusation of anti-Semitism and hidden negationism – despite being completely unfounded – tetanizes the majority of its victims. How should we explain this strange phenomenon?

A first reason lies in the brutality of the accusation, very unusual in a society bathed in a polite consensus – at least among well-behaved people. Suddenly, in a procedure reminiscent of the logic of fascism in which insult overshadows argument, we are dealing with a genuine provocation: an accusation so serious and so incongruous that we can well imagine it leaves some people speechless.

And then, it's very difficult to defend yourself against such an accusation: 'No, I'm not anti-Semitic' being a double negation ('I'm not one of those people who don't like Jews') with the fragility this implies. How, indeed, can one prove that *one is not* something? Say that one has Jewish friends? That's the worst of all. ('Ah! He's got his good Jews.') Remind people, in certain cases, that one is Jewish oneself? We have seen how that is an aggravating factor. Launch a legal action? Lost in advance, as the accusers are clever enough to use terms that shelter them from prosecution for defamation, which has its precise rules. They will never say that you're anti-Semitic; they'll even say that 'of course, you're not', letting their argument, their tone, their comparisons and their historic references do the slandering work while they remain protected.

In the end, it is both impossible and unnecessary to defend oneself. The only effective reaction is attack. We have to dismantle the mechanism, show what position the accusers are speaking from, what their past is, what their political reasons are, what personal benefits they draw from their lies, what their connections and associations are. We have to make clear, and this is the object of the present essay, a question whose importance is not negligible: what the real and reactionary function is today, in the arena of the incessant combat that has divided the French intelligentsia for three hundred years – for or against popular revolutions – of this violent and shameless word 'anti-Semitism'.

The Philo-Semitic Reaction

The Treason of the Intellectuals

Ivan Segré

Introduction

The West presents itself, in the charming words of the editor of *Le Nouvel Observateur*, as the universal civilization. I prefer to call a cat a cat, the West the West, and as for universal, I leave it an enigma for the time being.

          – Benny Lévy, *Le Livre et les livres*

Meanwhile, let us remind young people that for several decades the political use of the word 'West' was confined to the racist far-right, actually serving as the name of one of its most violent groupings [i.e. *Occident*].

          – Alain Badiou, *Polemics*

Giving my book the title *The Philo-Semitic Reaction*, and subtitling it 'The Treason of the Intellectuals', meant opening a perspective of expectation. The start of the twenty-first century had seen the birth of an important ideological current in France, represented in particular by the historian Alexandre Adler, the sociologist Emmanuel Brenner, the cineaste Eli Chouraqui, the philosopher Alain Finkielkraut, the lawyer William Goldnagel, the linguist Jean-Claude Milner, the philosopher Robert Misrahi, the political scientist Pierre-André Taguieff, the sociologist Shmuel Trigano and the philosopher Yves-Charles Zarka. The launch of the Second Intifada in September 2000, and the perception of a renewal of anti-Semitism in France, led these intellectuals to produce a number of publications, documentaries, accusations and justifications in support of the twin slogans of the 'struggle against anti-Semitism' and the 'defence of Zionism'. Their detractors referred to these intellectuals as 'communitarian' or 'communitarist', accusing them of exacerbating an identitarian particularism – in the event, a Jewish one. We know, moreover, how Julien Benda justified the title of his famous work:

> Like the ancient prophet of Israel, the modern intellectual teaches: 'Deploy your zeal for the Lord God of hosts.' This has been for half a century the attitude of those men whose function should have been to oppose the realism of peoples, yet who, with all their power and in full awareness, have worked rather to inflame; an attitude that I venture for this reason to call the treason of the intellectuals.[1]

It would seem self-evident, then, that my argument would undertake to renew that of Julien Benda, in other words to display the betrayal of universalism that guides the thinking of these 'communitarian' intellectuals. And as their object is in fact to 'inflame' a Jewish particularism, this treason of the intellectuals would seem to be what it literally is for Benda, i.e. a return to the 'ancient prophet of Israel', to a particularist form of divinity (or of thought). Yet this is precisely not my argument, as my concern in this book is to refute the claim of this thought to be 'communitarian'. This is also why this adjective is systematically placed in quotes. What I maintain, in fact, is not just that this ideological current is *reactionary* rather than communitarian (here in its proper sense), but also that it actually involves the betrayal of a Jewish particularism – i.e. a treason of the intellectuals understood in a strictly opposite sense. And I shall show, by means of detailed examination of a selection of representative texts of this so-called 'communitarian' current, that what I have called the 'philo-Semitic reaction' is the cornerstone, in contemporary France, of a broad ideological operation aiming to impose the slogan of 'defence of the West'.

★   ★   ★

Since the political use of the word 'Occident',* particularly under Vichy France, had been disqualified by its historic compromise with Nazism, reactionary thought had to renew this use in such a way that the 'defence of the West' would appear – 'after Auschwitz' – as a rampart against Nazism or its contemporary avatars. It was necessary therefore to integrate the 'struggle against anti-Semitism' into the value system of an ideological current that was historically hostile to Jews. Such at least is my premise. The question then is the following: Is this the act of a reactionary line of thought which, having taken note of the criminal paths onto which political use of the word 'West' led, has subsequently worked to reconceive its identity, to the point that the words 'Jews' and 'Israel' no longer denote an alterity to subjugate and destroy, but rather 'the stranger, the widow and the orphan'? Or is this simply a well-concealed operation of seduction that needs to be exposed, so that the 'defence of the West' will appear today just as it was yesterday, i.e. basically an imperialist vision of the world, a xenophobic ideal of society, and a policing concept of knowledge?

In order to reply to this question, I have examined the texts produced by these 'communitarian' intellectuals in the early twenty-first century – the period following the 2000 Intifada and the perception of a revival of anti-Semitism in France, but also, and above all, following '9-11', the Bush era in the United States, and finally, the appearance of a line of political argument in France, one of whose slogans has been to struggle against the 'new anti-Semitism' and another to 'put an end' to May 1968, to 'progressivism' and its sociological and philosophical representatives. My interest in these 'communitarian' intellectuals is thus readily understandable: they are, more than any others, in the vanguard of a contemporary philo-Semitic reaction, and their intellectual, social and institutional vocation is to present an authorized discourse. Examining the discourse of the 'communitarian' intellectuals thus means taking cognizance of what

---

* 'Occident' was the name taken by a fascist student group in the 1960s, some of whose members were later to hold ministerial posts.

the most reactionary thought today authorizes, sometimes rec-
ommends and more often demands, in terms of the 'defence of
Zionism' or the 'struggle against anti-Semitism'. And it means
showing its ridiculous character.

1

The 'Communitarian' Ideology (Critique of Recent French 'Communitarian' Thought)

There has always been a certain imperial triad. In first place, the conquering soldier. In second place, the trader opening up markets. In third place, the missionary who converts. Whether the task is to convert to Christ-the-King or to preach the 'rights of man', it is unworthy of a philosopher to occupy this third position.

– Alain Badiou, Polemics

The Zionist intellectuals are those who rebel against the ghetto, deeming it chilly and alienating, but equally reject Western-style assimilation.

– Eli Barnavi, Sionisme, sionismes

In an article posted on the internet in autumn 2003, the Swiss intellectual Tariq Ramadan proposed a 'critique of the (new) communitarian intellectuals', targeting 'the works of Pierre-André Taguieff' which he presented as 'highly revealing' for this current of thought, in particular 'his polemic' *La Nouvelle judéophobie*, published in 2002, and 'above all' Alain Finkielkraut, whose book *Au nom de l'autre. Réflexions sur l'antisémitisme qui vient* 'revealed', according to Ramadan, 'a communitarist attitude that falsifies the terms of debate'. Ramadan equally cited, as examples of those 'French Jewish intellectuals who had up till now been viewed as universalist thinkers', but who 'had begun, on both the national and the international level, to develop analyses increasingly governed by a communitarian concern that tends to relativize the defence of universal principles of equality and justice', Alexandre Adler, Bernard Kouchner, André Glucksmann and Bernard-Henri Lévy. In actual fact, according to Ramadan, 'whether on the domestic level (struggle against anti-Semitism) or on the international stage (defence of Zionism), we are witnessing the emergence of a new attitude', which he denounced as follows: 'the political position they adopt responds to a communitarian logic, whether as Jews, as nationalists, or as defenders of Israel'.

This article of Tariq Ramadan's was rejected by a number of French daily papers before appearing on the internet, when it immediately aroused indignation.[1] The author was actually criticized for linking up with an old anti-Semitic tradition by drawing up a list of Jews, or supposed Jews, who had taken up public positions allegedly oriented by the defence of 'Jewish interests' to the detriment of national – or in this case, republican – ones, accusing them of a 'dual loyalty', on the one hand to their 'adopted' country (in this case France) and on the other to their unshakeable 'country of origin', i.e. to Israel and the Jewish people. But what precisely did Tariq Ramadan mean by 'communitarian'? In the article in question, he justified his position in the following terms:

> The recent war in Iraq had a revealing effect. Intellectuals as different as Bernard Kouchner, André Glucksmann and Bernard-Henry Lévy, who had taken up courageous positions over Bosnia, Rwanda and Chechnya, curiously supported the US–British intervention in Iraq. We might wonder why their justifications so often seemed unfounded: to eliminate a dictator (why not earlier?), for the democratization of that country (why not Saudi Arabia?), etc. The United States certainly acted in support of its own interests, but we know that Israel supported the intervention and that Israeli military advisers were involved with the troops, as noted by British journalists who were present in the

operations (*Independent*, 6 June 2003). We know that the architect
of this operation in the Bush administration was Paul Wolfowitz,
a well-known Zionist, who has never hidden his view that the
fall of Saddam Hussein would offer Israel greater security as well
as definite economic advantages.

According to Ramadan, the curious support of 'French Jewish
intellectuals' for the US–British intervention in Iraq was explained
by their support for the state of Israel. But beyond this, support
for Israel was its ultimate origin, the proof of this being that the
'architect' of this military intervention was Paul Wolfowitz, a 'well-
known Zionist', while American 'interests' are only introduced
here by a concessionary 'certainly'. Yet it seems just as rational, in
terms of the American 'interests' at stake in Iraq, or more widely in
the Persian Gulf, to envisage an exactly opposite hypothesis here:
in other words, that the argument of 'greater security' for Israel
was a rhetorical camouflage, while American political orientations were essentially based on exclusively national considerations
that had nothing to do with Israeli national interest or the Zionist
project. Suggesting that the positions taken on the Iraq intervention by 'French Jewish intellectuals' could be explained by their
support for Israel, then explaining the intervention itself in terms
of Israeli strategic interests, Ramadan thus informs us of what
he understands by a 'communitarian' position, i.e. support of or
identification with American foreign policy, on the understanding, it seems, that the United States is in the hands of the Jews, or
at least those of the 'well-known Zionist' Paul Wolfowitz. And if
I can accept Ramadan's thesis – having myself noted and criticized a 'communitarian' drift on the part of a certain number of
French intellectuals – this is with the qualification that I see this
drift as having a quite different significance, since for me it is
not a matter of denouncing the betrayal of 'universalism' to the
benefit of Jewish particularism, but rather something quite different – America not yet being, as I see it, in the hands of Jews.[2]
I should also explain that, if my own 'list' is not exactly the same
as that suggested by Ramadan, the reason is the five authors I

focus on here – Raphaël Draï, Shmuel Trigano, Alexandre Adler, Alain Finkielkraut and André Kaspi – by dint of their writings and in some cases their institutional responsibilities, seemed the best examples of 'analyses increasingly oriented by a communitarian concern that tends to relativize the defence of universal principles of equality and justice'. But the prejudice that ascribes to this current of thought a 'communitarian' orientation, more precisely a Jewish or Zionist one, will be all the more confounded.[3]

RAPHAËL DRAÏ, *SOUS LE SIGNE DE SION*

Raphaël Draï's* book *Sous le Signe de Sion. Le nouvel antisémitisme est arrivé* (2001) was written – apart from its postscript – before the attacks of 11 September 2001, and focuses on the political situation in the Middle East, more precisely on the 'Second Intifada' launched in September 2000 following the failure of the Camp David negotiations, and its repercussions in France, particularly in the media, where Israel, in the view of the author, was the victim of a 'thrashing'. The main interest of Draï's text for us, and his own main object, was to provide the French reader with a Zionist perspective on the Israeli–Arab conflict, in a general context that the author sees as very hostile to Israel, if not openly anti-Semitic, given anti-Zionism and anti-Semitism are strictly equivalent in his eyes. Draï's position on what the 'defence of Zionism' means will form the starting-point of our analysis, but also a reference point in relation to which we shall display the shifts and slippages other so-called 'communitarian' analysts effect on this question. We shall therefore call this the position of the orthodox Zionist.

---

* Raphaël Draï: born in Constantine, Algeria in 1942. Professor of political science at the University of Aix-Marseille III. Author of numerous books which combine political science and psychoanalysis.

The first pronouncement of the orthodox zionist

Raphaël Draï expresses the position of the orthodox Zionist on the subject of the Israeli–American strategic alliance with a key phrase in his book, one that we have first of all to situate in its context. On pages 103–4 of *Sous le signe de Sion*, the author refers to 'the investment of the Israeli-Arab conflict by the Western imaginary', and the way in which, following its 1967 victory, Israel was presented 'as a regional – even world – military superpower, against whom the Palestinians were represented as a population of destitute refugees subject to the pitiless yoke of their conquerors' – this forming, according to the author, a 'permutation' and 'transformation of roles' in the Western and particularly the French imaginary, since it meant equating 'the state of Israel with an illegitimate occupying power, fated sooner or later to be defeated, and the Palestinians with a form of resistance that irresistibly evoked Free France in the face of the Nazi occupation'. This reversal of positions is what the author calls 'the substitution of Jewish by Palestinian victimhood', i.e. the way in which the Palestinians came to occupy, in the Western, European and French imaginary, the position which had been that of the Jews during the Second World War – Jews who now as Israelis occupied the position of the Nazis, in other words that of a racist imperialism. And the author adds that this substitution in the victim role 'was reinforced by all the schemas, slogans and stereotypes of the Cold War, of anti-colonialism and anti-American Third Worldism, under neo-Stalinist influence'. It is here that orthodox Zionist thought finds its key and distinctive formulation. In fact, if progressive anti-Zionism structurally identifies Israel and the United States, in other words reduces Zionism to a form of regional imperialism serving the interests of global imperialism (in the best of cases), there are then two distinct ways of rejecting this anti-Zionism: the first proposes a reversal of values, while the second sets out to refute this identification.

a) The reactionary reversal: this first path consists in validating the identification made by progressives between Israel and the United States, but reversing its axiology, so that *imperialism* becomes, in the non-progressive and reactionary discourse, *civilization* (civilization, human rights, international law, economic and social prosperity, etc.). Progressive and reactionary analyses agree in fact about this identification between Israel and the United States, i.e. in their common assumption. This is for example what the book by the Palestinian intellectual Camille Mansour, *Israël et les États-Unis. Histoire d'une alliance stratégique* (1995), seeks to explain, conferring on this identification the dignity of an argued and logical conclusion, since the main thesis of his book, at the end of his analysis, is that the strategic alliance between Israel and the United States is not ultimately based either, (1) on a coincidence of well-understood interests, or (2) on the ideological and moral issue represented by the 'memory' of Auschwitz, or (3) on a 'communitarian' American-Jewish lobbying – but on nothing less than a common cultural and ideological identity. And since everyone agrees about this, all that remains is to decide, depending on the ideological option chosen, whether this identity is politically imperialist or civilizing.

b) Refutation of the thesis of a cultural and ideological identity: this second route is precisely that of orthodox Zionism, in this case represented by Raphaël Draï. His main concern here is to break with the figure of reversal that we have shown above. In fact, after having relocated progressive anti-Zionism in the ideological configuration of the post-War years ('the Cold War', 'anti-colonialism' and 'anti-American Third Worldism'), Draï explains the Zionist position on the question of the Israeli–American alliance as follows: 'The state of Israel, allied to the United States because no other diplomatic choice was available for it to defend its existence, was presented, on the grounds of an "influential Jewish lobby", as its "evil genius", as an expansionist, colonialist, and before long a racist state.' Tackling the history of international relations 'under the sign of Zion', Draï sees no cultural or ideological predisposition to a strategic Israeli–American alliance, but a simple coincidence of well-understood interests, even making it clear that, in the Israeli case, this was for lack of an alternative and for vital existential reasons. If the reasons for such an alliance must still be examined from the American point of view, or if the hypothesis can be ventured of a cultural or ideological identification with Israel, from the orthodox Zionist point of view the state of Israel is no more predisposed, culturally and ideologically, towards an Israeli–American alliance than an Israeli–Indian one; this is only for geo-strategic reasons that are eminently pragmatic and in this sense contingent. This is why, according to Draï, the identification between Israel and the United States amounts to no more than a fantasy identification that inevitably ends with the guilt of Israel and the innocence of the United States, whose 'evil genius' Israel is and has to be. In fact, we find here one of the most traditional anti-Semitic themes, since at the time of the British Empire the Jews were already its 'evil genius', as witness for example the formulation of the Hungarian anti-Semite Zoltán Bosnyák, translated from the Hungarian and cited by Imre Hermann in his *Psychologie de l'antisémitisme* (1986): 'According to Bosnyák, "the two world imperialisms", "the holy alliance of England and Israel" that "has showered so many ills on Humanity", must disappear at the same time from the surface of the Earth.' According to the anti-Semitic eschatology offered here, the disappearance of Israel is synonymous with the disappearance of world imperialism, which at that time meant British imperialism, and vice versa. But whereas the imperial position of Great Britain was a function of history, in the sense that it occupied a position that was not intrinsic to it, as far as Israel is concerned its imperialism is not something constructed in and by history, but is indeed intrinsic. That is why, in this 'holy alliance of England and Israel', Spain, France, England and the United States, and tomorrow China, can successively occupy the role of imperial power, or leading member of the imperial alliance – but

Israel always remains in second place, since the very essence of Israel, its unchangeable nature, is to instrumentalize world power, whatever its cultural and ideological identity, and to use this for its own designs of regional or world domination; in sum, to be its 'evil genius'.

The second pronouncement of the orthodox zionist

This key phrase in Draï's text is in no way isolated, its effects run through the whole of his analysis, and it particularly involves a second distinction specific to Zionist orthodoxy: that Israel belongs irreducibly to 'the West', and not just to the United States. On pages 151–2, the author sets out to demonstrate the necessity, and accordingly the legitimacy, of Zionism in the light of twentieth-century history, but by adopting a standpoint of a Jewish nationalism that is precisely distinguished from 'the West':

> The enemies of the state of Israel criticize it for exploiting the Shoah for propaganda purposes, in order to justify the creation of the 'artificial' Zionist state. The Shoah would thus be both pledge and shield of this state, which would otherwise lack any acceptable justification. In reality, if the state and people of Israel have well integrated the Shoah into their history and their acts of memory, it is certainly not in this way. From 1917–18 on, everything happened as if what is generically called the West had wanted to demonstrate that Judaism could only survive by exercising its right to self-defence – unless by depriving it also of this right it was left no other outcome than to disappear. The anti-Jewish persecutions that ravaged the USSR under Stalin, and Germany in the course of Nazification, were bound to impel Jews to emigrate, and what countries were open to these refugees and exiles? The European countries, and America as well, restricted entry onto their territories, if they did not quite simply ban it.

To place oneself 'under the sign of Zion', for this author, thus means grasping the singularity of the Jewish people's history, divided between the Christian West and the Islamic East (a division that partly coincides with the distinction between Ashkenazi and Sephardic exiles), as the 'evil genius' of each (the Jewish situation fluctuating between forced conversion, expulsion and annihilation in the Christian West, while stabilizing in the Arabic and Muslim countries into the status of *dhimmis*), with the outcome that, in the Israeli formula – '*aïn brera*' – there was no choice: the survival of the Jewish nation involved Jewish political sovereignty, which for historical, cultural and ideological (or religious) reasons could only, in the eyes of the Jewish masses of Eastern Europe, be realized in Palestine (as opposed to Uganda, eastern Poland or some territory of the Soviet Union). And if the countries of the Americas, in particular the United States, might be a preferred destination for Jews fleeing Germany and then Europe 'in the course of Nazificiation', the local authorities did not see things in these terms – the United States being no exception to the rule in terms of restricting Jewish immigration, a restriction motivated largely by anti-Semitic prejudices that were just as manifest in the New World as in Old Europe. The author can therefore conclude:

> Is this not how we should understand the real link between the Shoah and the creation of the state of Israel? From 1895 to 1917, then from 1917 to 1948, through 1933 and the Nuremberg laws which the whole world was aware of, through 1940 and the anti-Jewish decrees of Vichy, it seemed that the Western world, whether totalitarian or democratic, sought to persuade defenceless Jews that only one path was open to them, that of annihilation. (p. 154)

According to Raphaël Draï, therefore, the Zionist project is based on a unique cultural and ideological identity, irreducible in particular not just to American cultural and ideological identity, but also to Western identity in general, 'whether totalitarian or democratic'. The orthodox Zionist position then consists in presenting Jewish political sovereignty in Palestine as a historical or existential necessity for the Jewish nation, and in this sense as legitimate. This legitimacy has been formulated by the Israeli historian Zeev Sternhell in the following terms:

> Israel was a historical necessity. For me, the legitimacy of the conquest of Palestine by the Jews and Zionism meant the conquest of land. It lies in this necessity of having a home. And someone had to pay the price of this conquest. The founders, who were far less cowardly than many born Israelis, did not conceal this fact. They knew that they had come to conquer this land by the strength of their work, by all means possible and imaginable, including force of arms. This is what Zionism was, the conquest of land. I have never had any doubts as to the legitimacy of Zionism. I believe that Zionism is fundamentally just, justified and legitimized by the existential necessity that Jews found themselves in of finding a bit of land for themselves. But this vision also marks the limitations of Zionism. For me, Zionism is justified on these premises and not on historical grounds. This means that, from the moment that the objective has been achieved, the moment that a state where Jews are at home has been founded, a final end is made to the process of conquest. This is why, speaking concretely, the 1949 borders, which are commonly called the 1967 borders – I prefer to say the 1949 borders, as they were the borders at the end of the war of independence – constitute the final point of the conquest of land.[4]

It would then appear that, according to the orthodox analysis – of the pioneers but also of Zeev Sternhell and Raphaël Draï – the original root of Zionism is equally foreign to the Christian West and to the Islamic East, to both the 'free world' and 'totalitarianism', and finally to America as much as any other empire or civilization. Its coupling with one of these more than another can accordingly result only from reasons that are quite contingent in relation to its ultimate rationale, which is the project – the existential necessity – of 'a state where Jews are at home'. In the conclusion to his book, Draï can thus reaffirm the singularity of Zionism in relation to both 'the West' and 'democracy':

> The movement of national liberation that undertook to deliver the Jewish people from the hatred, pogroms and genocide of a West that rejected being called barbaric at the same time as it extended the realm of barbarism to unimaginable lengths – this movement named itself Zionism by reference to Zion. Two millennia of exile spared it the ridicule of calling itself the 'democratic and popular republic of Israel'. It did not want to imprison itself in any preconceived idea of nation or state. Let us simply accept that the stigma regained its true meaning. (p. 239)

The orthodox Zionist position consists, in fact, of asserting the singularity of a name – Zionism, Zion – against its assimilation to other names, whether those of America, the West or Democracy.

SHMUEL TRIGANO, *LES FRONTIÈRES D'AUSCHWITZ*, OR THE ART OF METAPHOR

Shmuel Trigano's* book *Les Frontières d'Auschwitz* (2005) is situated, like that of Raphaël Draï, in the wake of the polemic stances that followed the media coverage of the 'Second Intifada' in France. In this sense, his work continues that of Draï – his colleague and co-director of the College of Jewish Studies of the Alliance Israélite Universelle – since he is equally concerned to denounce the bias of the media, their disinformation and even their anti-Israeli propaganda. I am not concerned here with the relationship between the two authors. What must hold our attention in Trigano's book, however, is his

---

* Shmuel Trigano: born in 1948 in Blida, Algeria. Professor of religious and political sociology at the University of Paris X Nanterre, Director of the College of Jewish Studies of the Alliance Israélite Universelle and author of many books on religion and Judaism.

significant divergence from Draï's position regarding the particular point we are concerned with here – the singularity of the name of Zion.

The 'true beacon of freedom in the world'

In a chapter titled 'Israel's global exclusion', Trigano deals with the international condemnations this state regularly faces, concluding with the following lines:

> Certainly, this diversion of the international body [the UN] is the result of the corrupting impulse given to its operation at the start by the Arab-Communist bloc and its Third World acolytes. Yet the nations of the democratic world have remained within it and continued to take part in its work. The European bloc is its most fervent participant. France has made the UN the pivot of its foreign policy. The Arabs have succeeded de facto in assigning Israel to the rank of a pariah state, the condition of *dhimmi* into which Islam has always cast non-Muslims, and they have done this with the assent of the democratic nations, except for the United States, which is decidedly the true beacon of freedom in the world ... By this token, the status of Israel within the UN is the measure of the morality of its member states. (pp. 200–1)

These lines initially seem similar to Draï's claims in many respects, as well as many other intellectuals who defend Zionism, since the object is to denounce the exclusion of Israel and its 'pariah state' condition among nations, so 'the status of Israel' becomes 'the measure of the morality of states' – just as the status of Jews was the measure of the morality of individuals (the Dreyfus affair remaining the historical paradigm of this dividing line between anti-Semites and anti-anti-Semites). And yet a closer analysis immediately reveals points of divergence that continue to produce their effects in 'communitarian' discourse. First of all, Trigano's text distinguishes between a 'corrupting influence' and what is or are corrupted. In other words, so long as the UN was under the influence of the 'nations of the democratic world' there was no need to fear anti-Zionism or anti-Semitism, but with the introduction of the 'Arab-Communist bloc and its Third World acolytes', Israel found itself threatened and outlawed from the nations. We thus have on the one hand those who corrupt – the Arabs, the Communists, and their Third World confederates – and on the other hand those who have been corrupted – the democratic nations. Secondly, this original distinction divides into two sub-categories for each of the two first categories distinguished ('the corrupting influence' on the one hand, the corrupted body on the other). As far as the 'corrupting influence' is concerned, in fact, 'the Arabs' are distinguished from other agents of corruption, namely the Communists and Third Worldists (since Arab anti-Zionism preceded and succeeds the 'Arab-Communist bloc'), whereas in the case of the corrupted body, 'Europe' is distinguished from other democratic nations as being particularly susceptible to the 'corrupting influence'. Thirdly, this text distinguishes between two extremes among the democratic nations: France and the United States. France, by 'making the UN the pivot of its foreign policy', becomes the spearhead of a Europe ready to resort to a corrupt international body, whereas the United States resists by supporting Israel within the UN, or even de-legitimizing the UN by way of a unilateral policy. The author concludes from this that the United States is 'decidedly the true beacon of freedom in the world'. These distinctions, however, beyond their evident affiliation to the Zionist cause, are a long way from Draï's statements on the subject of the singularity of the name of Zion. In effect, the distinction that Trigano introduces between a healthy body (the democratic West) and a corrupting influence (the Arabs, the Communists and the Third Worldists) is a heterodox one in relation to orthodox Zionism, with its assertion that Zionism is the singular name of Israel among the nations, or precisely what Draï maintains to be 'under the sign of Zion'. And this first shift immediately leads to a second, since the support of the United States for

Israel no longer follows from an empirical, geo-strategic or pragmatic analysis, as in Draï's text, but from a ('decidedly') confirmed
vocation of the United States to be 'the true beacon of freedom in
the world' – in other words, from an American cultural and ideological disposition to be the support of Israel among the nations.

The 'American rock'

The passage analyzed above is followed by the start of a new
chapter: 'The European Empire Against Israel'. This text reworks
the previous distinctions with reference to historical development,
and radicalizes certain aspects:

> The de facto exclusion of Israel from the international stage
> would not have been possible without the hostility of Europe,
> both individual states and the Council of Europe. The bloc vote
> of the European countries and the Arab-Islamic states in inter-
> national arenas, on questions connected with Israel, is in fact the
> cornerstone of this exclusion. Until the collapse of the Soviet
> Union, this exclusion was the act of the Arab-Islamic bloc. Today
> it takes a new form. This new situation has a profound meaning
> for both Europe and Israel. The old dream of Theodor Herzl
> to make the Jewish state the vector for democratic Europe's
> accepting the Jews it was unable to integrate, has here collapsed
> with a crash. If it were not for the American rock, Israel's isola-
> tion would be almost total, it would stand at the edge of the
> abyss. (p. 202)

According to Trigano, though the collapse of the Communist
bloc after 1989 had suggested a weakening of the 'corrupting influence' and a strengthening of the resistance capacities of
the democratic nations, what transpired in reality (as the title of
his chapter indicates) is the 'European empire' took the place of
the Soviet Union in what was formerly the 'Arab-Communist
bloc' against Israel, so with Europe now allied to the Arabs there

remains only America on the side of the democratic nations. In other, more metaphorical terms, once Europe had passed body and soul to the side of the 'corrupting influence' and 'hostility' towards Israel, the only healthy body that remained was an America whose original predisposition to support Israel is stated but left obscure. In the Israeli Declaration of Independence of 1948, however, the 'rock' metaphor is applied to Israel itself, and not to America. In his *Histoire moderne d'Israël*, Eli Barnavi makes clear that by expressing its trust in the 'rock of Israel', the text of this Declaration offers 'an elegant compromise formula between the religious, who wanted to anchor the Jewish state in divinity, and the agnostic, concerned with freedom of conscience and secularism' (p. 32). In other words, religious minds could interpret the 'rock' metaphor as divine providence, but it was free for secular spirits to understand something else, for example the capacity and determination of the Jewish people to take their political destiny in hand, 'in and through history', to take up the formulation of Daniel Bensaïd, citing Marx.[5] But if Trigano interprets the 'rock' metaphor as applying just as well to America, how do things stand with this 'compromise'?

What's in an image?

The metaphorical register that accompanies the occurrences of the name America in these two texts tells us something about the rhetorical effects of a shift that in itself has nothing rhetorical about it, since it makes it possible to distinguish between Zionist orthodoxy and Zionist heterodoxy. In fact, while according to Raphaël Draï the Israeli–American alliance does not follow from any original predisposition, for Shmuel Trigano the United States is first of all 'the true beacon of freedom in the world' when it takes the lead in the democratic nations' support for Israel, and then – after Israel has been abandoned by Europe, i.e. once America has become the sole support of Israel – it becomes 'the American rock'. These two metaphors in no way appear by chance in Trigano's text, but seek to grasp the singularity of America in the contemporary history of anti-Zionism. The metaphor that presents the United States as the 'true beacon of freedom in the world' refers to America when it stands at the head of the democratic nations, hence a metaphor that refers us to the age of Enlightenment; the 'rock' metaphor then denotes America when it is the sole support of Israel, a metaphor that refers us this time to the Bible, very precisely to the 'rock of Israel'. The author's metaphorical register accordingly introduces a historical, cultural and ideological distinction between Europe and America that could be stated as follows: Europe's hostility to Israel signals a betrayal of the Enlightenment ideal, whereas the solitary support of America for Israel signals an identitarian faithfulness to biblical values; the American reference to the Bible is thus a pledge of support for Israel that is far more solid than the European reference to Enlightenment ideals. And we then understand how the American predisposition to support Israel is explained, according to this author, by its privileged relationship to the Good Book.

The distinction between Zionist orthodoxy and heterodoxy, between the texts of Raphaël Draï and Shmuel Trigano, can now be formulated as follows. Whereas Zionist orthodoxy applies a materialist conception of international relations, Zionist hetero-doxy applies an idealist conception of these same international relations, i.e. an opposition between the register of political prag-matism and that of original predisposition. Draï in fact relates the Israeli–American alliance to a purely political necessity (Israel scarcely had a choice, whereas for America, though the author does not offer any explanation of its support for Israel, there is nothing to suggest that resort is needed to an original predisposi-tion that the author moreover explicitly rejects). Trigano, on the other hand, relates the Israeli–American alliance to a purely ideal-ist, religious or biblical necessity. Thus, whereas Jewish religious orthodoxy considers the biblical metaphor of the 'rock' to refer for example to the thrice-daily Jewish prayer that 'We praise thee

G-d, our G-d and the G-d of our fathers, our rock, the rock of our life', and Zionist orthodoxy proposes the compromise formula of placing trust in 'the rock of Israel'; Zionist heterodoxy, for its part, believes the 'rock' metaphor decidedly applies to America, since it is precisely this that explains its unflinching support of Israel, i.e. its original predisposition to support Israel – in a word, its alliance with Israel.

Analysis of a text by Alexandre Adler will enable us to examine the political implications of a shift observable in Trigano's metaphorical register. As for deciding where the boundary lies between the Zionist heterodoxy of the latter and pure heresy, that is a different question – certainly a more specifically literary one, but specifically biblical as well, since it touches on the relationship between the letter and the spirit.

ALEXANDRE ADLER, *L'ODYSÉE AMÉRICAINE*

In a brilliant essay of international geopolitics and contemporary history, covering all five continents around a central problematic, Alexandre Adler's* *L'Odysée américaine* (2004) seeks to reject the reductionist and in his opinion erroneous view of an American empire imposing its law on the world, and substitutes for this the view of an emerging multipolar world in which American democracy constitutes, sometimes despite itself, a regulating axis and an inextinguishable source of inspiration. In fact, as the author maintains, 'America is, has been and will be the essential land of human freedom in this world' (p. 277), an assertion he has previously illustrated by recalling its historic role as

---

   * Alexandre Adler: born in Paris in 1950. Journalist, commentator, historian and international relations specialist. A member of the French Communist Party from 1968 to 1979 and assistant editor of the Communist-aligned journal *La Pensée*. Now known for his links to neoconservative circles in the US, his support for the Iraq War and Nicolas Sarkozy, as well as for pro-Israeli positions. Author of numerous books on Communism, Israel and geopolitics.

promised land and refuge for people of all origins: 'America has seen the almost legendary integration of all those persecuted in the Old World, from the Irish through the Greeks to the Armenians' (p. 269). This centrality of America, not as imperial power but as 'essential land of human freedom in this world', should be studied in its articulation in the author's argument, along with the Zionist convictions he formulated in a text published a short time before this essay: 'Le Sionisme et le monde contemporain'.

Zionist and anti-zionist

In a collection of texts edited by the Union des Étudiants Juifs Français, and published under the title *Le Sionisme expliqué à mes potes* (2003), Alexandre Adler wrote:

> The Zionist project is nothing more than the attempt to gather Jews together – or at least, those who desire this – to give them back a common identity and establish this common identity in the very birthplace of the people of Israel in the Middle East; this project eventually succeeded beyond all expectation. ('Le Sionisme et le monde contemporain', p. 226)

By this formulation, the author indicates the surprising success of the 'Zionist project', as the reassertion of a sovereign Jewish national identity in 'Palestine'. Then, after having set out the major contemporary reconfigurations of a 'Zionist project' today realized, Adler deals with the development of relations between Israel and the Jewish diaspora, which have been in some sense 'normalized' just like Zionism itself, and he concludes: 'In one and the same movement, the existence of Israel is accepted by all Jews as a central dimension of their identity, while Israel abandons the idea that the future of all Jews lies necessarily, for today, on Israeli territory' (pp. 238–9). None the less, the relationship between the existence of Israel and the diaspora remains, according to this author, essentially asymmetrical, since he closes his contribution to the 2003 book with the words: 'Zionism is a prerequisite for the influence of the Jewish people as a whole. The Jewish people had an imperative need for this material support in humanity, this *makom* or "place", i.e. a state, a language, and a nationality. Israel is thus the site of a modern Jewish project' (p. 242). The author maintains the primacy of Israel over the diaspora, in the sense that the Jewish identity – or the 'modern Jewish project' – uniting Israelis and diaspora Jews has today as its 'place' the sovereign existence of Jews in 'Palestine' – a state, a language, a nationality. And so it is precisely by virtue of this determining influence of Israel on the diaspora that the author could venture, earlier on in his text, the following observation:

> In the difficult times we are going through today, those within the Jewish community who proclaim their anti-Zionism run the risk of breaking in a definitive fashion the tie that unites them with other Jews of the diaspora. In other words, it becomes ever less imaginable to conceive a Jewish identity that would not include a strong Zionist component. (pp. 240–1)

The primacy of Israel as the place where Jewish sovereignty is exercised is therefore, according to Alexandre Adler, such that it becomes impossible for a Jew to proclaim his anti-Zionism without risking a break with Jewish identity or with Jews as a whole – both Israeli Jews and Jews of the diaspora. His assertion of the success of the 'Zionist project', likewise of a necessary ideological and existential fidelity to this project, is then bound to instruct his approach to Israeli–American relations.

The ambivalences of American democracy

The author expresses his fidelity to the 'Zionist project' in *L'Odysée américaine* first of all by a certain number of reminders concerning the ambivalences of American democracy towards the Jews, reminders that seem definitively to rule out the metaphorical register Trigano deploys on the subject of the Israeli–American alliance. First of all, Adler mentions American anti-Semitism, particularly on page 283 where he recalls that in several American states Jews did not enjoy full civil rights until 1850, and more explicitly still on page 128, when he discusses American isolationism and the ideologies with which this was historically associated: 'racism, philistine contempt towards Europe, principled anti-Marxism and anti-Semitism, particularly in its final phase, after 1936, when men such as Henry Ford, an admirer of Hitler, and Charles Lindbergh, were joined, as in France at the same time, by certain currents of the populist left that defended "real Americans" against the "New York immigrant" socialist demagogues' – a passage that concludes by recalling that Henry Ford 'distributed the *Protocol of the Elders of Zion* in the United States', and his 'portrait adorned the vestibule of the Nazi party office in Berlin'. Secondly, Adler recalls at several points (pp. 49, 291–2, 294, 296) the active support of the CIA, not only to Latin American dictators, but also to former Nazi bigwigs that it sheltered from international – and in particular, Israeli – pursuit, and brought to South America by the 'rat line' set up with the help of the Vatican. Finally, after citing the 'famous quip' of the powerful New York senator Jacob Javits that 'an orientalist is basically an anti-Semite who has learned some difficult languages' (cited on p. 68), without in any way seeming to reject these terms, the author recalls at several points the reality of American Arab policy, for example on page 127:

> In passing, it is impossible to say that Islam could in any way complain of a reticent approach on the part of the United States. American aid to Egypt has been constant since 1978. The US favoured Jordan with a free trade agreement before Israel or Turkey. It established peaceful relations with Syria after the 1991 war. And it never challenged Saudi policy … until 11 September 2001.

He equally emphasizes 'the longest incarceration ever inflicted on a spy' was 'of the Jewish-American Jonathan Pollard', a prisoner of conscience of the Saudi lobby at Langley, who was beginning his eighteenth year of detention at a time when all the Eastern bloc spies of his day arrested in the United States had long since been released, one of them even becoming a Polish government minister under Walesa. (p. 295)

Proclaiming his fidelity to the 'Zionist project' on the one hand, and recalling some historical truths about American ambiguities towards Jews or Israel on the other, Adler would seem unlikely to embark on such lyrical flights as those that punctuate Trigano's text, at least when he deals with Israeli–American relations, and might rather be expected to share Draï's perspective on this subject. Let us see now whether his geopolitical approach to Israeli–American relations confirms or refutes this hypothesis.

The concept of 'total alliance'

Surveying the various geopolitical questions that govern the major orientations of American policy, Adler discusses the Israeli–American strategic alliance in the following terms:

The neoconservatives have given the signal for a total alliance with the Hebrew state, which finds the old Republican right wing more reticent than the old pacifist left of the Democratic party. Certainly, the Israeli aspiration to maintain a certain strategic independence, and privileged connections for example with Turkey, Russia, India and China more or less independent of Washington's diplomatic plans … may sometimes slow down the convergence between the two states, the greatest on the planet and one of the smallest. And yet, following the constitution of an inevitable Palestinian state and a more or less unilateral retreat by the Israelis from the West Bank and Gaza, the Hebrew state will only be able to find a stable foundation by accepting a kind of supervising mandate, which will clearly limit its sovereignty … Today, there are already more Israeli special forces fighting in Iraq in American uniform than there are on the West Bank and Gaza in their own uniform. Soon one of America's frontiers will lie on the Jordan, but this will be an electronic, cybernetic, ballistic frontier, leaving Jewish and Druze border guards the job of acting as police on the ground, vis-à-vis a Palestinian state that, closely tied to the most determined nationalist and Sunni forces, will always be part of the problem in the Middle East and not part of the solution. (pp. 97–8)

The author thus presents a picture of the major future orientations of the Israeli–American alliance, and the lasting changes it will imply in terms of the nature of the 'Zionist project'. His main thesis is the desire for national, political and strategic independence on the part of the Hebrew state, precisely the substance of the 'Zionist project', will have to be reformulated in the context of a 'total alliance' with American democracy as championed by the neoconservatives. And we can distinguish, in reading this text, three key reformulations of Jewish national independence, apparently made necessary both by the 'inevitable Palestinian state' and by the inevitable 'total alliance' with the United States that seems to be a correlate of this:

1) The Hebrew state's aspirations to multilateralism (Turkey, Russia, India, China) will have to fit into the strict framework of American national interests. In fact, once the 'inevitable Palestinian state' is established, 'the Hebrew state will only be able to find a stable foundation by accepting a kind of supervising mandate, which will clearly limit its sovereignty'. In other words, the state of Israel will be obliged to accept what America proposes for example to Iraq and Afghanistan today, a supervising mandate that clearly restricts their sovereignty in exchange for military protection.

2) The author goes on to make clear the nature of this limitation of Jewish national sovereignty in Palestine by asserting that 'there are already more Israeli special forces fighting in Iraq in American uniform than there are on the West Bank and Gaza in their own

uniform'. (And we note here he is far better informed than the London *Independent*, which only mentions 'military advisers', as cited by Tariq Ramadan, who can scarcely be suspected of minimizing this question.) In other words, the second constitutive requirement of the Zionist project, a Jewish national army charged with defending Jewish national sovereignty, is reformulated in terms of a 'total alliance' with the United States. The vocation of Israeli armed forces will be to fight outside Israel in American uniform.

3) Finally, the third constitutive requirement of the Zionist project, secure and recognized borders, is equally reformulated in this text, since the author informs us that 'soon one of America's frontiers will lie on the Jordan', so that Jewish national independence will consist in supplying the American democracy not just with 'Israeli special forces', but also with 'Jewish and Druze border guards' to survey the so-called American frontier on the Jordan, in other words, to 'act as police on the ground'. All the same, since this 'American mandate' over Palestine will be only supervisory, it seems these border guards will serve until further notice in Israeli uniform.

In the light of this prophetic picture drawn by Alexandre Adler, the successful project of Jewish national sovereignty in Palestine has no other future than the concept of an Israeli–American 'total alliance', 'a kind of supervising American mandate', the dispatch of Israeli special forces to other sites where this mandate is exercised (Iraq, Afghanistan, etc.) and a service as 'police on the ground' on America's frontier along the Jordan – all this in exchange for a guarantee to the Hebrew state of being under American military protection.[6] And the question then is to investigate how compatible this prophetic vision is with the Zionist convictions that the author elsewhere displays, particularly when he maintains: 'Zionism today is becoming as much an attachment tying the Jews of the diaspora to Israel as a national idea specific to Israel' (p. 238).

Heresy

In concluding his 2003 essay, Adler returns to the multifarious beneficial influence that American democracy exercises across the world, and particularly its relationship to the Jews and its support for Israel:

> There is finally a support for Israel, given that Jews from the world over have converged on the United States for a century and more, and these 'huddled masses', joined by the likes of Albert Einstein and the family of Thomas Mann, created in the space of two generations a culture that is determinant today for the Jewish people as a whole, a second Israel perhaps more important than the first in the Middle East. Everyone knows that the capital of the Jewish world today is neither Jerusalem, which remains a town encircled by the Arab world immediately outside its gates, nor even Tel Aviv that represents almost an intermediate step, but rather New York. (pp. 279–80)

On reading this text we can observe two shifts, which make it possible in retrospect to explain the manner in which Adler combines fidelity to Zionism on the one hand with promotion of the concept of an Israeli–American 'total alliance' on the other: (1) America has been a land of acceptance and refuge for generations of Jews from Central and Eastern Europe fleeing persecution (in particular Tsarist, then Soviet, and finally Nazi), hence the appearance of an American Jewish culture, and more specifically of a New York one. (2) This Jewish culture has become 'a second Israel perhaps more important than the first', by virtue of its determining character 'for the Jewish people as a whole' (first shift, in the form of a hypothetical: 'perhaps'). (3) 'Everyone knows that the capital of the Jewish world today is neither Jerusalem ... nor even Tel Aviv, but rather New York' (second shift, this time in the affirmative form of self-evidence: 'everyone knows'). The author thus passes from noting the birth of a Jewish–American culture in the twentieth century (as there have been many other

Jewish cultures throughout Jewish history, from Baghdad via Granada to Vilnius, from the Judeo-Arabic texts of Maimonides to the Yiddish theatre of Peretz, by way of Judeo-Spanish, etc.), to the conclusion that we are witnessing the birth of a 'second Israel' which he says is 'perhaps' more important than the first in the Middle East. There is an abyss, however, between noting a Jewish-American culture and the assertion that there is a second Israel possibly more important than the first, i.e. everything that distinguishes a Jewish minority in the diaspora from a Jewish sovereignty in Palestine – or more precisely, from the 'Zionist project' as defined by Golda Meir (a young Zionist militant in America before she settled in Palestine) in the following dialogue with a member of the last Anglo-American commission to investigate the situation in Palestine in 1946: ' "If the Jews as a minority had the same privileges that you promise the Arabs as a minority, do you consider they would be satisfied?" "No, sir", Golda Myerson replied. "There has to be a place in the world where the Jews are not a minority." '[7] But instructed now in the concept of an Israeli–American 'total alliance', the reader will understand that the vocation of Jewish national sovereignty provides the transition to a kind of American mandate over Palestine, that the demand formulated by Golda Meir is no longer pertinent, and indeed that the question arises as to which of the two Israels is the more important in terms of influence over the Jewish people as a whole. And once it is agreed that the vocation of Israeli soldiers is to fight in American uniform, even to serve as 'police on the ground' on America's frontier along the river Jordan, this question is purely rhetorical. In fact, it is assumed that Jerusalem remains the 'capital of the Jewish world' only for a few cranks who are attached to Jewish tradition, and that Tel Aviv has primacy over New York only for some other people, no less cranky, who still believe in the success – 'beyond all expectation' – of the 'Zionist project'. For everyone else, i.e. more or less 'the whole world' now converted to the Israeli–American 'total alliance', it is a publicly known fact that the capital of the Jewish world is New York, and the prime minister of Israel is … Paul Wolfowitz, 'a well-known Zionist'.

In the course of an interview with Elisabeth Schemla broadcast on the *Proche-Orient.info* site on 13 October 2003, Adler strongly asserted his Zionist convictions and expressed more vigorously still his feelings about 'those within the Jewish community who proclaim their anti-Zionism', and thereby 'run the risk of breaking in a definitive fashion the tie that unites them with other Jews of the diaspora'. He actually maintained to the interviewer:

> At bottom, Tariq Ramadan is neither terrifying nor sympathetic. I am far more shocked by Jewish traitors such as [Rony] Brauman and his kind. As for M. Mermet the Brezhnevian journalist, M. Langlois, director of *Politis*, and a few others, they know how to put things differently. And that's why it's impossible to trap those people. They seem to me infinitely more contemptible, infinitely more repugnant.[8]

According to 'Brauman and his kind' whom Adler refers to here, the policy that should be promoted in Israel-Palestine is the creation of a bi-national state, Jewish and Arab – but also Jewish, Muslim and Christian, since as they see it, so long as the conflict is dominated by ethnic or religious allegiance, no just and equitable peace is possible or sustainable. Against this vision of a bi-national state, Adler opposes the vision of an American mandate over Israel. We can immediately conclude that, in the eyes of an orthodox and consistent Zionist for whom only Jewish sovereignty in Palestine can fulfil the Zionist project, between these two visions that of 'Brauman and his kind' is clearly the lesser evil. In fact, nothing indicates 'the American odyssey' should be a priori homogeneous to the Zionist project, nor again to Jewish or biblical history – and this is the view of the author himself, who, though far from an orthodox Zionist, does know his classics. And it is only a short step from here to worshipping the Statue of Liberty.

ALAIN FINKIELKRAUT, *AU NOM DE L'AUTRE*,
OR THE MEMORY OF AUSCHWITZ

In a posthumous text titled *L'Europe et les Juifs*, taken from an
event at the Institut d'Études Lévinassiennes where he conversed
with Alain Finkielkraut* (reproduced in *La Confusion des temps*,
2004), Benny Lévy spoke of his 'unease' at reading his interlocutor's most recent work, more precisely the pages that explain
'the basis of what Alain Finkielkraut calls European consciousness
as bad conscience, as consciousness of its demons, as consciousness of the embodiment of evil, as consciousness of Auschwitz
as a kind of moral caution for the democratic process' (p. 31).
Lévy was referring here to Finkielkraut's book *Au nom de l'autre*.
Réflexions sur l'antisémitisme qui vient, and in particular to the paragraph beginning on page 13 and ending on page 15. With a view
to explaining the 'unease' Finkielkraut's prose seems to cause in
certain circles, it is useful therefore to put the passage in question in
its context.

Finkielkraut makes three assertions in this passage. The first is
that 'the memory of Auschwitz ... is *engrained*' (original emphasis), meaning engraved in stone, as immediately explained by a
quotation from François Furet which maintains that the memory
of Auschwitz 'has always stood out in sharper relief as the negative
accompaniment of democratic consciousness and embodiment of
the evil to which its negation leads'. In other words, 'the memory
of Auschwitz' has become the moral law of democratic consciousness, i.e. precisely its defining feature. The second assertion
is that only 'the memory of Auschwitz' can adequately fulfil this
function, which the author justifies by explaining that 'the criminal credo of the Nazis, and it alone, explicitly took as its target
universal humanity'. A quotation from Habermas is then given to

---

* Alain Finkielkraut: born in 1949, Paris. An essayist and philosopher, he
currently teaches at the École Polytechnique as professor of the 'history of
ideas and modernity' in the department of humanities and social sciences.
Author of many books and often visible in the media, he is known for his
provocative and conservative sallies.

explain this assertion, since 'as Habermas writes: "Something happened in the death camps that no one up till then would simply have been able to believe possible. This touched on a deep sphere of solidarity between all that bears a human face."' And this deep sphere of human solidarity, attained at Auschwitz as nowhere else, is what Alain Finkielkraut named earlier in his book as 'democratic man' or 'man with abstraction made of his origins' (p. 14), and finally, as 'universal humanity'. The third and final assertion here is that it is important to distinguish, on the subject of the 'memory of Auschwitz', between America and the rest of the world, since:

> The methodic and unprecedented assault on the other person that took place in the European theatre reflects onto America, more than any other political collectivity, an inverted image of itself. What is specific about democracy in the New World, in fact, is that it is not simply constitutional: it is *consubstantial* with the nation. No distinction can be made, in this country without an ancien régime, between the political regime and the country: the form *is* the content of national sentiment; the identity is embodied in the Statue of Liberty. [Original emphases]

To which the author immediately adds:

> Certainly, and this is the least one can say, America has not always matched up to its own definition: a museum of slavery would have a rightful place in Washington. It would, however, be picking a quarrel with the United States to suspect it of seeking to avoid recognizing its own crimes by the comfortable evocation of a distant genocide. A sincere stupor and a sacred horror inspired the building of this memorial [the Holocaust Memorial in Washington, DC].

America thus becomes, in Finkielkraut's text, 'the inverted image' of Auschwitz, witnessing to a democratic identity that is 'consubstantial' with the nation. Which is why, for Finkielkraut, only

America could be embodied in a Holocaust memorial or a Statue of Liberty, whereas for Lévy, this claim is precisely the embodiment of 'the consciousness of the modern Jew living in Europe after 1945' (*La Confusion des temps*, p. 31) – to which we should add: living in Europe, indeed, but equally of course in America. And the question for Lévy is to prescribe a remedy for his 'unease', drawing here on the Platonic analogy that the doctor is to the cook as the philosopher is to the orator – the point being that what Lévy prescribes with a view to satisfying the demand of 'an internal critique of this modern Jewish consciousness' is the rabbinical study of texts. In other words, Lévy's response to Finkielkraut is that there is no 'inverted image' of Auschwitz, there is only the uninterrupted continuity of the scholarly genealogies of Israel. These two positions are irreducible to one another: on the one hand a 'memory of Auschwitz' embodied in the Holocaust memorial or the Statue of Liberty, on the other hand the genealogical transmission of a knowledge embodied in rabbinical study of texts. Yet because our subject here is not the singularity of rabbinical knowledge, we shall tackle the question raised by Lévy from two other points of view: on the one hand that of the Zionist, on the other that of the Jewish champion of universalism.

The Zionist's critique of this 'modern' or 'communitarian' Jew, depending on the terminology adopted, seems at first sight as evident as could be, since it was a major ideological issue from the Eichmann trial in Jerusalem through to the last shot in Steven Spielberg's film *Schindler's List*. In effect, it precisely consists in presenting the state of Israel, rather than any other political collectivity, as the 'inverted image' of Auschwitz, and for the simple reason that the Nazis did everything to put into effect the 'final solution of the Jewish problem', whereas the American nation remained 'unharmed'.[9] And yet this would mean missing the essential point where the Jew of study (devoted to the Name), the Zionist (devoted to Jewish national sovereignty in Israel) and the Jewish champion of universality (devoted to the emancipation of all) come together. In fact, the Jew of study, the Zionist, and the Jew of universality all object, to the argument of Alain Finkielkraut, that America is no more 'consubstantial' with democracy than is France or Russia, since with regard to its necessarily egalitarian 'definition', the condition of their black population under slavery was no more democratic than that of the French or Russian peasants under the ancien régime – and this without 'picking a quarrel with the United States', but simply out of concern for a rigour that is at least logical, not to mention ethical. In all logic, the Zionist would add, if the question is to measure the degree of consubstantiality between a nation and democratic egalitarianism, it is the Israeli nation that takes the palm here, not America – even the America of 'this consciousness of the modern Jew living in Europe after 1945' – since, until the contrary is proved, Jewish national sovereignty here is based neither on the ruins of an ancien régime, nor on those of slavery, so that it can well claim a certain consubstantial relationship with democracy. (Apart from the fact that, to use a comparison dear to the historic leader of the PLO, Yasser Arafat, the 'Indians' of Palestine have grown increasingly numerous since the arrival of the first Zionist settlers, whereas the American Indians, close to 26 million when the first colonists arrived, were no more than a few tens of thousands by the end of the nineteenth century.) The sacralization of the name of America, inasmuch as it indicates a symptom, thus does not escape either the Jew of study, or the Zionist, or the Jew of universality, which allows them to pronounce, on the subject of the 'modern' or 'communitarian' Jew, if not a single remedy, then at least a single diagnosis. We suggest calling it the 'smug admiration of a statue'.

It remains none the less that a hypothetical alternative reading would permit the full coherence of Finkielkraut's text to be restored, and this without recourse to its value as a symptom. If he is actually maintaining (1) that Nazism took universal humanity as its target; (2) that democracy is not a political form historically *consubstantial* with Israeli national identity; and finally, (3) that slavery does not invalidate the idea that a democratic nation has of itself (in other words, 'blacks don't count'), he can indeed conclude that 'the methodical and unprecedented assault on the other person that took place in the European theatre reflects onto America, more than any other political collectivity, the inverted image of itself'.

ANDRÉ KASPI AND THE SINGULARITY OF 'ANTI-AMERICANISM'

In his book *Les États-Unis d'aujourd'hui* (1999), subtitled *Mal connus, mal aimés, mal compris*, the historian André Kaspi proposes to make the present-day United States better known, better loved and better understood.*

With this perspective in mind, his book is addressed above all to all those, particularly in France, who so readily and so unjustly succumb to the siren calls of anti-Americanism. This does not however mean he opposes these with the vision of those professing a 'smug admiration' for America, whose 'critical sense is enfeebled to say the least' (p. 27). What the author proposes is rather an instructed, nuanced and fair view of the country that is, has been and will be a land of liberty: 'America!'

André Kaspi writes that 'the inverse [of this "smug admiration"] has the name anti-Americanism', adding:

> But if equally to be condemned, this is less easy to define. The word dates from 1968, if we can believe the *Petit Robert*. Until then there existed only 'Americanism', defined as: 'Manner of being that imitates that of the Americans, in particular the inhabitants of the United States.' Ernest Renan illustrated it by observing that 'the world is heading for a kind of Americanism, which injures our refined ideas'. Anti-Americanism goes together with a

---

* André Kaspi: born in Béziers in 1937. Historian of the United States and from 1998 to 2006 professor of North American history at the University of Paris I, Sorbonne, and director of the Research Centre on North American History. Author of numerous books on the history of the US and of the Jews, as well as on international relations.

crowd of other antis, such as anti-Christianism, anti-racism, anti-clericalism, anti-Dreyfusard, anti-French, anti-naturalism, etc. The *Grand Larousse* dictionary of the French language lists thirty-two of these. What is perplexing is that none of these antis, except anti-Americanism, involves a foreign nation. It goes without saying that anti-Sovietism, which no longer has an object, had the function of opposing a regime, a political philosophy, and not the Russia that long embodied the Soviet system. (p. 28)

If 'anti-Americanism' is one of thirty-two nouns in the French language constructed with the prefix 'anti-', the author shares with us his perplexity at the appearance of this neologism, dating from 1968, since 'none of these antis, except anti-Americanism, involves a foreign nation'. And he justifies this remark by forestalling in advance the objection that 'anti-Sovietism' characterized opposition 'to a regime, a political philosophy' and not to a nation, even if 'Russia long embodied the Soviet system'. 'Anti-Americanism', on the other hand, according to Kaspi, targets not a 'regime' or a 'political philosophy', but a nation – hence his perplexity. Yet the date this neologism appeared, '1968', inevitably evokes the 'ideological revolt' of May 1968 and its international context,[10] the struggles of national liberation (Vietnam being the exemplar), the radical movement in America, and finally and above all, the Cold War opposing the two 'blocs': America at the head of the 'free world' on the one hand, Soviet Russia at the head of 'communism' on the other, so that it seems we must indeed relate the anti-Americanism in question 'to a regime, a political philosophy' more than to a nation, or at least in the same degree as anti-Sovietism, no matter the precise terms in which these are defined: democracy versus totalitarianism, imperialism versus communism, etc. Moreover, in the lines that immediately follow, Kaspi lists the four forms of anti-Americanism distinguished by Jean-Baptiste Duroselle (in *La France et les États-Unis, des origines à nos jours*, 1976). None of these four forms of anti-Americanism, as related by Kaspi, aims at the American nation rather than at a 'regime' or a 'political philosophy':

There was the systematic anti-Americanism of the Communists who were still denouncing the crimes of capitalism; that of the Gaullists struggling against the hegemony of the allied superpower; that of the defenders of the colonial empire who condemned the Americans' philosophy of liberation; that of the neutralists who maintained an equal distance from the Soviet Union and the United States. These all had in common that they made the United States an enemy to oppose. American culture put France in peril. Political and economic imperialism prejudiced our national independence. (pp. 28–9)

Whether the object was to denounce, (1) 'the crimes of capitalism', (2) 'the hegemony of the allied superpower', (3) 'the Americans' philosophy of liberation', or (4), like the neutralists, 'to maintain an equal distance from the Soviet Union and the United States', none of the four forms of anti-Americanism Kaspi lists, following J.-B. Duroselle, justifies his assertion that only anti-Americanism 'involves a foreign nation', as distinct from a 'regime' or a 'political philosophy'. Conversely, if there is a notion that seems to give a national identity to a 'regime' or a 'political philosophy', it is indeed that of 'anti-Americanism', in the four variants listed, to which 'pro-Americanism' precisely opposes the identification of 'America' with the 'free world', i.e. the homeland of liberty, or again, in Finkielkraut's expression, the country where 'identity is embodied in the Statue of Liberty'. We need then to elucidate the author's assertion, at first sight enigmatic, that 'none of these antis, except anti-Americanism, involves a foreign nation'.

Among the examples of words constructed with the prefix 'anti-', marking a strong opposition, Kaspi cites 'anti-Christianism' that challenges a religion, 'anti-racism' that challenges an ideology, 'anti-clericalism' that challenges the power or influence of the church, 'anti-Dreyfusard', which challenges the innocence of Dreyfus, 'anti-French', which does indeed challenge a nation, but not a foreign one, and finally 'anti-naturalism' that challenges the aesthetic and literary school that formed around Émile Zola and stood for exploration by the novel of society in all its aspects, precisely in the manner of a naturalist. But the question that a reader is bound to raise is how the words 'anti-Semitism' and 'anti-Zionism' should be characterized, for if these two 'antis' do not bear on a 'foreign nation', what exactly do they refer to? Let us examine this question.

a) *Anti-Semitism*. 'Anti-Semitism' is a neologism that appeared in the late nineteenth century (generally attributed to the journalist Wilhelm Marr), denoting a current of thought, opinion or prejudice hostile to Jews and ascribing to them negative racial characteristics allegedly specific to the 'Jewish nation' or 'Jewish people'. Historically, there have been two ways of opposing anti-Semitic ideology. The first is to oppose to the notion of national identity (German or French) that of citizenship, consequently dispatching ethnic origin and religious confession to the sphere of private particularism. An ethnic approach to national identities was thus opposed by a civic or political approach that combined under the concept of 'nation' French people of Jewish, Italian, Polish, German or other origin, or alternatively French people of Jewish, Protestant, Catholic or other confession. (This first option was particularly supported by the assimilated Jews of democratic Western Europe, in France above all.) The second option, supported particularly by the Jews of Central and Eastern Europe, consisted in struggling for Jewish national independence in Palestine – *Eretz Israel*. When Theodor Herzl, a Central European Jew who had largely assimilated – or rallied to – universalist and republican ideals, covered the 'Dreyfus affair' for a Viennese newspaper and discovered that revolutionary France, France of the 'Rights of Man and the Citizen', was pervaded by a fanatical anti-Semitism, he concluded that the regime or political philosophy of a country like France could not obscure the reality of a national identity that was historically hostile to Jews: the project of Jewish national independence was born, uniting the Viennese bourgeoisie and the Polish proletariat around the same objective, 'a place in the world where Jews are not a minority'. By this very token, Herzl seemed to maintain that anti-Semitism targeted 'a foreign nation', since it was in this sense that he formulated the Zionist project. Against Herzl, however, Kaspi seems to maintain that the Jews of France, Germany, Poland and Russia do not constitute a 'foreign nation', precisely in the sense that the citizens of a modern democratic state are all from different ethnic, national or religious origins, and that this identitarian origin relates exclusively to the private sphere. American citizens, on the other hand, by virtue of their national sovereignty, clearly comprise a 'foreign nation'. And the reader can now understand how, as distinct from an anti-Americanism that targets a sovereign 'foreign nation', anti-Semitism targets Jews who are assimilated among sovereign nations. The singularity of anti-Americanism, then, among all the other 'antis' that Kaspi lists and that leave him 'perplexed', is that only anti-Americanism involves a sovereign foreign nation.

b) *Anti-Zionism*. Anti-Zionism is an ideological current opposed to Zionism, i.e. opposed to the project of a Jewish national sovereignty in Palestine, but also to the effectiveness of this project, its success 'beyond all expectations' (Adler). Anti-Zionism has had, and still has, a number of different variants, including the anti-Zionism of the Jews of the Bund, partisans of a Jewish proletarian revolution in eastern Poland; that of internationalist Jews, partisans of a proletarian revolution knowing no national or identitarian claims; or again that of English Jewish notables, the main opponents of Chaim Weizmann in London when he sought to convince Lord Balfour and the British government to support the establishment of a 'Jewish national home' in Palestine – the decisive step on the road to Jewish sovereignty in the place, and replacing the mandate of the British empire over this land then populated principally by Arabs.[11] From the time of the military victory of 1967 and the conquest of Jerusalem by the Hebrew state, then from the 'ideological revolt' of May 1968, sympathy towards Israel – the state of the victims of Nazi genocide, the little progressive state confronting the reactionary Arab world – not only evaporated but turned into its opposite, and the victims of yesterday became 'a people sure of itself and dominating' (de Gaulle). Anti-Zionism was no longer principally an issue within the Jewish milieu, as in the early twentieth century, but an ideological current with several variants that were sometimes violently hostile to the state of Israel and openly anti-Semitic. For anti-Semitism, i.e. hatred of the Jews as a foreign nation exiled among sovereign nations, also found an extension in anti-Zionism, the challenge to Jewish sovereignty in Palestine. And so, if there is a 'foreign nation' that is distinct from a 'regime' or a 'political philosophy', it is indeed the Israeli nation, at least to the precise degree that anti-Zionism is (or can be) an extension of anti-Semitism. Hence the question: where does anti-Zionism come in, when 'what is perplexing is that none of these antis, except anti-Americanism, involves a foreign nation'? To answer this question, we need to grasp the successive shifts that we have noted on reading the previous authors, all involved in the current of thought known as 'communitarian'.

The position of Raphaël Draï, that of an orthodox Zionist, consists in maintaining the singularity of the name of Israel, located at the point of juncture, or exclusion, between the Christian West and the Islamic East, but also between democracy and totalitarianism, imperialism and communism, etc. This is because, in the last instance, Zionism rests on a singular utterance: that of Golda Meir who maintained in 1946 that 'there has to be a place in the world where Jews are not a minority', in other words, Jews are not ruled by a government whose identitarian or national substratum might at any moment resuscitate anti-Semitism from its ashes, leading to forced conversion, (geographical or legal) exclusion, extermination.

Starting from this axiom, we have shown the progressive slippages towards complacency that orient so-called 'communitarian' prose, in the event, four stages of one and the same process. The first slippage appears under the metaphor of the 'American rock', and consists in having the name of America appear in the place and instead of the divine Name which, at the origin of this metaphor in the Jewish Bible, is denoted by the 'rock of Israel'. In other words, the hypothesis of an original predisposition of America to support Israel, in the manner of the divine rock for Jacob, locates America in the place of God (in the biblical alliance). Hence the statement: Israel is under American providence. The second slippage consists in maintaining that 'everyone knows' that New York is today 'the capital of the Jewish world', which amounts to drawing the political conclusion that imposes itself in the wake of the first (religious) shift, i.e. that there is no sovereignty outside of God, as everyone knows. Hence the statement: Israel is under a kind of American mandate. The third slippage consists in deducing from this the theological–political law that then imposes itself on every democratic consciousness, i.e. that absolute Evil 'reflects onto America, more than any other political collectivity, the inverted image of itself'. Hence the statement: the Statue of Liberty embodies the memory of Auschwitz. Finally, the fourth slippage consists in investigating the singularity of the word 'anti-Americanism' in the place of and instead of the word 'anti–Zionism', a lapsus that sums up the three previous ones in a stripped down and laconic fashion: 'replacement of a sovereign Jewish nation by the smug admiration of a statue'.

Appendix: Origin and Continuity of 'Communitarian' Ideology from May 1968 to Today

The book by the psychoanalysts and political scientists Béla Grunberger and Janine Chasseguet-Smirgel, *L'Univers contestationnaire*, was published in 1969 under the pseudonym André Alexandre and reissued in 2004 under the authors' own names. In it they propose an analytic interpretation of the student movement of May 1968 that will enable us to explain, if not to elucidate, the origin of French 'communitarian' discourse.

THE NEW STUDENT ANTI–SEMITISM OF MAY 1968

Written in the heat of the events of May 1968 and the enthusiasm these aroused among many intellectuals, *L'Univers contestationnaire* presented as an exercise of analytic and political lucidity as to the true (psychic) nature of the student revolt. According to Grunberger and Chasseguet-Smirgel, the student movement of May 1968 represented contestation for its own sake: 'It is manifest that what matters to the contester is contestation' (p. 64). What does this 'contestation for its own sake' mean? The authors' thesis is that challenging bourgeois society is actually 'an attempt to eradicate the father, not to take his place but to maintain his non–existence'. This is also called by these authors an 'avoidance of Oedipus' as structuring complex. Their psychoanalytic interpretation sets out in fact to display a 'denial of the existence of generations', which necessarily takes the form of a challenge to the 'discourse of the father'. According to these authors, the 'father's' discourse is equally 'bourgeois' discourse and 'Jewish' discourse, an equivalence that immediately reveals the true issue in this exercise of applied psychoanalysis: to display the anti-Semitic wellspring of the ideological revolt of May 1968; hence a '*univers contestationnaire*' that echoes the title of David Rousset's 1946 memoir *L'Univers concentrationnaire.**

The analytical hypothesis of an identity between 'Jewish' and 'bourgeois' discourses is based on the following analogy: the student contesting of bourgeois discourse characteristic of May 1968 had its original prototype in the gospel's contesting of Jewish discourse, and translates analytically into contesting the discourse of the father as the discourse of law. In other words, the bourgeois is to the student of May 1968 what the Jew is to the Christian of the gospels, in the sense that both 'bourgeois' and 'Jew' are figures of the 'father' that rebellion seeks to deny. The Christian abolition of the Jewish law would thus be a manner of abolishing the structuring function that the father exercises for any desiring subject: Christian discourse is based on asserting the self-foundation of the son against the father, whereas Jewish discourse is based on the assertion and the memory of generational procreation. The preface to the new edition of *L'Univers contestationnaire* illustrates this on the basis of biblical genealogies taken from the book of *Genesis*, to reveal the importance of filiation in the structuring elaboration of the Oedipus complex. But this argument was already central to the authors' thesis in their original publication. Thus on page 73 they write:

If we examine the opposition between Judaism and Christianity alongside the parallel opposition between the religion of the father

---

* 'The Concentration-Camp World', translated into English by Yvonne Moyse and Roger Senhouse as *A World Apart*, London: Secker and Warburg, 1951.

and the religion of the son, it is easy for us to show the difference between the two confessions seen from the standpoint of education: the God of the Bible, a severe father, gives his people a strict regulation extending to all acts of life, and chastises them each time they turn away from the right path … As for Christianity, we maintain that it has freed the believer from the yoke of the Law, demanding Faith from him for all religious activity: his sins are pardoned in advance … (p. 73 n. 27, in the section titled 'Avoidance of the Oedipus complex and Christianity')

This 'difference' between Christianity and Judaism is based on what distinguishes the 'religion of the son' from the 'religion of the father', so that the analytic correspondence between the contester of May 1968 and the Christian of the gospels can be emphasized as follows:

The contester … contests the very existence of his historic and corporeal father … He cleaves the image of his father by cathecting a father who is more abstract and often evoked as a moral or aesthetic ideal, but who is in fact disembodied, obliterated and distant, more of a concept than a reality. Christianity, for its part, is indeed the story of a contested corporeal father. (p. 84)

Positing this analogy, the authors seek to demonstrate the effectiveness of their interpretative framework by proposing other transpositions of the analytic father/son paradigm, as in their interpretation of a passage from *Quelle Université? Quelle Société?* (a collective volume published by Éditions du Seuil in 1968):

The author who says about the riots in the Latin Quarter: 'raised in the culture of symbols and values, the students choose first of all to attack symbols and values: the tricolour flag, the national monument as place of pilgrimage', makes us think that the national monument is the tomb of the father. This reminds us that Nazi anti-Semitism began by profaning Jewish cemeteries, and that one of the main activities of the Chinese Cultural Revolution consisted in destroying funeral monuments and everything pertaining to the cult of ancestors. (pp. 52–3)

Attacking the 'national monument' as the 'tomb of the father' was thus symptomatic of a challenge to the discourse of the father, which these analysts discovered not only in the student revolt of May 1968, but also in Nazi anti-Semitism and the Chinese Cultural Revolution, with the difference that in the case of Nazism, as distinct from the cultural or student revolutions whether Chinese or French, the Jew was only the 'father' of the anti-Semite on the assumption that an identification between 'Jew' and 'father' was made, i.e. that 'Jew = father'. It was on this condition that the authors could conclude (or diagnose) that the student of May 1968 was to the bourgeois what the Nazi anti-Semite was to the Jew, as without this, such an analogy would be immediately invalidated by the fact that, even if it is granted that the bourgeois was indeed the 'father' of the contesting 1968 student in France or in China, it is much harder to accept that the Jew was the 'father' of the Nazi anti-Semite of 1933 in Germany. The methodological issue involved in this applied psychoanalysis would thus be to maintain the primacy of the analytic spirit over genealogical literalness, whatever the authors of biblical genealogies might say. We find an illustration of this, moreover, in the interpretation the authors offer here of the contesting imaginary: recalling that the law is an introduction to reality (of the other, of the world), they note that the bourgeois is identified with the impurity of matter and money (anality) in 'contestatory' literature, and conclude that the imaginary of May 1968 refers us to a logic of purification that was already at work in the psychology of the Nazi anti-Semite, in the sense that bourgeois 'vomit' embodies what is to be rejected as impure and excluded from student being-together. A quotation from Gilles Sandier is used to illustrate the analytic wellspring of hatred for the bourgeois in the contestatory psyche:

Sandier (*Combat*, 3 June) vilifies the supporters of de Gaulle in the following terms: 'All those who profit, exploit, repress and kill, all those who laugh, *pleasure* and *feast themselves*, all those who died of fright … these are the hordes that the fashionable districts have *vomited* onto the Champs-Élysées for this carnival … these battalions of rats still damp with sweat are a plague, the hordes of Poujade and Pétain, *discarded* soldiers, grocers, cashiers and daddy's boys, they're all here. The plainclothesman and the nun, the Gaullist party boss, the rentière from Passy, the parachutist on half-pay, the *scum* of the OAS and Occident, scabs, dealers of all kinds, pimps, decorated braggarts, *residues* of the old world.' (p. 119)

The words that the authors emphasize are designed to display the desire for purification that inspired the discourse of contestation and situates it in the imaginary of racist mythologies and the discourse of sadism.[12] The desire to destroy the Jews (at work in Nazism) and the desire to destroy the bourgeois (an ineffective fantasy in May 1968) would thus arise from the same psychic mechanisms. And since the bourgeois and the Jew are hated as figures of the father, and the psychic mechanisms observable in the contestatory discourse of the students of May 1968 are identical to those observable in the collective psychology of Nazism, it follows that the ideological revolt of May 1968 is, analytically speaking, an anti-Semitic revolt. Hence the paradox that, while the students demonstrated under the slogan 'We are all German Jews', the authors of *L'Univers contestationnaire* diagnose a crisis of acute anti-Semitism.

Rather than avoiding this paradox, the authors are eager to explain it, with recourse to the analytic concept of denegation. In other words, under the assertion 'We are all German Jews', the authors propose to understand 'We are not anti-Semites', as an instance of denegation. They write, in fact:

The objection could be made that the students demonstrated to shouts of 'We are all German Jews', which would prove they were expressing their sympathy with Jews and were thus not anti-Semitic. We have to reject this argument, since the contester continues to contest the father, and as the Jew is in the unconscious the prototype of the father, sooner or later, in one way or another, their projection will reappear and with it their anti-Semitism ... It is simply that on this occasion they revivify a direct paternal conflict that is still more or less unconscious, and there is no need to displace it onto the Jew, the real Jew being the father. The student's father, an ordinary bourgeois Frenchman, does not like the '*boches*' [Krauts], and despite everything remains in the best of cases a bit anti-Semitic. 'We are all German Jews' is nothing else in this sense than a challenge aimed at the father. (p. 91)

The students' slogan, then, despite appearances, is nothing other than the expression of a hatred that is analytically anti-Semitic, 'the real Jew being the father'. The proof is put forward as follows. Assume: (1) that the hatred of the father is the unconscious well-spring of the student movement of May 1968; (2) that 'the real Jew is the father', and not the German Jew; and finally (3) that 'the student's father ... remains a bit anti-Semitic' (towards German Jews). It then follows (4) that the slogan, 'We are all German Jews', is an anti-Semitic slogan. QED.

However, if *Genesis* is a story of filiation, it also serves to remove the parental function from the realm of myth and to enable the son to question the words of a living father, rather than the 'national monument' or the 'tomb of the father'. This is what Benny Lévy emphasizes when he raises the same objection that Freud raised on re-reading the biblical text: *Genesis* is the tale of a living father.[13] Consequently, to attack the symbols of France and its republic in 1968, or to attack the 'site of national pilgrimage', undoubtedly means contesting the discourse of the father, but this contestation has nothing to do with hatred of the Jew as analytic category of the 'father', except by failing to question the history and speech of a living father. And in this sense, the first lesson to draw from the tale of generations in *Genesis* is that the question

that the authors of *L'Univers contestationnaire* censor, not without
a certain denegation, is: who was the father that was contested
in May 1968 in France? Which is to say: who is 'the student's
father, an ordinary bourgeois Frenchman', but also (and in 'the
best of cases') 'a bit anti-Semitic'? Contestation of this very living
father, who moreover manifests himself as such,[14] is however the
literal sense of the long quotation from Gilles Sandier taken from
Combat magazine, whose anal imaginary the authors delight in
emphasizing – according to them a real anti-Semitic symptom –
while carefully avoiding the ideological imaginary that the letter
of this text combats, and that is evidently the ideological imaginary of the 'father'. The interpretation that substitutes the analytic
category of 'father' as discourse of the law for the contested historic father here acquires its unchallengeable therapeutic value, i.e.
the father who was 'a bit anti-Semitic' in June 1940 becomes the
'real Jew' in May 1968.[15]

The eighteenth Brumaire of the 'communitarian' intellectuals

In their preface to the reissue of *L'Univers concentrationnaire* in
2004, Grunberger and Chasseguet-Smirgel write: 'We noted how
the bourgeois and the Jew are more or less congruent in the criticism and hatred that is made of them (likewise the American
and the Jew, and this long before the very existence of Israel)'
(p. 28). This remark emphasizes the continuing topicality of this
essay in applied psychoanalysis. A book by Shmuel Trigano, *La
Démission de la République. Juifs et Musulmans en France* (2003) is
revealing in this respect about what links the so-called 'communitarian' intellectuals with the theses developed in *L'Univers
contestationnaire*, and by that same token, what links the contemporary philo-Semitic reaction with the analytic paradigm of May
1968. Trigano's main thesis is that the anti-Semitic violence that
has resurfaced in France must be placed in an ideological context
of the abandonment of the concept of national identity in favour

of that of citizenship. The 'dereliction' discussed in this work is in fact that of a republic whose national or identitarian wellspring has supposedly been abolished. It is this that Trigano calls a 'dereliction of identity' by the French republic (p. 104). The only way of resisting a dereliction of this kind, however, is to restore the discourse of the father. And this is precisely, according to him, 'the sacral function' of the Jew.

Chapter 7 of Trigano's book has the title 'The Moral Disarmament of French Society: What 11 September Revealed' (pp. 55–62). In this chapter, the author proposes a psychoanalytic interpretation of the 2001 attacks, and according to him, in fact, 'the attack triggered the manifestation of a syndrome that only psychoanalysis can explain'. As he immediately goes on to state, the analytic wellspring of these attacks – or this 'syndrome' – is that, so he explains, 'the figure of the powerful father who structures reality was then found to be broken'. In Trigano's eyes – those of a 'communitarian' psychoanalyst – the Pentagon and the World Trade Center inevitably evoked the 'figure of the father', an analytical hypothesis that is developed further on in the following terms:

> Parricide is fundamentally inscribed in an action of this kind. For it is the figure of the father that maintains the tension between these two principles [i.e. the reality principle on the side of the father, and the pleasure principle on the side of the mother], a tension without which return to the mother (and thus the domination of the pleasure principle) would be irresistible. (p. 58)

The hatred of the West that, according to the author, characterizes 'Islamo-progressives', is allegedly a hatred of the father, in other words a desire for emancipation from the reality principle embodied by the Pentagon and the World Trade Center, and, by way of these symbols, by Western civilization.[16] While taking up, extending and bringing up to date the theses of Grunberger and Chasseguet-Smirgel in *L'Univers contestationnaire*, Trigano casts a new light on the subject, since once hatred of the bourgeois and hatred of the Jew 'are congruent', just as are hatred of America and of Israel, it follows that in the contemporary – say, post-11 September – configuration, Islamo-progressives occupy the position that was formerly held by the Christian-leftists in May 1968. In other words, the analogy is now as follows: French or Western identity is to the 'Islamo-progressive' what the bourgeois was to the 'contestationary' student in May 1968. The analytic paradigm of May 1968 is thus refashioned to contemporary taste, having been relieved of its anti-Christian aspect, which is all the more awkward in that the new enemy is designated by the formula 'the Islamo-progessive clan' (title of chapter 5 in Trigano's book). The essential core of the analytic thesis of *L'Univers contestationnaire* remains intact, however – what threatens French society, 'seen in the light of the "Father"', is a 'moral collapse' that goes back to May 1968. Trigano writes: 'The misleading of collective consciousness is taking place in a French society where what Gérard Mendel describes as the "revolt against the father" has been under way for thirty years, since the rupture of 1968, breaking all the symbols of authority' (p. 60). To recast the broken symbols of authority is then the work to be accomplished, the point being to reconnect in all equanimity with the assertion of French identity. And this requires an investigation of the position of both Jews and Muslims, as in the book's subtitle, 'Jews and Muslims in France'. It seems, in fact, as if this position has always been a question or a problem. The author reminds us, moreover, in an aside to his text (as he recalls his particular vigilance on this subject):

> Entry into this identity that is called 'France', which I do not develop any mystique about (as such a mystique was often anti-Semitic), but which I consider as a given, necessary to its emotional and political stability, presupposes on the part of Muslim Arabs a complete remaking of their identity, their religion, and also their psychology. (p. 91)

The question thus arises as to what the 'entry' of Jews 'into this identity that is called "France"' involves, in past, present and future.

Trigano's response to this question is chiefly to be found in chapter 16 of his book, titled 'The Issue', which opens with the following words: 'The problem with which we are faced is simple … The dereliction of French identity places democracy, liberty and equality in danger. If it is buried, it paves the way for chaos and mediocrity' (p. 119). This 'problem', or 'dereliction', is referred to further on as a 'syndrome', the author maintaining that there is 'a psychoanalytic dimension in the syndrome that we shall analyze', which immediately refers us to 'what was revealed by 11 September'. And in point of fact, Trigano analyzes the 'syndrome' of French identity as he analyzes the 'syndrome' of Western identity, diagnosing a challenge to French identity by an 'Islamo-progressive clan' that in this way contests the discourse of the father: 'When the image of authority (the father) is overthrown, there follows a situation of disorder and war of all against all (the war of the sons), until the moment that the need for authority to settle differences (the law of the father) is restored.'

Overthrowing the image of the father is decidedly what the Islamo-progressives and other '68ers were about, threatening France and the West in this way with falling into chaos. And it is here that the function of the Jew enters the scene:

> In this perspective, appeal to Jewish figures acquires an unsuspected meaning, since in the imaginary of Islam and Christianity the Jew represents the figure of that which precedes, of anteriority, i.e. of the father – the father who has been eliminated in the interest of self-assertion. The father who is hated because he embodies the Law that is necessarily experienced as repressive since it separates you from the proximity of the mother. He is envied and desired because without this Law there is only chaos and desolation. Separation is the constitutive principle of subjective identity. Here we see the source of the sacral function assumed by the Jews today. (pp. 120–1)

The author's response is therefore to introduce the analytic thesis of Grunberger and Chasseguet-Smirgel: that Jewish discourse is the discourse of the father, of the law, and here we have 'the sacral function assumed by the Jews'. And when the authors of *L'Univers contestationnaire* resort to biblical genealogies, Trigano, for his part, resorts to the register of metaphor to signal what the capital letter in the word 'Law' owes to this same Bible, spelling out that 'without this Law there is only chaos and desolation', words that evidently echo the famous *tohu wa bohu* of the first verses of *Genesis*, which the author proposes here to translate as 'chaos and desolation'.

The conjunction in the subtitle of Trigano's book, linking 'Jews and Muslims in France', thus conceals a key distinction between Jews and Muslims, since the Jews have already given the word 'Law' its capital letter, thereby conferring on the image – or images – of the father a sacred aura, whereas the Islamo-progressives have the unconscious desire of an incestuous return to the mother. All the same, the sense of the word 'Law' in Trigano's text – as in the writings of 'communitarian' intellectuals in general – should not be misconstrued. In no way does 'Law' here refer to the Hebrew word *torah*, which means teaching and indicates the observation and study of rabbinical doctrine, but rather to a historic founding moment in French Judaism, as distinct from Arab Muslim immigration:

> The entry of Jews into the French nation – no matter that they had already been geographically in France for centuries – was effected under the aegis of an assembly convened by Napoleon in 1807 to respond (in a quasi-communitarian way) to twelve extremely vexing questions, designed to judge their capacity (and their desire) to become French. These questions covered all areas of existence, from personal status and the laws that governed this to their relationship to France and the French, including the power of the rabbis and economic morality. (pp. 122–3)

And at the end of this assembly, the author reminds us, the Jewish notables summoned by Napoleon

> together took decisions that were religiously binding and amounted to disassociating religious laws from the civil and political laws of Judaism, declaring the latter null and void in favour of French law, and going so far as to proclaim that obeying the laws of the state was a religious duty for Jews. (pp. 123–4)

It would seem, then, that if the capital 'L' for Law in the texts of the 'communitarian' ideologists in no way supports a rabbinical study of biblical verses, any more than the assertion of Jewish sovereignty in Palestine, it does on the other hand indicate a protestation of allegiance to the Empire or some other 'image of authority': 'a complete reform of their identity, their religion, and also their psychology'.[17]

2

On Ethno-Cultural Sociology

We are so little accustomed to treating social facts scientifically, that certain propositions contained in this book may surprise the reader. However, if a science of societies exists, one must certainly not expect it to consist in a mere paraphrase of traditional prejudices, but rather cause us to see things in a different way from the ordinary man, for the purpose of any science is to make discoveries, and all such discoveries more or less upset accepted opinions.

– Émile Durkheim, preface to the first edition of *Rules of the Sociological Method*

Just as the state evangelizes when, although it is a state, it adopts a Christian attitude towards the Jews, so the Jew acts politically when, although a Jew, he demands civic rights.

– Karl Marx, 'On the Jewish Question'

September 2002 saw the publication of a collection of testimonies from secondary-school teachers in state education: *Les Territoires perdus de la République. Antisémitisme, racisme et sexisme en milieu scolaire.* The book came with an introduction and conclusion by Emmanuel Brenner,[1] and this first volume produced by Brenner was followed by a second, *'France, prends garde de perdre ton âme …' Fracture sociale et antisémitisme dans la République*, which was this time written entirely by himself. The second book, published to coincide with the re-issue of the first in 2004, extended the original argument that the categories of socio-economic analysis are inadequate to tackle the 'reality on the ground' in the school environment, and that the 'sociological illusion' inherited from Émile Durkheim needed nowadays to be replaced by the ethno-cultural sociology of Emmanuel Brenner.[2] As Thomas Deltombe wrote in *L'Islam imaginaire*:

> *Les Territoires perdus de la République* ... was to have great success with the media and the political class in the course of 2003. References to the *Territoires perdus* turned up in speeches by Roger Cukierman, Jean-Pierre Raffarin and Jacques Chirac. The rapporteur of the Stasi commission on secularism, Rémy Schwartz, also confessed that he had been much inspired by this book, so the claim could be made on the book's re-issue in 2004 that it had 'turned around the debate on secularism in education'. (pp. 304–5)

This was similarly emphasized by Alain Gresh in his book *L'Islam, la République et le monde*:

> *Les Territoires perdus de la République* contributed to defining the 'world view' of many teachers and many politicians. 'I have been struck by the testimonies collected in the book on the lost territories of the Republic', Jean-Pierre Raffarin maintained in a speech of 24 September 2003, on the sixtieth anniversary celebration of the CRIF, while Jacques Chirac, in a speech at Valenciennes on 21 October, called for the 're-conquest of the lost territories of the Republic'. (p. 315)

Given the fact that the democratic consensus of the National Assembly on what is popularly known as 'the law on the veil' – officially a law prohibiting the wearing of an 'ostensible sign' of religious allegiance on the premises of a state school – sanctioned this turnaround in the debate on secularism, what is involved here is clearly a real social process, combining a historical situation (the 'school environment' in contemporary France), a political slogan (re-conquering the 'lost territories of the Republic'), and its legislative sanction (the consensus in the National Assembly on a law banning pupils of any sex or religion from covering their hair on the premises of the French Republic's schools).

EMMANUEL BRENNER'S SOCIOLOGICAL THESIS

The sociological thesis of Emmanuel Brenner* is that the resurgence of anti-Semitic speech, action, and more generally behaviour in the school situation is essentially attributable to children of Maghrebian origin, and that this 'ethno-cultural origin' of the pupils accused is a key element – or a factor determinant in the last instance – in explaining the cause of the 'new anti-Semitism' in France. Brenner's sociological argument basically involves: (a) a set of observed facts from the testimonies of teachers collected in *Les Territoires perdus de la République,* from which he concludes that anti-Semitism in the school environment is mainly, if not exclusively, a Maghrebian phenomenon; (b) his sociological explanation of this phenomenon that Maghrebian culture is traditionally an anti-Jewish culture; and finally, (c) the methodological conclusions he proposes to draw from this, which take the form of a critique of the 'sociological illusion'.

The facts observed

The essentially Maghrebian origin of anti-Semitism in the school environment is presented first of all as an observed fact. And indeed, several of the testimonies gathered in *Les Territoires perdus*

---

* Emmanuel Brenner: pseudonym used by the historian Georges Bensoussan, born in Morocco in 1952. Bensoussan is the director of the *Revue d'histoire de la Shoah du Mémorial de la Shoah* and author of several books on the Holocaust, Israel and a major intellectual and political history of Zionism.

de la République go out of their way to stress the Maghrebian origin of pupils identified as guilty of anti-Semitic actions or speech.[3] The first of the teachers' testimonies in the volume, 'Sur l'antisémitisme des élèves de collège à Saint-Denis (Seine-Saint-Denis)', by Iannis Roder, senior teacher of history and geography, is particularly significant in this respect, since it opens and closes with such an assertion. His opening sentence runs as follows:

> In the course of teaching for the last several years in the department of Seine-Saint-Denis, more particularly in Saint-Denis itself, I have had cause on many occasions to note an anti-Semitism that is often present, and sometimes virulent, on the part of students who mainly originate from Maghrebian immigration. (p. 81)

And the author concludes his testimony with a sentence that returns once again to the Maghrebian origin of the pupils accused: 'A few corrections will not now be enough to stem the proliferation of anti-Semitic talk and allegations, particularly among our pupils of Maghrebian origin' (p. 91). The volume's subtitle, *Antisémitisme, racisme et sexisme en milieu scolaire*, is thus related right from the start to the Maghrebian component in the French 'school environment'. Moreover, the other testimonies collected by Emmanuel Brenner seem largely to confirm this first one, since either the origin (French, Maghrebian or other) of the accused pupil is not mentioned, or else it is implicitly mentioned by giving the first name (Muslim-Arab) of the pupil involved, or it is mentioned explicitly. By way of illustration, we can take the following testimonies: (1) On pages 94–5, a letter from teachers at the Lycée Bergson mentions two girls singled out by fellow pupils, who were humiliated, insulted and molested because of their Jewish origin, but without the identity of the aggressors being made clear other than by the words 'pupils' or 'their tormentors'. (2) On pages 144–7, a testimony relates the anti-Semitic words of a pupil called 'Tarek'. If ethno-cultural identity is not otherwise specified, it is thus implicitly emphasized by the first name of the pupil, as it is by the account that follows and presents the hostility of 'Muslim' pupils to a fellow-pupil who was herself Muslim but had the non-Muslim name 'Joëlle'. (3) Pages 109–12 contain five testimonies from teachers in the department of Val-d'Oise. Four of these five explicitly mention the ethno-cultural identity of certain pupils, and with the first three of these it is left to the reader to conclude that they are guilty of (a) negationist statements made in a *terminale* (final year of secondary school) class in which 'there are several Muslim pupils' (p. 109); (b) anti-Semitic statements recurrently made in another *terminale* class 'including several pupils of Maghrebian origin' (p. 110); then (c) a teacher explains that 'violent attacks on Christianity and Judaism on the part of several pupils of Maghrebian origin forced him to cover the section of the syllabus on religions very briefly and summarily' (p. 111). On the other hand, (d) the fourth testimony only reports that, 'according to some pupils', Dreyfus was 'a cunning Jew who deserved to end up in prison' (p. 112). Finally, (e) the last testimony relates 'the words pronounced by an unidentified pupil among a group of boys of Maghrebian origin: "Hitler was right, we should have continued his work!"' (p. 112). These five testimonies from teachers in the Val-d'Oise thus signal the very high proportion of anti-Semitic (and sometimes anti-Christian) incidents that to all appearance involve pupils of Maghrebian origin, in this case four out of five. They equally suggest that when ethno-cultural origin is not specified, as in (d), it is either implicit, particularly by the repetitive character of the tag 'Maghrebian origin' that precedes or follows the testimony, or else that in the case of a pupil or individual of non-Maghrebian origin, their ethno-cultural origin (French, European, Asian or other) is not significant. Finally, these testimonies present being of Maghrebian origin and being Muslim as equivalent, since the mention 'Muslim' follows the mention 'of Maghrebian origin', implying an equivalence between Maghrebian origin and African origin, at least when the object is to point out the Muslim religion of the accused pupils, as shown by a further testimony that mentions the refusal of certain pupils to observe a minute's silence on the day after the attacks of 11 September 2001, these being described as 'all pupils of Maghrebian or black African origin, and Muslim' (p. 108). It is then taken as established fact, something observed, that anti-Semitism in the school environment is 'mainly' the act of pupils issuing from Maghrebian or Muslim–Arab immigration, or more generally pupils of Muslim religion. Once these observed facts are noted, they then have to be explained. The introductory section by Emmanuel Brenner, titled 'A Nation in Disarray' and preceding the testimonies of these teachers, sets out to offer an analysis of the causes of the anti-Semitism, racism and sexism that are rampant in the school environment today.

The ethno-cultural explanation

The explanation that serves to illuminate this whole series of observed facts runs as follows, put forward by Brenner in the very first lines of his argument:

> In January 2002, Majib Cherfi, lead singer of the musical group Zebda – associated with the Toulouse '*motivé-e-s*'* – declared in an interview with *Le Nouvel Observateur* (no. 1942): 'When I was small, we didn't like Jews. My parents were anti-Semitic like people are in the Maghreb. The word "Jew" in Berber is an insult. It wasn't about Palestine or politics, it's just how it was. You didn't like Jews except for those that you knew.' Did the journalist distort Cherfi's statements? As it happens, many young Maghrebians confirm that there is a long tradition of anti-Judaism in the Maghreb, consisting more often in contempt rather than hatred, and occasionally flaring up into bouts of violence. It is this kind of anti-Semitism that Arab-Muslim immigration into our country has introduced in France. (p. 14)

* This political movement created in Toulouse by Zebda was of a broad left character, standing for 'political democracy' and reaching out particularly to young people of immigrant background.

The testimony of this singer of Maghrebian origin thus confirms the existence of 'a tradition of anti-Judaism in the Maghreb', since as Majib Cherfi put it: 'The word "Jew" in Berber is an insult.' And the cause of anti-Semitism in the school environment is thereby elucidated: the origin of this resurgence of anti-Semitism has to be sought in Maghrebian culture. Brenner stresses this still more forcefully when he asserts that 'it is this kind of anti-Semitism that Arab–Muslim immigration into our country has introduced', suggesting in this way that the tradition of 'contempt' for the Jews, 'occasionally flaring up into bouts of violence', is foreign to 'our country'. Nevertheless, on page 71 Brenner qualifies this position, since he now writes that Maghrebian anti-Semitism 'is reintroducing into France the anti-Semitic plague that educational effort has taken more than half a century to stem and then push back'. The implication here is that contemporary anti-Semitism, or the 'new anti-Semitism', has a different origin from the anti-Semitism observed in France in the past (the 'old anti-Semitism'). The case remains, however, that according to Brenner what we see today is a specifically Maghrebian anti-Semitism to which France or citizens of non-Maghrebian origin are supposed to be largely immune. Thus on page 32 he cites the testimony of a teacher of French who reports that, during a lecture on Primo Levi's *If This Is a Man*, 'the only opposition came from two Maghrebian pupils who refused the work proposed: "We don't like it, it's stories about Jews."' And the reason for this refusal, according to Brenner, was therefore the Maghrebian origin of these two pupils.

Critique of the 'sociological illusion'

Once the facts are observed and explained, conclusions can be drawn regarding the debate between two sociological approaches, illustrated here by Stéphane Beaud and Michel Pialoux on the one hand, the authors of *Violences urbaines, violences sociales. Genèse des nouvelles classes dangereuses* (2003), and Brenner on the other.

One of these approaches (Beaud and Pialoux) privileges socio-economic determinations, the other (Brenner) ethno-cultural ones. Brenner compares these two sociological approaches, then proposes a critique of Beaud and Pialoux's 'sociological illusion', a critique that gives its title to the first part of his second book, *'France, prends garde de perdre ton âme …'* After evoking the socio-economic roots of the *'banlieue* malaise' (unemployment, urban, economic and social exclusion, racism) and accepting the undeniable character of all this as shown by a number of studies, Brenner seeks to refute the idea that these socio-economic causes are determinant in the last instance, and to focus rather on what socio-economic categories help conceal, i.e. the ethno-cultural causes of this 'malaise' (p. 30). And indeed:

> If the social roots of the disarray, not to say despair, of a large number of these young people of Maghrebian origin are patent, those who rightly bring them to light are unfortunately just as guilty of the sociological illusion and ultimately of political naivety. (p. 30)

The 'sociological illusion' and 'political naivety' that, according to the author, characterize the study of Beaud and Pialoux, are then spelled out as follows: 'In analyzing the deviant behaviour of a fraction of young people of Maghrebian origin (almost exclusively boys), Beaud and Pialoux refuse to proceed to a cultural analysis, which to their minds is undoubtedly suspect of essentialism, thus basically of racism' (pp. 31–2), and it is accordingly this refusal 'to proceed to a cultural analysis' that leads the two sociologists to the conclusion: 'Nothing here would signal a cultural background, rather than simply a "counter-violence opposed to the social violence that has been done to them"' (pp. 39–40). A methodological position such as this, however, is precisely what Brenner rejects:

Apropos behaviour that they themselves characterize as 'deviant' and 'provocative', hostile to the 'White world' and the 'established order' (sic), the two sociologists, in 425 pages, do not once utter the word 'anti-Semitism'. Yet everyone knows the extent to which hatred of Jews obsesses a large part of these *banlieues*, and more specifically a section of the Maghrebian population that live there.

In fact, according to Brenner, this hostility to the 'White world' and the 'established order' should have led these two sociologists to investigate the anti-Semitism that is rampant today in the *banlieues*, 'more specifically' among Maghrebians. Finally, given the reason for the 'sociological illusion' is the desire to distance oneself from a culturalist approach suspected of 'essentialism' or even 'racism', ethno-cultural sociology takes as its watchword the intention of breaking taboos, a watchword that serves as a programme and targets both sociologists and politicians:

A section of the political class seems paralysed in the face of this tendency, since the new configuration of danger forces it to jettison so many intellectual schemas that have become obsolete. Anti-Semitism of Maghrebian origin is one of those awkward subjects that people scarcely speak about. (p. 62)

Replying to 'the Islamist Tariq Ramadan', Brenner therefore calls on the political class and 'Western intellectuals' to open their eyes to 'the reality on the ground' and free themselves from 'obsolete intellectual schemas':

Now, far from putting an end to the hypocrisy that brings our citizens into disrepute, the Islamist Tariq Ramadan, the object of adulation in the '*cités*', declared on 8 November 2003, despite the reality on the ground: 'Anti-Semitism in France is supposedly the work of Muslim Arabs, and so a community is stigmatized in an unacceptable manner. This is a staggering analysis.' It is only by naming the reality that a diagnosis can be made of the anti-

Semitism that is winning over our country, only on this condition that solutions can be drawn up … Everyone knows the reality, but in the house of France, they all prefer to keep silent even though the flames of the fire are already licking their walls. The fear of being labelled 'Islamophobic' and classed as a 'covert supporter of Le Pen' is only equalled in our contemporary history by the cowardice … with which so many Western intellectuals bowed the knee to Communist tyranny. (*'France, prends garde …'*, pp. 79–80)

Yet it is the reference to Munich as symbol of the resignation of the Western democracies in the face of Nazi peril that remains Brenner's privileged point of reference throughout both these books, even providing the title for the second, 'France, guard against losing your soul …', a reference to the title of a Resistance text written in 1941 by the Jesuit Gaston Fessard. And indeed, Brenner describes the situation in France as 'a tendency that evokes the climate of the 1930s'.

Basing himself on the testimonies of teachers faced with the 'reality on the ground', on the confessions of a single Maghrebian and on an ethno-cultural methodology, Brenner concludes that the anti-Semitic behaviour observed in the school environment today, and by extension in the whole of French society, is mainly, if not essentially, the act of Arabs, and that it is urgent to have the sociological and political courage to recognize this. And yet the conclusions Brenner draws are in no way presented as the results of a sociological construction, marking the transition from a pre-conceptual approach to the methodical construction of a social fact, but as already common knowledge, since 'everyone knows the extent to which hatred of the Jews obsesses a large part of the *banlieues*, and more specifically a section of the Maghrebian population that live there' – 'everyone knows the reality'. In other words, Brenner's sociological study essentially consists in saying out loud what 'everyone knows'. We only need Monsieur

Jourdain to conclude: 'So I was doing ethno-cultural sociology without knowing it!'

The echoes of this exercise in ethno-cultural sociology, right up to the highest circles of state, do indeed attest to its wide audience. The scandal that followed the statements Alain Finkielkraut made to the Israeli newspaper *Haaretz* (17 November 2005) then appears only the more unfair, simply revealing the 'intellectual Munich' that Brenner denounces, since Finkielkraut did no more than substitute an 'ethno-religious' sociology of his own coinage for Brenner's 'socio-cultural' sociology. In this interview,[4] in fact, Finkielkraut explained:

> In France, they would like very much to reduce these riots to their social dimension, to see them as a revolt of youths from the suburbs against their situation, against the discrimination they suffer from, against unemployment. The problem is that most of these youths are blacks or Arabs, with a Muslim identity. Look, in France there are also other immigrants whose situation is difficult – Chinese, Vietnamese, Portuguese – and they're not taking part in the riots. Therefore, it is clear that this is a revolt with an ethno-religious character.

Further on, moreover, Finkielkraut concludes that the causes of these riots, which he describes as a real 'anti-republican pogrom', have to be sought in Muslim culture:

> We are witness to an Islamic radicalization that must be explained in its entirety before we get to the French case, to a culture that, instead of dealing with its problems, searches for an external guilty party. It's easier to find an external guilty party. It's tempting to tell yourself that in France you're neglected, and to say, 'Gimme, Gimme'. It hasn't worked like that for anyone. It can't work.

This is precisely the same as Emmanuel Brenner's ethno-culturalist approach, applied this time to the urban riots of October–November 2005: (1) observation of the fact that this violence is not characteristic of all populations that are socio-economically disadvantaged, but particularly 'of blacks and Arabs, with a Muslim identity'; (2) explanation by ethno-cultural origin that in Arab–Muslim, or more broadly, Islamic culture, the 'other', the 'foreigner', is identified as the cause of all problems; and finally, (3) the necessary critique of 'sociologism' that follows from this, of the explanations put forward by all those 'who would like at all cost to reduce these riots to their social dimension'.[5] Brenner and Finkielkraut thus coincide in an ethno-cultural or ethno-religious analysis that relates anti-Semitism, racism and sexism in the school environment, along with the urban riots of winter 2005, to the presence of populations originating from the Maghreb, or more broadly from Islamic countries, on the territory of the French Republic. And once it is established that to attack Jews, the forces of order, or private property (cars parked on the public highway) are all so many ethno-cultural or ethno-religious attitudes specific to populations originating from the Islamic countries, then the term 'pogrom' is able to serve as a link between different forms of violence attributable to 'blacks or Arabs'. Should we then conclude that Brenner's sociological analyses, and those of Finkielkraut, signal 'a culture that, instead of confronting its problems, seeks an external guilty party'? In answering this question, we shall impose on ourselves the rule of resorting only to documents Brenner cites in his two books, therefore the testimonies collected in *Les Territoires perdus de la République*. Does any reading of these testimonies that is at all critical reasonably permit the conclusion to be drawn that anti-Semitism, racism and sexism in the school environment – and by extension, in the whole of French society – are essentially or in the main the act of populations of Maghrebian origin? Or is this just a xenophobic exaggeration?

MAGHREBIAN ANTI–SEMITISM: TWO CASE STUDIES

A collection of testimonies is an analytical tool whose particular character lies precisely in the notion of 'testimony', since, as distinct from statistical data, the testimony of a teacher is first and foremost the word of an actor engaged in the reality he or she describes, which makes for both its strength and its weakness: strength in the sense that teachers are the individuals best placed to inform us about the development of anti–Semitic behaviour in the school environment; weakness in that their testimony necessarily bears an aspect of subjectivity, arbitrariness and personal conviction. With a view to reducing the necessarily subjective dimension of a testimony, while making best use of the valuable light it casts on the 'reality on the ground', the sociologist will then set out: (1) to collect a wide range of testimonies from teachers with a view to ensuring the greatest possible plurality of experiences and subjectivities; (2) to gather testimony from other actors involved in the reality on the ground (for example *surveillants*,* pupils, and their parents); and (3) to approach the testimonies collected with a critical eye, particularly inquiring as to what the testimony shows in the way of subjectivity, and therefore what it tells us about the witnesses themselves and the prism through which they inform us about *their* reality on the ground.

The cover of this book proclaims: 'edited by Emmanuel Brenner', adding the names of a number of authors: 'Arlette Corvarola, Sophie Frehadjian, Élise Jacquard, Barbara Lefebvre, Iannis Roder, Marie Zeitgeber', as well as 'other secondary school teachers'. Out of a total of 238 pages, the actual testimonies from teachers make up only 120 (pp. 86–206), the first part of which are divided into fifteen texts each headed by a title (in bold type) and with the name of the author placed at the end; this series is then followed by a long testimony from Élise Jacquard (pp. 161–206), which is

---

* The *surveillant* in a French school is responsible for maintaining discipline in class, and supervising pupils in the absence of a teacher. This is translated below as 'monitor'.

presented as a case study on the deterioration of working conditions at a technical *lycée* in Paris: 'A Case of De-schooling'. This kind of presentation confers on the whole ensemble the effect of plurality. But that remains largely a mere 'effect', since the names of the same teachers recur regularly in the course of the fifteen testimonies, so much so that three of them – Barbara Lefebvre, Sophie Ferhadjian and Arlette Corvarola – together supply nine of the fifteen testimonies, more than half of those collected. A detailed study of two of these will thus supply a great deal of information as to the tenor of this work.

First case study: Barbara Lefebvre, 'On the Ambiguous Role of Certain Mediators'★

We propose to show, by a thorough and exhaustive commentary on one of the testimonies from Barbara Lefebvre (pp. 95–9), a senior teacher in history and geography, the subjective aspect that governs every testimony, and thereby the manner in which the notion of 'anti-Semitism in the school environment' is an unclear and confused notion, as long as it is not subject to critical analysis. The question of the resurgence of anti-Semitism, like that of its attribution to a population of Maghrebian origin, presupposes in fact a preliminary agreement as to what should be classed as 'anti-Semitism' (likewise 'racism' and 'sexism'), as well as what justifies attributing it to this or that individual of Maghrebian origin.

This testimony from Barbara Lefebvre opens with the following words: 'Up till now, in this establishment in the department of Hauts-de-Seine, I have not been the victim of verbal aggression with an anti-Semitic character, and yet the climate is far from healthy in this respect.' It may seem somewhat surprising that this first sentence informs us that the teacher has 'not been the victim of verbal aggression with an anti-Semitic character', since

---

★ The 'mediator' (*médiateur*) in a French school has the function of facilitating communication between teachers, pupils and parents.

on the one hand, as she will make clear later on, nothing indicates that she is Jewish, while on the other hand the question is more of knowing whether she has *witnessed* 'verbal aggression with an anti-Semitic character' or more broadly anti-Semitic statements (on the occasion of a dispute between pupils, during a lesson, etc.). As it happens, she does not report having witnessed such incidents 'up till now, in this establishment in the department of Hauts-de-Seine'. The reader's attention, however, is aroused by the mention of a 'climate' in the establishment which is supposedly revelatory of a resurgence of anti-Semitism in the school environment, and her testimony promises to inform us about the nature of a 'climate' that is 'far from healthy in this respect':

> In the course of the year 2000–2001, the presence of two monitors of Maghrebian origin considerably undermined the educational work conducted by the administration and the teachers. These two young students recruited by the rectorate turned out to be particularly successful political and religious activists. Over the year, one of them even adopted in his choice of clothing signs that left no doubt as to his opinions: long white tunic, Islamic goatee, little white crocheted skullcap. This individual exerted a real fascination in the school on the 'budding headmen' of Maghrebian origin, developing a rigorist discourse towards them (no alcohol, no drugs, no sex), the 'lifestyle choice' of Islamic militants of Wahhabi obedience who dress up their political project in a social discourse with moralistic and pseudo-religious pretensions. Only a few Arab girls clearly expressed their rejection of this propaganda. Some of them, in fact, complained to the mediators (three youth jobs recruited by the school head for a five-year contract) and to certain teachers of Maghrebian origin: according to them, this monitor was harassing them psychologically by condemning their clothing and their behaviour, which he claimed was too Westernized for proper young Muslim women.

The 'far from healthy climate' then involves 'the presence of two monitors of Maghrebian origin'. Yet only 'one of them' showed, by his dress and discourse, a behaviour that could be classed as religious proselytism on the premises of a secular educational establishment, which first of all shows it is not 'Maghrebian origin' in question here, but rather the confusion that this person made between the state school and a (Muslim) religious school. And this is highlighted all the more by the fact that the 'Arab girls' who were unhappy with his 'propaganda' complained in particular to 'certain teachers of Maghrebian origin', which demonstrates perfectly that being 'of Maghrebian origin' in no way means that one confuses the role of monitor – or teacher – in a state school with that of religious educator, since it is precisely to teachers of Maghrebian origin that these 'Arab girls' denounced the harassment of which they believed themselves victims. Moreover, we note that this harassment, if indeed to be condemned, is not of the same order, let alone equally bad, as the harassment encountered in other occupational or educational environments (for example in certain private companies, or again in certain religious institutions), at least if one agrees the insistent condemnation of clothing claimed to be 'too Westernized' is not of the same order as sexual harassment, let alone the sexual abuse of a minor on the part of a person in authority. Finally, to qualify the 'propaganda' of this monitor as a 'rigorist discourse' on the grounds that he counselled the establishment's 'budding headmen' to abstain from alcohol, drugs and sex, teaches us as much about the system of values of this teacher as it does about those of the monitor. But to continue:

One incident will reveal the degree of this monitor's persistent activism: a colleague of mine went into our history storeroom in the mid afternoon (a windowless room where we keep our wall maps); on opening the door, she saw the light on and surprised the monitor at prayer. We chose not to inform the rest of our colleagues about this, in order not to create conflict. This incident led to the creation of a situation of tacit consensus between him and ourselves: he knew that we knew, and his respect for republican principles in the school was the condition of our silence.

'The degree of persistent activism' is revealed by the discovery of a 'monitor at prayer'. The fact of taking advantage of this 'window-less room' where wall maps are stored to accomplish his religious obligations (undoubtedly one of the Muslim's five daily prayers) is thus seen as convincing proof of his 'Wahhabi obedience'. And yet, if it is undoubtedly reprehensible to attend to one's personal concerns during working time (but was it his working time?), and debatable even to pray in a public building, i.e. a room that was not earmarked for this, it is quite contradictory on the other hand to see this as a form of active proselytism, since this monitor had very clearly *withdrawn* into the room to pray, hence the phrase 'she discovered the monitor at prayer'. Once again, this 'incident' teaches us more about the subjectivity of the teacher, and her propensity to identify a Muslim at prayer with an Islamic militant 'of Wahhabi obedience', than about any supposedly anti-Semitic, racist or sexist 'climate' rampant in the establishment. The main interest of this testimony, moreover, at least up to this point, lies above all in the way it refers to the discovery of a monitor of Muslim religion at prayer in a 'windowless room' as an 'incident'. In contrast to this teacher's reaction, what alerts the sociologist is the nature of the prevailing 'climate' in an establishment where such knowledge on the part of the teachers ('he knew that we knew') is implicitly presented as a symbolic power of life and death over the monitor ('the condition of our silence'); in other, more Shakespearean terms, this means they had him at their mercy. To continue, however:

> Both of the two monitors were quite unappreciative of the history and geography team made up exclusively of young women particularly attached to the republican school's principles of secularism and equality, on top of which they were faced with one teacher of Jewish religion and another of Armenian origin!

The hostility of these two monitors towards the history and geography teachers thus combines the three evils that give this book its subtitle: 'anti-Semitism, racism and sexism in the school environment'. In effect, the cause of this hostility was supposedly: (1) the presence of 'a teacher of Jewish religion' (anti-Semitism); (2) that 'of another of Armenian origin' (racism); and finally, (3) a team 'made up exclusively of young women' (sexism). Yet this is simply the sentiment of this teacher, since nothing is given to corroborate what she says about the reality of this hostility. Moreover, if there *was* hostility, it might have been caused not by the origin or sex of these young teachers, but rather by their particular personal interpretation of what it means to be attached 'to the republican school's principles of secularism and equality'. But to continue further:

> This was all the more intolerable to these two individuals because they were negationists. When they learned our respective origins, they came to us to request 'reliable historical information' on the subject of genocide, and the Shoah in particular. Naïvely, I believed at first they were seeking to reach an objective opinion of the facts.

The reason for the pronounced antipathy of these two monitors towards the young female team of history and geography teachers was therefore that they were 'negationists', hence one can deduce their anti-Semitism (towards Jews) and their racism (towards Armenians); hence, too, an atmosphere that was 'far from healthy'. And yet the expression of this antipathy, and of the 'intolerable' nature of the situation, is not immediately perceptible as such, since the two monitors, learning the respective origins of the teachers in question, immediately asked them about a historical subject that they were teaching, and that particularly concerned them because of their own origins. Is this really a sign of pronounced antipathy? First of all, what we see here suggests more a concern to obtain information and elements for reflection on the genocides in question, as indeed the author of the testimony herself remarks: 'Naïvely, I believed at first they were seeking to reach an objective opinion of the facts.' The sole proof of this

Wahhabi militancy and an antipathy tainted with anti-Semitism, racism and sexism thus remains their negationism. Here is how this is presented:

> In reality, it was rapidly apparent that they used all our conversations and the texts we offered them to refine their 'relativist' dialectic. They built up their negationist arguments by raising questions that were ever more detailed; my colleague, who had worked on the mechanisms of negationist discourse (on both the Armenian and the Jewish genocide), confirmed to me that they had already acquired the ideological and rhetorical reflexes of these.

The supreme proof of their negationism is thus that, under cover of obtaining information about the historical reality of the genocides from the two teachers, the monitors sought instead to 'refine their "relativist" dialectic', knowing it was necessary to have 'worked on the mechanisms of negationist discourse' in order to notice 'they had acquired the ideological and rhetorical reflexes of these'. In other words, it was a 'specialist colleague' who had revealed to her that they were negationists. In her conclusion to the first section of this testimony, the section that justifies its title 'On the Ambiguous Role of Certain Mediators', Barbara Lefebvre can thus maintain:

> Their degree of influence on young people in middle school as well as in the surrounding housing estates is all the more disturbing in that the perversion of their intellectual baggage is matched only by their skill in the methods of spreading ideas characteristic of fundamentalist movements. The state school that recruits them thus become both a tribune and a convenient cover for establishing their network of influence.

In the second part of this first testimony from Barbara Lefebvre, the teacher of history and geography mentions an 'identical atmosphere' the previous year at another *lycée*, but with the difference that this time words led on to action: 'Already in 1999, it was an identical atmosphere in a Seine-Saint-Denis school that led one of my pupils to write in the class's workbook for history and geography, where I set out the work to be done: "*sale Juif*" [dirty Jew].'

This fact sheds a retrospective light on the first sentence of her testimony, where she spells out that in the Hauts-de-Seine establishment where the two monitors previously mentioned had run riot, she had 'not been the victim of verbal aggression of an anti-Semitic character', as distinct therefore from this school in Seine-Saint-Denis. And yet the reader's attention, at this point in the account, is directed not to the manifestly anti-Semitic nature of the 'verbal aggression', but rather to the questionable identification of the teacher as the victim of this 'aggression', since in this case the words written in the book would have been '*sale Juive*' (dirty Jewess).[6] The following questions therefore arise: If it was the woman teacher whom this was aimed at, why did the pupil write 'dirty Jew' in the masculine form? And if it was someone else, why did the pupil commit this anti-Semitic verbal aggression in the history and geography workbook? We can propose the hypothesis that this incident attests to an equivalence in the mind and language of this student between this kind of 'verbal aggression' and an obscenity. In other words, the phrase 'dirty Jew' has the same significance in the mind of this student as words like 'prick', 'shit', 'fart', etc. (It is highly likely, moreover, that the capital 'J' for Jew was added by Barbara Lefebvre, and not by the pupil.) This incident does indeed signal an anti-Semitic prejudice deeply anchored in the psychic roots of this young school student, in the sense that the word 'Jew' and the prohibition that surrounds it amounts in his mind and his language to a form of taboo, a word that is not to be spoken, an obscenity. On the other hand, however, this does not strictly speaking amount to an aggression aimed at the teacher, since to all appearance she was no more targeted by the words 'dirty Jew' than she would have been by its equivalent terms in this pupil's value system ('prick', 'shit', etc.), so that the question becomes: What permits the teacher to believe herself the 'victim' of this anti-Semitic verbal aggression, when a simple grammatical analysis of the phrase in question manifestly contradicts this interpretation?

Let us carry on, then: 'My relationship with this pupil of Maghrebian origin had been stormy right from the start of the year, and it now came to a head.' The reader now learns that this incident followed on from others, even if their exact nature is not made clear. As for the 'Maghrebian origin' of the accused pupil, this does not enlighten us about the possibility of identifying the teacher as the 'victim' of this anti-Semitic verbal aggression (assuming that a middle-school pupil, even 'of Maghrebian origin', is capable of distinguishing between the masculine and feminine forms of the noun in question). The teacher continues: 'I do not know how this pupil learned that I was Jewish, since as a firm defender of the principle of secularism I do not wear any distinctive sign at my place of work; moreover, my family name does not make it possible to identify me as a member of the Jewish community.'

The difficulty of identifying the teacher as being the 'victim' of this aggression is now emphasized by the fact that nothing indicates she is Jewish, so the question clearly arises as to how this teacher knows the words 'dirty Jew' written in a workbook by a pupil who, in all likelihood, is unaware that his teacher is a 'member of the Jewish community', amount to verbal aggression of an anti-Semitic character aimed personally at her. In fact, everything leads us to believe that what we have here is an anti-Semitic prejudice which, in the mind and language of this pupil, is no more aimed at a particular target than any other obscene word (or drawing) written in another workbook would be, except for the fact that the words 'dirty Jew' were written in the 'history and geography workbook'. Doesn't this mean that while the history and geography teacher as an individual was indeed the target of the phrase in question, this was not in her capacity as an assumed member of the Jewish community? To continue:

I imagine that it was colleagues of mine, or well-intentioned members of the teaching staff (mediators?), who informed certain pupils that a Jewish woman teacher was concealed behind a perfectly French surname. The mythology of the Jewish plot (à la *Protocols of the Elders of Zion*) has a very real existence in Arab-Muslim culture; this pupil might well have imagined that he was confronting an agent of 'world Jewry' with only one objective in mind: to stuff his head with Zionist propaganda!

The teacher's answer as to how she knew this pupil was able to identify her as a 'member of the Jewish community' thus refers us to the supposed hypothesis of a list of Jewish teachers that certain 'colleagues' or 'mediators', not necessarily 'well-intentioned' but at least well-informed, conveyed to certain pupils, including the author of this anti-Semitic verbal aggression. And what justifies this hypothesis, in the eyes of this teacher, is that 'the mythology of the Jewish plot (à la *Protocols of the Elders of Zion*) has a very real existence in Arab–Muslim culture'. But a pupil able to identify his history and geography teacher as 'an agent of world Jewry' charged with 'stuffing his head with Zionist propaganda', by the sole fact of the presence of her name on a list of Jewish teachers concealed 'behind a perfectly French surname', should be equally able to distinguish between feminine and masculine forms of the noun in question, so that the question insistently remains as to how to identity Barbara Lefebvre as the 'victim' of this anti-Semitic verbal aggression, when everything leads us to believe that the writing of this pupil of Maghrebian origin was addressed to her role as a teacher and not to her ancestry? 'For the first time in my life', she continues, 'I was the victim of a deliberate anti-Semitic act; I was knocked for six, but immediately resolved to find the author of this inscription and punish him.' We can admire the courage of this teacher, determined not to give in despite her emotion, and 'resolved' that justice would be done:

I naively thought that the name of the guilty party would be rapidly revealed, that the pupils would be sensitive (if not

sensitized by my colleagues and the administration) to the seriousness of the insult. But to no avail: 'We're not sneaks.' 'Why do
you make such a fuss? It's not so serious.' Some pupils even said
to their classmates (who were trying to defend my insistence on
discovering the guilty party) that after all, 'We've got the right
to say what we like'; being anti-Semitic wasn't a crime, but 'an
opinion like any other'.

The reaction of the pupils to the teacher's 'insistence' enables the
reader immediately to distinguish three groups of pupils, in relation
to their perception of the incident and the attitude it generated
in them: A first group of pupils showed a reflex of solidarity with
the guilty pupil against the authority of the teacher or the institution. This attitude was not dependent on the act committed, it did
not take this into account at all; it was simply a tacit or unwritten
law of the imaginary community of a middle-school class that
'We're not sneaks'. A second group seems to have been prepared
to recognize that a serious offence could have been committed by
one of their classmates, but in this particular case the seriousness
escaped them: 'Why do you make such a fuss? It's not so serious.'
Is it because they were insensitive to the seriousness of a 'deliberate anti-Semitic act' towards their teacher? Or rather because, in
their eyes, the words 'dirty Jew' – in the masculine form, written
in the history and geography syllabus book – were not aimed
at anyone in particular, and certainly not at their teacher, who
was a woman with a 'perfectly French surname', but formed part
of a shared symbolic and imaginary value system in which the
word 'Jew' went together with 'prick', 'shit', etc.? A third group
of pupils appears on the other hand to have assimilated what
the adults understood by the words 'dirty Jew', i.e. an insult that
revealed the existence of anti-Semitic prejudices in the class and
aroused among the teachers the desire to punish such prejudices;
hence the first glimmerings of a 'relativist dialectic': you have
'the right to say what you like', it's 'an opinion like any other'.
Nothing permits us therefore to conclude that any of the pupils
identified the teacher as a 'member of the Jewish community',

and their statements even signal the contrary, since none of them seems to have envisaged that this inscription could have been aimed at the teacher personally, which would have explained her 'insistence'. (Perhaps they did not have access to the list of Jewish teachers circulated in the establishment?) And the question inescapably comes back as to how Barbara Lefebvre was able to conclude that she personally was the 'victim' of an anti-Semitic verbal aggression, and thus make denunciation of the guilty party a sine qua non of the exercise of her function as teacher, when everything leads us to believe the author of this inscription was unaware she was Jewish? Imperturbably, however, she goes on:

> The pupil felt the pressure exerted on the class (I refused to give lessons until the affair was cleared up), and the following day he tried to muddy the trail by writing the same insult in the work-book of another of my classes. It took all the patience of the principal teacher of this class, as well as my silent rage, to eventually obtain, at the end of a whole day of pressure and negotiation, the name of the guilty party.

The attempt at diversion by shifting suspicion onto a pupil in another class, despite being in vain, none the less attracts the reader's attention, since it insistently repeated a grammatical mistake ('the same insult') whose origin is hard to explain, all the more so since, in a class that showed such solidarity with 'a deliberate anti-Semitic act', there must surely have been one pupil who could instruct the guilty party in the minimum of grammar required to commit this kind of anti-Semitic verbal aggression. Yet the 'silent rage' of the teacher was in no way appeased by this diversion, and 'at the end of a whole day of pressure and negotiation' the guilty party was finally identified, though it seems after a kind of agreement having been reached between pupils and teachers – the 'negotiation' no doubt bearing, as is the custom in such circumstances, on the disciplinary sanctions that the guilty party would incur if he identified himself or was identified. Yet once this person was identified, the investigation seems to have been closed, and the exercise of the teaching function was able to recommence.

What is a 'Jew'? What is an anti-Semitic prejudice? What is a prejudice? These questions would certainly be raised for this middle-school class 'at the end of a whole day of pressure and negotiation', and be the object of at least one, if not several, lessons of history and geography. Yet we read:

> I went then to the police station, where the judicial officer encouraged me to register a complaint (and not simply have the matter recorded in the day book). The pupil was ordered in and informed of the complaint, and the prosecutor decided to make a deal with him: if he did not draw attention to himself in the next six months, the matter would be filed away.

The lesson in history and geography was thus deferred *sine die*, since it is clear that no one can insist a teacher does her work when her physical integrity is threatened. As for the 'negotiation' that made it possible to identify the guilty party, the reader will conclude that either the teacher did not feel bound by the agreement in which this resulted, or that the pupils agreed that in the circumstances a complaint to the police was her only resort. It remains that both the teacher and the judicial officer of the police seem to have been in agreement on what remains enigmatic to the eyes of the reader, i.e. what it is that justifies identifying an inscription bearing the words 'dirty Jew' in the masculine form with a threat aimed personally at this teacher, when everything leads us to believe that she is a woman and gave no indication of being a 'member of the Jewish community'? (Unless, of course, we conclude that since the pupil in question was of Maghrebian origin, it is too much to expect him to distinguish grammatically between masculine and feminine, even though he is likely to have in his hands a list of Jewish teachers concealed behind 'perfectly French surnames'.) Imperturbably, however, almost heroically, the narrative comes to a conclusion:

In the presence of his mother (deeply affected by her son's action), the pupil offered me his apologies and begged me to explain to him what a Jew was, so that he would understand better and not say stupid things like this in future. I was petrified by that statement.

Do the apologies of the author of the inscription and his request to be informed of the meaning of a word that he apparently did not understand, validate the hypothesis of the teacher, the judicial police officer and the prosecutor, according to which Barbara Lefebvre had been, 'for the first time in my life', the 'victim of a deliberate anti-Semitic action'? Or, on the contrary, do they validate the hypothesis that this inscription displays an identification, in the mind and language of the pupil, between the words 'dirty Jew' and other 'stupidities' of the same order such as the words 'prick', 'shit', etc. – except that these particular words were written in the class's history and geography workbook? In other words, what is it in such a circumstance that demands resort to the forces of order, rather than to a history and geography lesson introduced by the words: 'I do not want to know who wrote this, but I want to explain to you what it means'? At the end of her testimony, Barbara Lefebvre writes: 'I was petrified by that statement.' What more is there to say?

Second case study: Sophie Ferhadjian, 'racism, anti-Semitism and the abandonment of secularism'

Barbara Lefebvre's first testimony is immediately followed by one from Sophie Ferhadjian, titled 'Racism, anti-Semitism and the abandonment of secularism', from which we shall focus on some significant extracts. Evoking 'statements and attitudes that were racist, anti-Semitic, and infringing secularism' at her establishment in the department of Hauts-de-Seine, this second teacher of history and geography spells out that 'the greatest number of racist and anti-republican actions mentioned here are attributable to Maghrebian Muslim pupils who proclaim this identity, but also to monitors and mediators who are likewise Maghrebian and Muslim' (pp. 99–100). Her account of these 'racist and anti-republican acts' is as follows:

> In the course of the 2000–2001 school year, we witnessed the Islamization of a monitor without any adult in the establishment being prepared to intervene, despite repeated complaints by a number of pupils. He underwent a physical change in the course of the year, growing a beard and wearing long white shirts almost down to his knees. His behaviour gradually changed: he stopped greeting women teachers and refused to look at us. The school rapidly became his field of activity. He preached there, denouncing girls who were 'badly dressed', and even clashed with the school principal who had asked him without success to remove his skullcap when he'd finished his prayers. (p. 100)

The reader will immediately wonder whether this is the same school, and the same monitor, as it was indeed the school year 2000–2001 and a middle school in the Hauts-de-Seine. It turns out that Barbara Lefebvre and Sophie Ferhadjian were both teachers of history and geography at this middle school, and are relating the same facts. In other words, not only is half of this book of testimonies the work of just three teachers, but on top of this, two of them teach at the same college and tell us the same facts about anti-Semitism, racism and sexism – or more realistically, about the folkloric attire of a monitor and his 'rigorist discourse' towards the students. But here is the interpretation Ferhadjian offers:

> Given the aggravation of the situation, we decided by common agreement with a fellow teacher of history and geography to make approaches with a view to stopping him from this kind of activity, whether at our own school or another. But the way that the administration operates makes it impossible for a teacher to send a letter to the schools inspectorate or the rector's office

without informing the principal. Information was thus conveyed anonymously, a difficult and delicate choice, but one that was forced on us given the laxity or even dereliction of the administration in the face of such a serious infringement of the principle of secularism. (pp. 100–101)

Disturbed by the presence of a monitor who had adopted a folkloric outfit, Sophie Ferhadjian and a colleague, whom the reader will understand was Barbara Lefebvre, decided to inform the inspectorate without going via the principal, who to all appearance did not share their point of view, since he refused to immediately dismiss a monitor who wore 'long white shirts almost down to his knees'. They therefore wrote an anonymous letter of denunciation, to warn the schools inspectorate of 'such a serious infringement of the principle of secularism'. And the following sentence in her testimony also tells us something about the likely content of this letter: 'Why should we expect anything different, when the minister and his local officials are contributing to this policy of abandonment and resignation by encouraging the recruitment of monitors from the same community and religious environment as the pupils?' What is therefore denounced in the form of an anonymous letter to the schools inspectorate is thus nothing less than the 'ambiguous' ethno-cultural origin of certain monitors. Sophie Ferhadjian's account then continues with the entrance of the second monitor, whom we recognize as the already mentioned 'negationist':

In the course of the same school year, another monitor, also of Maghrebian origin and a science student at university, approached me in order to obtain information on the subject of negationism vis-à-vis the Jewish genocide. When I expressed surprise, he explained that anti-Semitic and negationist (he said 'revisionist') books and statements were current in the 'milieu' he frequented, questioning the number of deaths in gas chambers and their very existence. This conversation rapidly made me understand that he had quite a grasp of the subject. He knew the names of certain negationists, the titles of their books and even that a 'revisionist conference' was shortly to be held in Cairo. He was not therefore seeking 'information', but rather a way to trip up a history and geography teacher who taught a history that he saw as fallacious. A few days later, in response to his request, I brought him Jorge Semprun's *L'Écriture ou la vie*, as well as a comparative article on Armenian and Jewish negationism written by the American historian Richard G. Hovannisian, a professor at the University of California (UCLA). Turkish negationism vis-à-vis the Armenian genocide worried him far more than negationism of the Jewish genocide. (pp. 101–2)

Sophie Ferhadjian's testimony corroborates Barbara Lefebvre's on all points, i.e. that a monitor who had apparently developed in a 'milieu' in which negationist opinions were current questioned a teacher of history and geography about the historical reality of the Armenian and Jewish genocides, while a second monitor – 'curious' – listened in on the conversation. She brought this monitor books on the question 'at his request' and in order to increase his knowledge.[7] And she concludes: 'Turkish negationism vis-à-vis the Armenian genocide worried him far more than negationism of the Jewish genocide.' The proof of this monitor's negationism thus rests on the following facts: (1) he is aware of a current of thought that he calls 'revisionist' rather than 'negationist'; (2) he asks a teacher of history and geography about the reality of the genocides; and finally, (3) he appears to be more worried about Turkish negationism.

Analysis of these two testimonies, from Barbara Lefebvre and from Sophie Ferhadjian, has enabled us to display the fine dialectic that links the 'reality on the ground' as perceived by the authors of these testimonies with the same 'reality on the ground' as it might appear to a sociologist. In fact, on the subject of the prevailing 'climate' in these two schools, the sociological conclusion seems to us significantly different from that of Monsieur Jourdain, as we shall see. (1) It is disturbing, to say the least, that in the minds of teachers of history and geography, whom one might expect to be aware of the diversity of cultures and civilizations, the mere fact of wearing traditional dress or respecting religious obligations without impinging on anyone (for instance, praying in a 'windowless room' used to store wall charts) was enough to identify 'such a serious infringement of the principle of secularism'. (2) It is disturbing, to say the least, that a teacher should characterize as 'rigorist discourse' the act of persuading 'budding headmen' to abstain from alcohol, drugs and sex. (3) It is disturbing, to say the least, that a qualified teacher of history and geography suggests that informing a student subject to negationist influences in his 'milieu' is a way of giving him 'the means to trip up a teacher of history and geography', giving us to understand by this that the knowledge of this 'teacher' about the Jewish and Armenian genocides could be tripped up by the first supposedly negationist student to come along, and that the teaching of history is not an adequate response to negationism. (4) It is disturbing, to say the least, that a qualified teacher of history and geography has no other recourse than to complain to the police when a middle-school student displays anti-Semitic prejudices on the history and geography page of the class workbook. (5) It is disturbing, to say the least, that in an 'identical climate', she and her colleague deemed it healthy to write anonymous letters to the schools inspectorate denouncing the Maghrebian origin of the monitors recruited by the rectorate. (6) It is disturbing, to say the least, that none of the co-authors of this book, beginning with Emmanuel Brenner who 'edited' it, was disturbed by the publication of testimonies that reveal such prejudices and such lack of pedagogic and psychic maturity on the part of their authors. And finally, (7) it is disturbing, to say the least, that the highest state authorities in France maintain they have taken seriously the slogan of re-conquering the 'lost territories of the Republic', all the more so as it turns out that the ideological activism of these two women teachers had as its sole effect and intention a rejection of the fundamental principle of the republican school – that teaching is secular, and consequently, if a monitor's attitude towards pupils displays 'such a serious infringement of the principle of secularism', this is not by virtue of his dress, his 'rigorist discourse' or his secret prayers, but rather by the discrimination of which he is guilty by addressing himself only to pupils of Maghrebian origin. This is actually where the 'infringement' of the principle of secularism lies: in the fact that he did not address the same 'rigorist discourse' to all pupils (unless of course we opt for a pedagogy in state schools that is determinedly permissive in matters of alcohol, drugs and sex). For the principle of secularism demands that the teaching in state schools should be equally addressed to all. (As for the negationist propaganda of these two monitors – which consisted, in the one case, in asking a teacher of history and geography about the reality of the genocides, and in the other, in 'curious' listening – if it is a question of denouncing the fact that such a teacher is in their eyes the representative of 'a history he saw as fallacious', it is hardly acceptable to prove this by the fact that they view her as a privileged interlocutor and ask her for books on these questions.) That said, it is then reassuring at least to note that on the question of anti-Semitism, racism and sexism, these two Hauts-de-Seine middle schools, where 'the majority of pupils are children from Maghrebian and African immigrant background', have apparently had no other real difficulty than that of having to undergo the police-style and possibly xenophobic hysteria of two teachers of history and geography. And it is similarly reassuring to note that the 'budding headmen' are fascinated ('a real fascination', we are told) by a 'rigorist discourse' counselling abstinence with regard to alcohol, drugs and sex, and that young 'Arab girls' complain of a monitor who claims the right to dictate their style of dress. It is rather the opposite that would have been genuinely disturbing.

It still remains that, if one testimony is not sufficient to assert a social phenomena, the deconstruction of this testimony is likewise not sufficient to maintain the non-existence of this social phenomenon – in this case, anti-Semitism, racism and sexism in the school environment (not to mention negationism). This is why the conclusions that the sociologist can draw from these case studies bear chiefly on the social phenomenon of the book itself, *Les Territoires perdus de la République*. Its construction and its media audience, stretching up to the high circles of state, attest to an ideological re-conquest of the school and university space designed to confer 'Republican' legitimacy on a set of racist prejudices (against Maghrebians) and reactionary prejudices (the primacy of police repression over transmission of knowledge). We might add that 'the Jew' today assumes a particular and 'new' place in this ideological process, which I would explain as follows. Since Nazi anti-Semitism has been disqualified by history, in contemporary democratic consciousness, the struggle against the 'new anti-Semitism' has made it possible to resuscitate the ideological process of substituting an ethno-cultural question for a social question, to give this process political and academic legitimacy, since it is now presented as a struggle in the name of the Jews, the struggle against anti-Semitism justifying a re-conquest of the 'lost territories of the Republic' – and what is more, under a 'perfectly French' watchword. But where actually is the struggle against anti-Semitism in this book?

ISRAEL AND THE *LYCÉE* TEACHERS: THIRD CASE STUDY

Les Territoires perdus de le République reproduces, on pages 117–20, the text of an 'open letter from *lycée* teachers on racism and human rights', bearing the inscription '(*document*)' but no other signature apart from the geographical location of this *lycée* in the department of Val-d'Oise. This text is presented as a manifesto in support of secularism and a reminder of basic values made more necessary than ever by both the international context (the Middle East) and the national one (the Front National). It starts with the words:

The horrific situation in the Middle East reminds us more strongly every day that independence is an absolute for states, freedom for individuals, and peace for both. Our reference for everyone, our compass in this storm from which a number of waves are reaching us, must be the Declaration of the Rights of Man of 26 August 1789, complemented and extended by the Universal Declaration of 1948. Nothing sums these up better than the republican motto of '*Liberté, Égalité, Fraternité*', which we can read on the portal of every town hall, and which should have been explicitly recalled on the portal of our *lycée*, where, as in all teaching establishments, these three words translate into a single one: secularism. In our *lycée*, however, republican values are suffering.

The facts that these teachers report, and that justify the writing and publication of their 'open letter', are spelled out in the following passage:

> A Jewish pupil in the *terminale* class, after being the target of repeated anti-Semitic jibes, left the *lycée* to continue his studies in a Jewish school. Another problem is that in the corridors Muslim girls put on, if not Islamic headscarves, then at least headgear that is similar to this. Jewish pupils consider it normal not to have to appear for tests on a Saturday. (pp. 117–18)

These three facts, designed to show that 'republican values are under threat in our *lycée*', are thus all equally classified under the category of 'problem': (1) the persecution of a ('Jewish') pupil by others on account of his religious or ethno-cultural origin; (2) the wearing by certain ('Muslim') pupils of clothing that indicates, or may indicate, a sign of religious or ethno-cultural allegiance; and (3) the absence of certain ('Jewish') pupils on Saturday. And yet none of these three facts indicates, strictly speaking, an 'infringement of the principle of secularism' or of 'republican values', and the three also lack any common feature: (1) The anti-Semitic prejudices of certain pupils in this establishment do not infringe the principle of secularism; they indicate a need to put this principle into practice, first of all by protecting the pupil who is the victim of this abuse, then by sanctioning its authors, and finally by informing all pupils in the school about the nature and origins of anti-Semitic and racist prejudices. In other words, it is the struggle of teachers against these prejudices that attests to the effectiveness of the principle of secularism and of republican values, and it is only to the extent that teachers tolerate, convey or introduce such prejudices into the school that there is any 'infringement of the principle of secularism', or that 'republican principles are threatened'. The anti-Semitism of school students is thus no more an 'infringement of the principle of secularism' than would be the presence of an illiterate pupil; it is simply the sign of a certain failure. An illiterate teacher, on the other hand, would indeed be an 'infringement', and not just a failure. (2) The wearing of Islamic scarves, or 'headgear that is similar to this', is also not an 'infringement of republican values', since it is only teaching that is secular. Besides, the wearing of religious apparel by a pupil is no more and no less of an obstacle to secular teaching than are the religious convictions of the pupil in question, so that in all logic, either it is these religious convictions themselves that are the problem, and clothing or headgear that are a sign of these are only an accessory to this, or else the convictions are not a problem, and then neither are the clothing and headgear. (3) The absence of a pupil for religious reasons is no more of an 'infringement of the principle of secularism' than is any unjustified absence. In other words, given that school attendance is compulsory, or the object of a contract between the pupil and the school principal, any unjustified absence is irregular. It is up to the principal therefore to inform the pupil that the reason for their absence is deemed unjustified, and that they will incur the disciplinary sanctions envisaged by the regulations in the case of repeated and unjustified absences. And so, unless the implication is that the teachers at this *lycée* share the anti-Semitic prejudices of their pupils, that the sight of an Islamic scarf immediately leads them to teach the Koran instead of maths, and that the principal closes his eyes to the absence – unjustified, in his eyes – of certain pupils because they are Jewish, none of these three categories of facts suggests an 'infringement of the principle of secularism', or justifies the line of argument of this 'open letter'. On the other hand, presenting these three categories of facts as equivalent immediately suggests a certain number of associations – for example, that if this pupil has been identified as 'Jewish' it is because he is absent on Saturdays; or that if there is anti-Semitic prejudice in the school, this is not unconnected with the wearing of Islamic scarves, or even with the absenteeism of certain pupils. All these are free associations not unrelated to the book's overall proposition that in terms of struggle against anti-Semitism, racism and sexism, the role of the republican school is to repress the assertion of community identity on the part of the pupils, and not to guarantee them a secular education. But let us continue. Immediately after relating the above facts, the '*lycée* teachers' write:

> In varying degrees, these kinds of behaviour are intolerable. Several of the acts incriminated appear trivial. One might believe it is better to close one's eyes and wait for 'things to sort themselves out'. We believe that this is a short-sighted policy, which insidiously weakens the respect due to the law and gradually destroys the law itself. If the republican law, discussed and voted by the representatives of the people, known by all and taught at school, is brought into contempt and flouted without our defending it, then what will impose itself is the law of the group, of the community, with consequences that are all too visible: the law of the strongest, violence and anarchy.

First of all, it is very hard to see how the persecution of a pupil because he is Jewish is a trivial fact to which one might 'close one's eyes'. It is therefore the two other facts, the wearing of Islamic scarves or 'similar headgear' and the absence of pupils on Saturdays, that 'appear trivial', particularly because these facts, as opposed to the first one, in no way infringe anyone's moral or physical integrity. In other words, the first effect of this redefinition of the principle of secularism is to bring into a relationship of equivalence ('in varying degrees') facts that precisely do not have the same nature. (The persecution of a pupil because he is Jewish is not of the same nature as a Saturday absence deemed unjustified, just as the fact of Saturday absenteeism and the fact of coming to class the same Saturday wearing an Islamic scarf or similar headgear are not of the same nature, since one is an absence that needs to be justified, the other is not.) As for the teachers' comments on 'republican law' as opposed to 'the law of the strongest', 'violence' and 'anarchy', these would be timely, even healthy, if it were a question of denouncing teachers who preferred to 'close their eyes' to the subject of anti-Semitic persecution taking place in the school. But when teachers justify making an equivalence between facts with no common measure, we can only be disturbed at the serious confusions that they generate, since, according to them, the following three facts would all be illustrations of the 'law of the strongest': (1) the persecution of a pupil because he is Jewish; (2) the wearing of the Islamic scarf or 'similar headgear'; (3) absenteeism on Saturdays. The rest of the text spells out the conception of 'republican values' that governs the educational thought and intentions of these teachers:

> Let us recall the simple ideas that united French people, thanks to the Republic, after the era of civil strife that marked the whole of the nineteenth century. On the one hand, teaching is secular. In other words, without forbidding anyone to have a religious faith, the law demands that each person should keep this to themselves; what belongs in the private sphere (individual conscience, family life) must in no case encroach on the public sphere, and especially not on the school, the place of formation. I have the right to be Jewish, or Catholic, or Muslim, or whatever else; other people have the right to know nothing of this, or to know only what they want to; I do not have to impose on everyone, day after day, the mark of my Judaism, or my Catholicism, or my belonging to Islam, or whatever else … Religion is a purely individual

matter. What is forbidden above all is proselytism: to make propaganda for religion, to try to recruit followers for this religion; and
proselytism begins when explicit symbols are displayed, such as
the Catholic cross, the Protestant dove, the Jewish kepi or the
Islamic scarf. Each person, whatever the sincerity of their faith,
must understand that to display such signs in public is in itself an
infringement of the freedom of others, exerting a pressure that,
no matter how trivial, is intolerable because of the risk of gener-
alization. (pp. 118–19)

The point of departure of this text is the assertion that 'teaching is
secular'. The rigorous meaning of this statement, however, is precisely its literal one: *teaching* is secular, and possibly, by extension,
the teacher in the exercise of his or her functions; but certainly
not the pupils, who for their part come to class with the whole set
of prejudices, beliefs, customs and particularities that are specific
to them and that must be respected so long as they are compatible with their duty as pupils of a republican school. This means
for example that the expression of racist or anti-Semitic prejudice,
whether in an essay, or addressed to a teacher or a fellow pupil,
must be punished, and that since secular teaching is compulsory,
the absence of a pupil must be justified. But these *lycée* teachers
substitute for the letter of the law what they believe to be its spirit,
that 'I do not have to impose on everyone, day after day, the mark
of my Judaism, or my Catholicism, or my belonging to Islam,
or whatever else'; that as far as religion goes, 'proselytism begins
when explicit symbols are displayed, such as the Catholic cross,
the Protestant dove, the Jewish kepi or the Islamic scarf'; and that
each person 'must understand that to display such signs in public
is in itself an attack on the freedom of others' – propositions
that are addressed here not to teachers, but rather to pupils. This
interpretation of the principle of secularism involves a shift whose
effects are potentially unlimited – and fearsome. In fact, whereas
what they mention here is 'explicit religious symbols', their previous contention was about 'Muslim girls' wearing, 'if not Islamic
scarves, then at least similar headgear'. Does this mean, then, that

the 'proselytism' in question begins as soon as a pupil's headgear is susceptible of suggesting an Islamic scarf, at least when this pupil is identified as a Muslim girl? Moreover, although this 'open letter' seems at first sight to be addressed exclusively to schoolteachers and pupils, it talks about 'displaying such signs in public', explaining that 'the private sphere (individual conscience, family life) must in no case encroach on the public sphere'. Does this mean that the mere act of wearing 'in public' headgear susceptible of suggesting a religious sign 'is itself an attack on the freedom of others'? Analysis of this testimony displays once again the way in which the perception of the 'reality on the ground' depends on the interpretation of the 'principle of secularism' that is made. In effect, according to whether (a) the scope of this principle is confined to the teaching that is provided, or (b) the secular principle is extended to the clothing of pupils and other forms of identitarian assertion, one and the same 'reality on the ground' presents itself under two very different aspects.

Under hypothesis (a), the 'reality on the ground' is as follows. A pupil is the victim of anti-Semitic persecution and forced to leave the school. It is normal for an event of this kind to lead to a certain number of measures or investigations concerning (1) the existence of anti-Semitic prejudice among the pupils; (2) the inability of the teachers and administration to foresee, take note of and prevent the expression of this prejudice and the abuse that follows against a pupil of the school; and (3) the fact that the isolation of this pupil left him no other recourse against his persecutors than to leave the state school for a Jewish school. On the other hand, the wearing of a certain category of head-cover is a trivial, even ethnological, consideration, which does not require any specific measure or investigation; and likewise the unjustified absence of certain pupils, whatever the days and the reasons invoked, are part of the 'reality on the ground' common to all establishments at every place and time, and do not require an emergency pedagogic meeting. According to the first interpretation of the 'principle of secularism', then, the only noteworthy fact that infringed this principle and should have led to a collective response by the pedagogic team is that the teachers at this *lycée* were unable to prevent a pupil from being literally excluded by other pupils on the grounds of religious or racial considerations.

Under hypothesis (b), on the other hand, the 'reality on the ground' is as follows. A number of pupils at this *lycée*, indeed an increasing number, are not secular. Some are Muslim, particularly girls who wear 'if not the Islamic scarf, then at least similar headgear'; others are Jewish, particularly those who absent themselves on Saturdays for religious reasons, declared or disguised. All of these are behaviours infringe the principle of secularism and, 'as the terrible situation in the Middle East reminds us more strongly each day', could only lead to conflicts – one such conflict being between a Jewish boy and certain unidentified fellow pupils. The measure required is then an 'open letter from *lycée* professors on racism and human rights', which reminds everyone that 'the values of the Republic' are not 'the law of the strongest', and that if 'I have the right to be Jewish, or Catholic, or Muslim, or whatever else … I do not have to impose on everyone, day after day, the mark of my Judaism, or my Catholicism, or my belonging to Islam, or whatever else'. But on top of this, the legislature should act as quickly as possible to prohibit the wearing of religious symbols at school, whether explicit or implicit, and even oblige all pupils to present themselves on Saturdays and other Jewish holidays.

By legislating on the wearing of 'ostensible' signs of religious allegiance, the state opted to extend the domain governed by the principle of secularism and opted for hypothesis (b), as championed by the authors of this 'open letter', and for the perception of the 'reality on the ground' that their interpretation of the principle of secularism implies. But once such clothing is banned on the premises of state school establishments, what does one do when a Jewish pupil is 'the target of repeated anti-Semitic statements'? Does one decide, given the 'terrible situation in the Middle East', to banish Jewish and Muslim pupils from the premises of public institutions, or rather to raise the questions that the 'reality on the ground' imposes, namely why this pupil found himself alone against all? Why could the '*lycée* professors' not prevent anti-Semitic abuse from de facto excluding a pupil from their school? Why did this pupil say nothing, why did he prefer to leave the establishment rather than alert his teachers? To this last question, the sociologist will venture the following hypothesis: perhaps the pupil concluded that, 'if I have the right to be Jewish', 'other people have the right not to know anything about this', and 'I do not have to impose on everyone the mark of my Judaism'.

FOURTH CASE STUDY: THE SIGN POLICE

Once wearing the Islamic scarf, or any headgear close to it, is identified as infringing the 'principle of secularism' in the same way that anti-Semitic persecution would, then the attention paid to the clothing of pupils in the republican school becomes a major issue for the 'reality on the ground' of these teachers. 'Anti-Semitism', 'racism' and 'sexism' in the school environment then become plagues the teacher can diagnose in broad daylight from the way her pupils are dressed. In a testimony titled 'A Case of De-schooling', Élise Jacquard accordingly shows a sensitivity to questions of clothing that takes the form of an extremist conception of republican values, thereby informing us of the consequences to expect from this extension of the domain of secularism.

To start with, Jacquard considers that a scarf with Algerian colours, or any other clothing worn by pupils that might be related to ethno-cultural belonging, indicates an 'infringement of the principle of secularism':

> We have also seen the appearance of jackets with a large hand of Fatima embroidered on the back, and certain pupils stubbornly refuse to remove scarves with the colours and name of Algeria, as well as graffiti and the name of Bin Laden. (p. 199)

The writing of graffiti – i.e. an act of vandalism – is thereby equated with the wearing of clothes. Does this mean a 'hand of Fatima' embroidered on a jacket immediately signals, in the mind of this teacher, that the individual flaunting this symbol is ready to commit an act of vandalism? And likewise, an act of vandalism appealing to the terrorist Bin Laden is equated with 'scarves with the colours and name of Algeria'. Does this mean such a scarf immediately evokes the name 'Bin Laden' in the mind of this teacher? And *that* being the case, did she pull off this scarf that should not be seen?

A note by the author, precisely referring to the 'scarf with the colours and name of Algeria', informs us of the outcome of this particular dispute: 'This was finally removed after a very tough statement by a professor on Algeria's independence, a statement that would be disavowed in bourgeois milieus, but without any real debate on the underlying issues.' We are not told any more as to the exact content of this statement. The fact remains that a well-turned statement about the independence of Algeria apparently made it possible to restore republican order in a class whose students did not understand the extremist meanings of the 'principle of secularism'.

Secondly, the visible clothing of young and possibly Muslim pupils becomes, in the eyes of the author, an object of investigation that requires genuine specialist competence:

> As for the girls, they have to be observed over some time to understand that what seems first of all imaginative headgear artistically arranged is in fact a technique perfectly honed to produce a total covering of the head, whatever the name that is given it. It starts with ribbons and turbans that get wider, collars that climb and are combined with increasingly wide scarves, then with shawls that are more or less shaken under the noses of colleagues at a moment when, in a different context and culture, a word of opposition would be spoken. The next stage is the little scarf on the head, or an actual hat. It is not easy to get them to remove these; we might even say it is impossible. The teachers

are not obeyed, and the more clever among their number avoid having to give orders. In recent weeks, we have even seen gloves appear. (p. 196)

Under the appearance of 'artistically arranged' styles of clothing, therefore, the author construes, on the basis of her professional experience and an acute sense of observation, a concern to cover one's hair that is bound to evoke the scarf of Islamic obedience. And the situation in the establishment is such that it is almost 'impossible' to make pupils remove this 'imaginative headgear' – these 'ribbons', 'turbans', 'increasingly wide scarves' or even 'actual hats' – so much so that the 'more clever' among the teachers in this establishment 'avoid having to give orders', which would seem to indicate a real policy of resignation. Can a well-turned statement about Algerian independence really cope with this 'imaginative headgear artistically arranged'?

Thirdly and finally, the concern to free female school students, despite themselves, from the insufferable yoke of Islamic sexism should not, according to this author, stop short at the premises of the republican school, as her reflections on the wearing of the Islamic scarf, or of any artistically arranged headgear similar to it, indicate:

> It is impossible to get the champions of difference to criticize the Islamic veil: they are convinced that this is a symbol of the religious freedom inscribed in the Declaration of Rights of 1789. It is all the less possible in that the principal himself incites this tolerance, while the more forward are intimidated by the decrees of the Council of State, not taking account of the fact that this has delivered contradictory judgements, in particular forbidding the veil when there is a disturbance to public order. (p. 202)

The watchword of this teacher is thus not just 'criticizing' the Islamic veil, but 'having it criticized'. And yet her republican proselytism meets with the objections of certain 'champions of difference' among her colleagues, including the 'principal himself', who base themselves on 'religious freedom' and the judgements of the Counsel of State, which until the recent law confined the principle of secularism to the 'teaching' offered and only prohibited certain clothing on the part of pupils in so far as this was a 'disturbance to public order'. But what is this 'disturbance to public order'? That is evidently the question at issue in this establishment, since in the eyes of some of her colleagues and the principal, neither the Islamic scarf nor the artistically arranged headgear seem to have indicated such a 'disturbance':

> Suggesting to my colleagues that a disturbance to public order could be generated provoked a scandalized response. It was equally impossible to make them understand that this was not a question of religious freedom but a torture inflicted on women, and that it could be prohibited on the whole of French territory on the basis of the preamble to the Constitution that unambiguously proclaims equality between the two sexes. Given that feminism is practically non-existent in this country, such a discussion is impossible. It is however the touchstone and the stumbling bloc. (p. 202)

According to this teacher, the question at issue is the distinction between noting a 'disturbance to public order' and 'generating it', given that 'a disturbance to public order could be generated'. In other words, under cover of artistically arranged headgear, Muslim girls were supposedly 'generating' disturbances to public order, an extremist conception of the notion of 'disturbance to public order' that 'provoked a scandalized response' on the part of certain colleagues. Don't such 'scandalized responses' equally indicate the 'generation' of a disturbance to public order? And in the absence of a well-turned statement on Algerian independence, ineffective in a situation such as this, isn't an anonymous letter of denunciation necessary? In fact, it seems that neither Jacquard's colleagues nor the principal of the establishment had adequately internalized 'the republican values that we have to transmit'. As proof of this: they see no 'torture inflicted on women' in the guise of this 'imaginative headgear artistically arranged' which it is almost 'impossible' to get removed. And such 'torture', it goes without saying, is unacceptable not just on the premises of an educational establishment, but on 'the whole of French territory'.

From the demand for a teaching addressed to all, to the demand for clothing devoid of any explicit religious symbol; then from the clothing of the teacher or mediator to the clothing of the pupil; then from an explicit religious symbol to a headgear similar to the Islamic scarf; then from this scarf to a scarf bearing the colours and name of Algeria, and from this to everything that covers the female body in a suspect manner ('we have even seen gloves appear', she writes); and then, finally, from Jacquard's school premises to the whole of French territory – the extension of the domain of secularism, in the minds of the authors of this book, seems to know no limits once its original mooring is cast off. And it is precisely this freedom of interpretation that offers a special object of study for the sociologist. In fact, once the transition is made from the teaching offered in a republican school to the pupils' clothing, the free interpretation of the 'principle of secularism' is a privileged 'terrain' for the analysis of prejudices, beliefs and representations of the teaching body – and beyond this, of society as a whole. The following remark by Marie Zeitgeber, taken from her testimony ('A Year in a Middle School', pp. 129–47), undoubtedly gives us the last word in this story:

> Among the teachers, we wondered how to react to a pupil who came into class with a 'naked midriff'. Once again, opinions were divided, and we reached a fairly consensual conclusion at the suggestion of a woman teacher: 'I prefer our girls to dress this way rather than veiled, or hidden under gymslips like when I was young!' (p. 147)

Faced with changes in the school population, these teachers accordingly seem to stress that they belong to a Western modernity whose slogan could well be: 'Give us a naked midriff rather than covered hair or the gymslips of our youth!' And this is what the law forbidding the display of ostensible signs of religious allegiance, as voted by the National Assembly, was later to formalize with the same kind of consensus as is on record with this group of teachers in the state school system.[8]

At the end of this analysis of the extensions, shifts and obfuscations of the 'principle of secularism', therefore, the question is as follows: Does the republican activism of these teachers intend to substitute, for a principle of secularism that exclusively concerns the teaching they will offer, a 'sign police' that authorizes increasingly free and extreme interpretations of what is or is not an 'infringement of the principle of secularism'? And once the latter is sanctioned by legislation, does not a substitution of this kind precisely imply such an infringement? In effect, doesn't prohibiting pupils from covering their hair on school premises mean asserting the freedom for pupils of both sexes to parade with 'bare midriff'? Is such a display less 'identitarian' or 'religious' than another? The answer would seem that 'bare midriff rather than covered hair' is neither more nor less identitarian, ethno-cultural or religious than the contrary slogan. And if the notion of 'disturbance to public order' is to be introduced, it even seems that, from a Freudian point of view, the latter is rather more hysterical than the former.

THE REALITY ON THE GROUND

If the testimonies collected in *Les Territoires perdus de la République* reveal a certain number of representations or prejudices that seem to be common to all the authors discussed above, and consequently shape the rather didactic unity of their statements, they also have the specific property of being testimonies, and by virtue of this serve to inform the sociologist of a certain 'reality on the ground'. But does this reality justify the conclusions that Emmanuel Brenner draws from it? According to him, all the testimonies in this volume show that 'anti-Semitism', 'racism' and 'sexism' in the school environment is principally or even essentially the characteristic of populations of Arab–Muslim origin. However, if a certain number of facts incontestably indicate a situation 'in the school environment' that is worrying, to say the least, it remains the case that nothing justifies imputing responsibility for this situation to pupils of Maghrebian origin, unless certain testimonies or facts are taken out of their varied context – a variety that we therefore have to restore by highlighting what Brenner's analyses do their utmost to obscure.

First of all, pupils of Maghrebian origin are themselves victims of violence in the school environment. Thus on page 124, Sophie Ferhadjian relates how a female middle-school pupil of Maghrebian origin stubbornly refused to go on a school trip, upon which a subsequent inquiry by the teachers concluded:

> The information gathered from the woman mediator brought to light that a pupil of African origin sexually harassed a female pupil of Maghrebian origin in the class, as well as others, threatening her with rape, which he and some fellow pupils planned to carry out during the trip to the Auvergne.

As a consequence, unless these uncontrolled sexual impulses are ascribed to the ethno-cultural origin of the aggressor, we have to place the anti-Semitic violence of pupils of Maghrebian origin in a violent school context in which they are both protagonists and victims.

Secondly, this violence is not just among pupils, or violence of pupils against teachers; it is also the violence of teachers, or more widely of the institution, towards them. The testimony of Élise Jacquard is instructive on this count, since pages 169–72 of her testimony are devoted to the anti-Semitism and racism of teachers. She writes in particular about the 1980s:

> At the same time, changes in teaching, concerning both the recruitment of pupils and the objectives of the minister, led teachers to blame Arab pupils, and secondarily Blacks who were in a small minority at that time (mainly West Indians) for the unease

that began to make itself felt in classes, from a pedagogical point of view. Racism made it possible to avoid tackling the subject of declining standards, without having either to really discuss it or to raise questions about teachers themselves. It was race that explained poor educational performance. Any questioning was dismissed. There was a certain consensus about this. (p. 170)

This situation even led this author to seek to reinstate pupils of Maghrebian or African origin 'whose files had been deliberately shelved'. But she came up against 'anti-republicans' who finally did not hesitate to 'get rid of these pupils by main force' (p. 172).

Thirdly, this violence is not just between pupils, or that of teachers against pupils (for example in the form of institutional violence, as witness the discrimination in handling students' files); there is also violence between teachers. On page 192, for example, Jacquard relates that the unbridled character of certain pupils' sexual impulses paralleled that of certain adults who were in no way of Maghrebian (or African) origin:

Sexual violence against female colleagues was not just on the part of pupils. There were such things as hands placed on the buttocks of women while they were photocopying, which signalled the transformation of the egalitarian teaching ethics of the earlier part of my career into the traditional custom of office life. There was also aggression in the teachers' cloakroom, with a male colleague putting his hand down a woman teacher's blouse to touch her breast. Or the need to fend off with fists an administrator who had unambiguously clutched a woman in his arms.

Actions like these were presumably not unique in the school environment, and presumably did not involve either pupils of Maghrebian origin or indeed any pupils at all – which guides the sociologist towards a hypothesis never envisaged by Emmanuel Brenner: that 'violence in the school environment' is primarily an indication of violence in French society as a whole, before being attributable to any ethno-cultural category. And so one might ask

Élise Jacquard whether tomorrow, if women teachers found a full covering of their body a way to restrain the ardour of certain colleagues, would this be 'an infringement of the principle of secularism'?

Fourthly, anti-Semitism is no more a characteristic of pupils of Maghrebian origin, or of school pupils in general, than is racism or sexism. On page 142, Marie Zeitgeber reports this statement by a male teacher concerning the pedagogic attitude to adopt in the case of overt anti-Semitic behaviour: 'a teacher explains that if he heard anti-Semitic statements made by pupils of Maghrebian origin, it would be hard for him to intervene because he "doesn't know a lot about what's going on there ..."' But if we return to the rigorous definition of the principle of secular education – the principle that the transmission of knowledge, addressed equally to all, is the only valid authority in school – then the statement of this teacher is evidence that anti-Semitism arises from ignorance, and in this sense illustrates precisely what an infringement of the principle of secularism really means: a teaching that gives free rein to ignorance. (Moreover, we should note that this teacher had never previously heard 'anti-Semitic statements on the part of pupils of Muslim origin'.)

Fifthly, and lastly, anti-Semitic or racist speech and acts on the part of pupils have to be placed in the context of relations between pupils, i.e. one of immaturity. Thus on page 144, Marie Zeitgeber relates an exchange between two pupils and the dialogue with the teacher that followed:

> In the middle of a lesson, an African pupil, Salimata, said to the boy next to her: 'Shut up, you dirty Arab!' The teacher intervened and criticized the girl, who replied: 'It's nothing, miss, you can't understand. I call him dirty Arab because he's a mate, and anyway I can't be racist because I'm black. You take it out on me, but you never say anything to the real racists because they're French.'

And the author ends this anecdote by saying: 'A racist insult doesn't intend just to humiliate someone, it is deadly: it relates the Other to their origins, to nothing, as if the existence of some people involved the destruction of others.' But these concluding words confuse two different registers of language, that of the pupil and that of the teacher.

Contrary to what Emmanuel Brenner maintains, then, the testimonies he presents indicate that the facts observed, – 'anti-Semitism', 'racism' and 'sexism' – implicate all actors in the school system, irrespective of place and origin, each in their particular fashion. And the violence seen in the school environment is a function of French society as a whole.

CONCLUSION: AN IMAGINARY SOCIOLOGIST?

As we can see, the ethno-cultural sociology of Emmanuel Brenner has no explanatory value in the analysis of 'anti-Semitism', 'racism' and 'sexism' in the school environment, but rather confers an appearance of scholarship on xenophobic prejudice, in the same way that Molière's doctors dressed up their stubborn ignorance and murderous impulses in Latin words. So there is nothing new under the sun, apart from the fact that today, ethno-cultural ideology is articulated in an unprecedented fashion around the two watchwords of 'struggle against anti-Semitism' and 'defence of Zionism'. Looked at more closely, however, Brenner's sociology is perfectly compatible with a foreign policy which is hostile to the state of Israel. As witness the French far right, which has always combined its particular anti-Maghrebian xenophobia with overt hostility to Israel. In this sense, it is even very likely that if French citizens of Maghrebian origin are blamed for the anti-Semitism of French society, French anti-Zionism, relieved of this burden, will be that much freer in speech and action. As far as the 'struggle against anti-Semitism' is concerned, it is clear that Brenner's sociological thesis has nothing to say about it, given that it is not based on anything but anti-Maghrebian prejudice, and dispenses with any analysis. By refusing to use the appropriate tools to discern expressions of anti-Semitism in the school environment, it is unable to recognize this behaviour and therefore to combat it. It is particularly revealing that Brenner bases himself on testimonies that are in some cases quite fanciful. But what most strikingly refutes the idea that the ideological reaction Brenner champions can in any way help the 'struggle against anti-Semitism', is the salience of anti-Jewish prejudice in the identitarian and ideological framework on which his own thesis is based, as we have emphasized. The singularity of Emmanuel Brenner, none the less, in the field of so-called 'communitarian' ideology, is his concern to offer an analysis that distinguishes him from his peers, so that he substitutes for the 'Islamo-leftist', 'Islamo-communist' or 'Islamo-progressive' adversary of Trigano, Finkielkraut or Taguieff, a kind of Islamo-LePenism on which he alone has patent rights, thereby warding off all the more securely any ideological affinity with a French far right that remains too far outside the pale:

It seems, rather, that we should speak of an anti-Semitism as reactionary as ever dressed up in new guise … Anti-Semitic Islamism is ideologically close to the far right. The alliance between these two tendencies is not a passing coincidence, it is an agreement on fundamentals. Both spill into a common apologia for identity and roots. Both equally stand, despite appearances, for the same refusal to integrate foreigners in France … This is why the man who is regularly presented as Arabophobic, Jean-Marie Le Pen, is on the contrary very close to the Arab world in general. In 1990–91, during the first Gulf War, Le Pen was Saddam Hussein's firmest supporter in France. Thirteen years later, he was again on Hussein's side in staunchly opposing the US and British war in Iraq. It was Le Pen, again, who declared in 1990, at the height of the Islamist wave in Algeria: 'The FIS is the national *djellaba* against cosmopolitan jeans.' Islamism and the far right are linked at their foundations, and it is also on these foundations that they share their anti-Semitism and negationism, in the same denial of the real, the same denial of the Law, given that the real is the Law, and the Law is the real. (*'France, prends garde ...'*, pp. 110–11)

And this word 'real' that concludes a paragraph on the subject of the Islamo-LePeniste alliance, sealed by the 'same denial of the real', has an appended note that reads as follows: 'Negation of the Law is always central to the procedure of anti-Semitism, it is always linked in part with negation of the figure of the Father, i.e. of the Jew in the monotheist religions derived from Judaism.' We recognize here, besides the diagnosis of the 'communitarian' psychoanalyst, a constant in French reactionary discourse: condemning one aspect of far-right ideas in order to learn from another. The procedure here consists in diagnosing in Le Pen a particularly symptomatic case of 'negation of the Law', i.e. a 'denial' of the 'figure of the Father' – which 'Father', however, turns out to be the firm champion of a re-conquest of the 'lost territories of the Republic'. Hence also a portrait of Le Pen as 'rebel son', even *'porteur de valise'*,* which is undoubtedly Emmanuel Brenner's most singular contribution to contemporary historiography.[9]

---

 * The *'porteurs de valise'*, literally 'suitcase carriers', were the French helpers of the FLN during the Algerian War.

Appendix: A Counter-Analysis of Ethno-Cultural Sociology's Statistical Data

'People are not born with fear of the other; they acquire it.'
– Guillaume Erner, *Expliquer l'antisémitisme.*
Le bouc émissaire: autopsie d'un modèle explicative

In his introduction to *Les Territoires perdus de la République*, Emmanuel Brenner refers at two points to the results on an inquiry by the Sofres polling agency designed to measure the extent of anti-Jewish prejudices among young people between the ages of fifteen and twenty-four.[10] The interest in referring to the results of such an investigation is clearly that, as opposed to a collection of testimonies, the statistical data are obtained from operations that are rigorously defined with a view to constructing an objective representation of a social fact. Furthermore, the investigation in question not only offers a quantitative representation of anti-Jewish prejudices observable among young people aged fifteen to twenty-four, it also makes it possible to analyse the results obtained according to different criteria, including the ethno-cultural 'Maghrebian' (the category 'parental origin' is subdivided into three sub-categories: 'France', 'European countries', 'Maghreb countries'). Consequently, if the resurgence of anti-Semitism in the school environment is a function of the strength of Maghrebian prejudice, as Emmanuel Brenner maintains, then the measuring instruments at the sociologist's disposal should reveal significant, regular and concordant differences according to whether or not the individuals questioned are of Maghrebian origin. The question, then, is as follows: Do the results of the Sofres survey on which Brenner bases his ethno-cultural hypothesis validate it or not? Following the method explained above, we shall concern ourselves here only with the sections of the survey that the ethno-cultural sociologist has himself used, that concerning 'the image of Jews' and 'young people and the Shoah'.

The image of Jews among young people aged fifteen to twenty-four

On page 40 of *Les Territoires perdus de la République*, Brenner refers to 'the ideological embedding of anti-Semitism in a segment of Maghrebian immigrants', proposing to verify right away the rigorous objectivity of this by referring to the statistics in the first section of the Sofres inquiry:

> To the question: 'Do you believe that Jews have too much influence in the field of economics and finance?', 22 per cent of the individuals questioned replied 'Yes', but 35 per cent of young people of Maghrebian origin gave a positive response. To the question 'Do Jews have too much influence in the media?', 21 per cent replied 'Yes', but the figure rose to 38 per cent among young people of Maghrebian origin. On 'too much influence in the world of politics?', the figures were 18 per cent for young people as a whole, and 24 per cent for those of Maghrebian origin. But it was the question of personal relations that most clearly showed this cleavage. To the question 'Would you envisage living with a Jewish partner?', 8 per cent of the total replied 'Personally, no', but 24 per cent of young people of Maghrebian origin gave the same response.

The available statistical data that measure the strength of anti-Jewish prejudice among young people would thus confirm, according to Brenner, the chiefly Maghrebian origin of the anti-

Semitism rampant in the school environment today, the proof being that a significant gap is observable between the young people as a whole who were questioned and the young people of Maghrebian origin, this gap ranging from 6 points (18 per cent against 24 per cent) to 17 points (21 per cent against 38 per cent). But before concluding that an ethno-cultural reading of these figures is justified, we should first examine Brenner's method of analysis. His procedure is first to assert that anti-Semitic acts in the school environment are those of pupils of Maghrebian origin, basing himself chiefly on a one-sided reading of didactic testimonies; then to propose the hypothesis that anti-Jewish prejudice is more intense among young Maghrebians by virtue of their ethno-cultural origin; and finally to confirm that his explanatory hypothesis is justified by noting differences in the statistical data between all the individuals questioned and those of Maghrebian origin, differences that he deems significant. But a procedure of this kind, if it is to be sociologically rigorous, requires answering at least the three following questions: (a) What constitutes a significant difference? (b) Once such a difference has been defined, are there also other significant differences revealed by these statistical results, implying other analytical grids? And (c), are the most significant differences those between young people of Maghrebian origin and the rest, or might a different analytical grid prove just as pertinent, if not more so? According to Brenner, a difference of anything over 6 points between the total sample and a particular category is defined as significant, since he mentions results ranging from a gap of 6 points to one of 17. Let us then suggest an alternative hypothesis or counter-hypothesis, and see if we obtain similar differences – i.e. such differences as permit us to conclude that this alternative hypothesis is also justified, at least according to Brenner's assumption of what degree of difference is significant. Let us propose, for example, that anti-Semitism in the school environment is essentially the act of young people who classify themselves ideologically as 'right-wing', and see what results are obtained using the analytical category of 'party preference' which the investigation also provides: are the differences observed here of the same order as those observed using the analytical category that the ethno-cultural sociologist privileges? In other words, is a 'right-wing' political sensibility more susceptible to anti-Jewish prejudice, so that this could equally be the origin of the resurgence of anti-Semitism observed in the school environment?

On the questions about 'the influence of Jews' in the economy, the media and politics, the results obtained by comparing these two hypotheses – one ethno-cultural and the other ideological – are as follows:

For the 'area of economics and finance', 22 per cent of the total sample 'agreed' that Jews had 'too much influence', and Brenner points out that the figure among young people of Maghrebian origin was 35 per cent, a difference of 13 points. But the figure for young people who classed themselves as 'right-wing' was 33 per cent, a difference of 11 points from the total. This classification is therefore equally significant, or only a shade less so, than that noted by Brenner.

As regards the media, 21 per cent of the total sample believed that Jews had 'too much influence', and Brenner points out that the figure among young people of Maghrebian origin was 38 per cent, or 17 points higher. Among young people classing themselves as 'right-wing' the figure was 29 per cent, or 8 points higher than the total. If this latter figure confirms the hypothesis of a more pronounced anti-Jewish prejudice among the 'right-wing' young people, it is still less significant than that observed among young people of Maghrebian origin (17 points higher); here, Brenner's socio-cultural hypothesis works better.

For politics, 18 per cent of the total questioned believed that Jews had 'too much influence', and Brenner points out that the figure among young people of Maghrebian origin was 24 per cent, or 6 points higher. The figure for the 'right-wing' young people was 26 per cent, or 8 points higher than the total, which is therefore equally significant – in fact, a shade more so – than that for young people of Maghrebian origin.

Accordingly, if the question of Jewish influence in the media seems to signal an ethno-cultural singularity specific to young people of Maghrebian origin, rigorously identical results are observed for both the area of economics and finance and for that of politics, whether these results are obtained on the basis of Brenner's ethno-cultural hypothesis or our own ideological hypothesis. Statistical analysis of the prejudice that ascribes to Jews a hidden power in the decision-making fields of national life thus does not allow us to conclude that the ethno-cultural hypothesis about the origin of anti-Semitism in the school environment is justified, unless we keep strictly to the question of Jewish influence in the media (or unless, of course, we conclude that Maghrebians have 'too much influence' on the right).[11]

To the question 'Would you envisage living with a Jewish partner?', 8 per cent of the total questioned replied 'No, I couldn't envisage this for myself', and Brenner notes that this response was given by 24 per cent of those of Maghrebian origin (a difference of 16 points). The figure for those individuals classified as 'right-wing' was 16 per cent (a difference of 8 points). If this does indeed confirm a more pronounced anti-Jewish prejudice among young people who class themselves as 'right-wing', for the question on the media the difference is less significant on the basis of our own ideological reading. Furthermore, the advantage here is more distinctly in favour of Brenner's ethno-cultural hypothesis, which is not relativized by a high degree of equality on other questions (as above for the areas of politics and economics). This is why Brenner remarks that 'the cleavage is most clearly marked by the question dealing with the personal sphere', though we now have to correct this by making clear that *only* the personal sphere seems to mark such a 'cleavage', at least so far as validating his explanatory hypothesis is concerned. But the correction does not stop here. This would in fact mean forgetting that these figures do not offer any enlightenment at all as to the origin of this negative response on the part of young people of Maghrebian origin – at least, until we know how many of them would respond negatively to the broader question 'Would you envisage living with anyone who is not Muslim (or not Maghrebian)?' For it is only in so far as the percentage of young people of Maghrebian origin who would not envisage living with any non-Muslim (or non-Maghrebian) is clearly lower than the percentage of the same young people who would not envisage living with a Jewish person that the difference is significant. In other words, if 24 per cent of these same young people of Maghrebian origin would no more envisage living with any non-Maghrebian or non-Muslim, then the 'cleavage' would not be a sign of anti-Jewish prejudice, but simply the assertion of a Muslim or Maghrebian identity. Since this question was not asked, it is impossible to draw any conclusion.

We can now turn to the third and last question in this first part of the Sofres inquiry, a question that Brenner does not discuss. This question is intended to assess the degree of identification among these young people between 'a French person of Jewish religion' and an 'Israeli Jew', the question being asked in the following words: 'According to you, does a French person of Jewish religion have more points in common with a French person of another religion or with an Israeli Jew?' The identification of a 'French person of Jewish religion' with an 'Israeli Jew' might in fact be a specific feature of Maghrebian anti-Semitism. By projecting their own social frustrations onto the Israeli–Palestinian conflict, young people of Maghrebian origin would then be taking up the anti-Zionism of the Arab–Muslim world and – as an outlet – identifying the Jewish community living in France with the state of Israel. Brenner indeed devotes a long discussion, both in *Les Territoires perdus de la République* and in *'France, prends garde …'*, to an analysis of Arab–Muslim anti-Zionism and the reappearance of the most traditional themes of Western anti-Semitism in the media and the academic and political circles of the Arab world (distribution of *The Protocols of the Elders of Zion*, accusations of ritual murder, etc.). The interest of this question could therefore not escape him, and likewise the interest of the results of this study. How then should we interpret this omission?

Out of the total sample, 63 per cent of respondents equated a 'Jewish French person' with a 'French person of another religion', and 29 per cent with an 'Israeli Jew'. Among the young people of Maghrebian origin, the results obtained for this same question were respectively 68 per cent and 32 per cent. Thus, if young people of Maghrebian origin show a slightly higher percentage than the national average in terms of identifying a 'French person of Jewish religion' with an 'Israeli Jew' (32 per cent against 29 per cent), the percentage is also higher for those who identify a 'French person of Jewish religion' with a 'French person of another religion' (68 per cent against 63 per cent), and by a slightly greater margin. Brenner's chosen statistical data thus do not permit the conclusion that the resurgence of anti-Semitism in the school environment comes from a projection of Arab–Muslim anti-Zionism onto French people of Jewish religion, this projection being supposedly characteristic of young people of Maghrebian origin. If we turn to our ideological hypothesis, however: Among those young people classing themselves as 'right-wing', 57 per cent identify a 'Jewish French person' with 'a French person of another religion' (6 points below the national average), while 36 per cent identify such a person with an 'Israeli Jew' (7 points above that average). Significant differences thus appear if the ideological hypothesis is applied to the data, but not when Brenner's ethno-cultural hypothesis is applied.

The use that Brenner makes of the results of the first section of this survey bearing on the 'image of Jews' consists therefore in extracting two questions out of the three and comparing the percentage for all the young people questioned with that for young people of Maghrebian origin, from which he concludes that the statistical data justify his working hypothesis. Our own analysis of the same figures, however, reveals that his method does not consist in examining the results of the study, but rather in extracting his own views from them without any such analysis.

Young people and the Shoah

Brenner's second reference to this Sofres survey relates to its third section, on 'young people and the Shoah'. On page 33 of *Les Territoires perdus de la République,* he writes:

> Given these scenes, these statements and this still contained verbal violence, it is impossible to be surprised by the finding that it is among young people of fifteen to twenty-four of Maghrebian origin that we find the highest percentage of individuals convinced that 'there is too much talk of the Shoah in France' (11 per cent as against 4 per cent of young people of French origin).

The results of this section of the Sofres survey thus confirm, according to Brenner, 'the alarming observation by teachers in secondary schools ... who all report their difficulties in the last ten years or so in teaching the Shoah in classes with a high Maghrebian component' (back cover of *Les Territoires perdus*), allegedly due to a gap of 7 points between 'young people of French origin' and those of Maghrebian origin. Yet the figure of 11 per cent is scarcely alarming in itself, and cannot explain the difficulties that 'all teachers' encounter when tackling the Shoah 'in classes with a high Maghrebian component'. In fact, the remaining 89 per cent of young people of Maghrebian origin do not believe that 'there is too much talk of the Shoah in France'. But out of an overriding concern to show a specifically Maghrebian origin of anti-Semitism in the school environment, Brenner sees even this as a confirmation of his thesis. The essence of his method, however, is something else. Given these testimonies from teachers who 'all' speak of their difficulties in 'teaching the Shoah in classes with a high Maghrebian component', the ethno-cultural sociologist is understandably interested in the Sofres survey's question as to whether young people are willing or not to hear about the Shoah. But he is interested only in one way of putting the question, or rather of responding to it: Do you think there is too much talk of it? But wouldn't it also be interesting, for both Brenner and his readers, to know the percentage of young people of Maghrebian origin who think that 'there is not enough talk' about the Shoah, and then to compare this with the percentage of 'young people of French origin' who think the same way? We thus need once again to fill the gap that Brenner overlooks, and it turns out that 54 per cent of young people of Maghrebian origin believe 'there is not enough talk of the Shoah in France', whereas only 49 per cent of 'young people of French origin' believe this.

Finally, how do things stand with the ideological hypothesis as far as this question about the Shoah is concerned? Does a comparison of the percentages obtained for the total sample, for those of Maghrebian origin, and for young people classing themselves as 'right-wing' enable us to confirm the relevance of our own hypothesis on a subject where Brenner's hypothesis finds no confirmation? For the total sample, 5 per cent believe that 'there is too much talk about of the Shoah' in France, while the figure is 11 per cent for young people of Maghrebian origin (a gap of 6 points), and 7 per cent for young people classing themselves as 'right-wing'. But out of the total sample of young people, 52 per cent believe that 'there is not enough talk of the Shoah in France', a figure rising to 54 per cent among young people of Maghrebian origin, but falling to 42 per cent among young people who are 'right-wing' (10 points less than the average).

The most significant difference, then, appears here on the second formulation of the question: 'Do you think that there is not enough talk of the Shoah in France?', since on this question, the gap observed with young people classifying themselves as 'right-wing' is 10 points (in relation to the total sample), and 12 points (in relation to young people of Maghrebian origin). It appears, then, from these results that those young people defining themselves as 'right-wing' are significantly less motivated than others when it comes to listening to a lesson on the Shoah, from which we conclude – on the basis of the statistical results available – that the difficulties encountered by history teachers do not come so much from pupils of Maghrebian origin as from those defining themselves as 'right-wing'.

After this methodological test of the two references to the Sofres survey in Brenner's text,[12] it is apparent the conclusions he draws from it are unfounded. The statistical data that the ethno-cultural sociologist produces do not justify making the ethno-cultural origin of pupils responsible. On the other hand, a summary analysis of this data does indeed confirm our alternative hypothesis, that Emmanuel Brenner is no more a proper sociologist than Doctor Diafoirus was a proper doctor.[*]

---

[*] Diafoirus is a ridiculous 'doctor' in Molière's play, *Le Malade imaginaire* (The Hypochondriac).

3

Anti-Taguieff: Pierre-André Taguieff's Revolution in Science

But whether one has the same present, or the same future, depends on whether one has the same past. We do not have the same language.

> – Henri Meschonnic, *Modernité! Modernité!*

When you leave the Sorbonne by the rue Saint-Jacques, you can go uphill or down. If you go up, you reach the Panthéon, where a number of great men are preserved; but if you go down, you are surely heading for the prefecture of police.

> – Georges Canguilhem, *Qu'est-ce que la psychologie?*

With his book on *La Nouvelle judéophobie*, Pierre-André Taguieff* seemed, in the eyes of certain French-language intellectuals such as Tariq Ramadan, 'to be developing analyses increasingly governed by a communitarian concern that tends to relativize the defence of universal principles of equality and justice'. Others, however, including Janine Chasseguet-Smirgel, have seen him as

---

* Pierre-André Taguieff: born in Paris in 1946. Sociologist, political scientist and historian of ideas, Taguieff is a director of research at the CNRS. Originally close to the Situationists, his early work was on racism and the *Nouvelle droite*. Taguieff later became an editorial board member of the pro-Iraq War journal *Le Meilleur des mondes* and has multiplied his works on the 'new anti-Semitism', dubbed 'Judeophobia', and his criticisms of intellectuals critical of Israel. Author of many books.

one of the few non-Jewish intellectuals in France who has taken up the defence of Jews. In her contribution to the collective work *Les Habits neufs de l'antisémitisme*, she remarks:

> In fact, as far as I am aware, very few non-Jewish intellectuals in France with regular access to the media have taken up the Jewish cause. Besides Éric Marty, we can cite Pierre-André Taguieff, author of the leading book on anti-Semitism in France, *La Nouvelle judéophobie*. (p. 77)

It is still the case, for both sides, that by publishing *La Nouvelle judéophobie* in 2002, followed by *Prêcheurs de la haine. Traversée de la judéophobie planétaire* (2004), Taguieff has in some sense become the leading light in the 'defence of Zionism' and the 'struggle against anti-Semitism' in France. We shall take a look at his much-remarked – and remarkable – contribution to so-called 'communitarian' discourse.

THE DEFENCE OF THE WEST '(INCLUDING ISRAEL)'

According to the author of *La Nouvelle judéophobie*,[1] the progressive, nationalist (Palestinian) and Islamic versions of anti-Zionism all display the same political intent to destroy the Jews, since every form of anti-Zionism 'in the strong sense of the term' comes down in the last instance to a form of 'eliminationist anti-Semitism':

> We can define anti-Zionism in the strong sense of the term as 'the strategy aiming to eliminate the state of Israel' (Bat Yeor). This kind of 'anti-Zionism' can be interpreted as the most recent form taken by what certain historians have called 'eliminationist' anti-Semitism (Goldhagen). (*La Nouvelle judéophobie*, p. 38)

In other words, 'eliminationist' anti-Semitism, according to Taguieff, is an ideological disposition that has been transposed unchanged from Nazi Germany to contemporary anti-Zionist advocacy, and the author rejects any distinction between Nazi anti-Semitism and anti-Zionism 'in the strong sense of the term', whatever its ideological character (progressive, nationalist or Islamic). This is his thesis, or his interpretation. But there is another distinction that the author avoids, even though this has an essential bearing on his thesis of Judeo-*phobia*. The various documents Taguieff cites need in fact to be distinguished according to whether they designate Zionism or the state of Israel as the paradigm of Evil (the world Jewish plot), or whether they equate it with a regional or secondary form of imperialism, the shift from one to the other being highly significant if we are concerned with the question of anti-Semitism and its resurgence in the form of a Judeophobic anti-Zionism. Arguing that the state of Israel is responsible for the misfortunes of the Arab world as a whole, even of all humanity, suggests a very different kind of 'Judeophobia' than arguing that Israel is responsible for the misfortunes of the Palestinians. And if the different political forms of anti-Zionism may well all be anti-Zionism 'in the strong sense of the term' – in other words, a challenge to the very principle of Jewish sovereignty in Palestine – it remains that this challenge does not have the same meaning, and consequently does not demand the same analysis, according to whether it resorts to the rhetoric of the world Jewish plot or rather to a political analysis of the Israeli–Palestinian conflict. The rhetoric of the world Jewish plot was displayed, for example, by the president of the Libyan bar, A. Sharafuddin, in a speech at a 1976 conference in Tripoli which is cited by Taguieff in *La Nouvelle judéophobie*:

Zionism, with its inhuman ethnic and racist principles, its devilish plans that spread chaos throughout the world ... [and] its ramifications that play an almost decisive role in the political leadership of the greatest countries in the world, must be viewed not just as a threat to this region, but rather to the world as a whole. (p. 136)

There is however a different anti-Zionist rhetoric that does not resort to the anti-Semitic imaginary of a world Jewish plot. On the same page, Taguieff remarks that the Palestinian intellectual Edward Said also attended the 1976 Tripoli conference intending to compromise him with Sharafuddin's anti-Semitic rhetoric, yet in a note Taguieff quotes this as an example of Said's anti-Zionist argument:

> Zionism and imperialism feed off one another … The struggle against imperialism and racism in modern Europe is a struggle for civilization, and we can only wage it successfully if we understand the system of ideas of the adversary and the origin of these ideas … In theory as in practice, Zionism is a subordinate form of European imperialism. (p. 136 n. 221)

Thus if Taguieff produces well-documented examples of anti-Zionist discourse, in this case Arab, he fails to distinguish between its different rhetorics. Yet an elementary analysis of the two above quotations requires a distinction to be made, according to whether the assertion is (1) that Zionism is a threat to the whole world (Sharafuddin), even *the* imperialist threat par excellence, or (2) that Zionism is a regional, derivative or 'subordinate' form of imperialism (Said), in a sense that is geographical (i.e. limited), historical (i.e. subsequent) and structural (i.e. subordinate) in character. By rejecting this distinction, Taguieff rules out using an analytical tool that would be very valuable for studying the metamorphosis of anti-Semitism into anti-Zionism, if analysis of this metamorphosis indeed depends, as he says, on showing that one and the same 'phobia' is involved.

What is more, not only does Taguieff fail to distinguish between these different anti-Zionist lines of argument, but the way he develops his theme tends to confuse them. Thus on page 228, Taguieff illustrates the refrain of a world Jewish plot by citing the 'supreme leader' of the Taliban, Mullah Omar, who maintained, on the subject of the 11 September 2001 attacks:

I am convinced that those who committed these attacks came from within America … Why did the investigations not take into consideration the absence of 4,000 Jews from their work at the World Trade Center on the day of the attack?

He comments on this statement by highlighting what Léon Poliakov called 'diabolic causality', writing: 'The practised eye of an Islamist is able to discern a Jewish cause behind any event.' He then adds: 'But the Islamist visionary here is only the most visibly grotesque figure of an army of agents of anti-Jewish hatred … fanatical Israelophobes and Americanophobes active in France as in other European countries …' There follows a quotation, 'by way of illustration', from the sociologist and editor-in-chief of the publishing house Éditions Fata Morgana, Bruno Roy:

Certain humanists hoped that the fair warning addressed to the USA on 11 September would lead it, given its moderation (the 5,500 deaths were less than 1 per cent of the victims of the blockade imposed on Iraq), to change its policy. A vain illusion: the worst of terrorist states, founded on genocide, enriched by slavery, prospers only on crime, from Mexico to Hiroshima, from Guatemala to Vietnam, from Colombia to Palestine. If today the Afghan people are the direct victim of bombings (and Palestine the indirect victim, as the Zionist power has taken advantage of the situation to intensify its massacres), it is all the more impossible for us to remain indifferent when the French government, a valet of the Americans, seeks to involve us in this crime.

And Taguieff concludes this quotation by mentioning the effort it takes him, as an intellectual and a reader of Primo Levi, not to give in to 'hatred'.[2] But in making this effort, he does not make clear that these two arguments proceed in strictly opposite directions. For the Taliban leader, it is the Jews or Zionists who act through American power and use this despite itself, even against itself – an example of the most died-in-the-wool rhetoric of the Jewish plot. For Roy, on the other hand, it is the United States that acts through Zionism ('from Mexico to Hiroshima, from Guatemala to Vietnam, from Colombia to Palestine'), signalling a different form of anti-Zionist rhetoric (the second form in the distinction we made above), with Israel as the 'subcontractor' of the United States in the Middle East. Examining this distinction means examining the different ways in which the identification between Israel and the United States is at work in anti-Zionist argument. And what this question brings to light, when it is raised, is a second and still more fundamental question of this identification itself. In fact, an identification between Israel and the United States seems to be what provides the common denominator between these two distinct anti-Zionist rhetorics. On the one hand, we observe the thesis of the Jewish plot (Sharafuddin and Mullah Omar, or again Saddam Hussein – cited on page 18 – maintaining in October 2001: 'Security for America and for the world could be obtained if … America freed itself from its damaging alliance with Zionism, which has constantly plotted to exploit the world and plunge it into blood and darkness, using America and other Western countries to this end'); and, on the other hand, the progressive thesis that presents Zionism as a secondary or derivative form of imperialism (Edward Said or Bruno Roy) – their common denominator being that both cases refer the Jewish or Zionist fact to a Western imperialist matrix, whether the former is cause (world Jewish plot) or effect (a 'subordinate' imperialism). Thus in obstinately confusing what it is important to distinguish and then to analyze, Taguieff dismisses one of the main axioms of anti-Zionism – the identification of Israel with a Western imperialist matrix – his reason being that this axiom is not, according to him, something to be questioned, but rather to be reversed. By maintaining that this matrix is not imperialist but civilizing, the 'defence of Zionism' then becomes akin to a defence and illustration of the universal vocation of Western civilization. And in fact, after having removed 'eliminationist' anti-Semitism from its historical matrix and making it the essence of anti-Zionism 'in the strong sense of the term', and in the process confusing what should be distinguished, the key operation for our analyst is then to posit America as the target of the new 'eliminationist' anti-Semitism – an operation that takes the form of a correction made to Annie Kriegel's thesis:

> Annie Kriegel maintained that 'anti-Zionism is to Communism what anti-Semitism was to Nazism'. Today this formula needs to be revised and corrected: accusatory anti-Zionism and demonizing anti-Americanism are to neo-Communism and neo-leftism what 'redemptive' anti-Semitism (Friedländer) was to Nazism. (p. 74)

Whereas Kriegel, though assimilating the question of Jewish existence to that of the state of Israel, maintained the singularity of the name of Israel in order to understand the contemporary avatars of anti-Semitism, Taguieff, for his part, corrects her thesis on one particular point (leaving aside the rhetorical enthusiasm), namely that for him 'anti-Americanism' is likewise an avatar of anti-Semitism. The main argument or centre of gravity in his book is thus the following: 'The criminalization of Israel went together with that of the West as a whole: the history of the West was simply one continuous crime, the moving image of the eternal and immobile crime, its essence' (p. 141). And a note relating to the 'history of the West' is appended to the word 'essence' (n. 232), in which Taguieff indicates one of the sources of this 'criminalizing argument', i.e. 'a number of publications of the Nation of Islam, a Black-American organization led by Louis Farrakhan', and particularly one titled *The Secret Relationship Between Blacks and Jews*, which he describes in these terms:

> [This work is] devoted to describing the capital involvement and responsibility of Jews in the African slave trade, on the assumption that this was the real 'holocaust', the major genocide, in the history of the world (the number of victims being given as 100 million). We read here for example: 'Jews were undeniably connected with the greatest criminal operation ever undertaken

against an entire race: the holocaust of Blacks from Africa. They
took part in the capture and forced export of millions of citizens
of Black Africa into a life of inhuman and degrading servitude,
for the profit of Jewish financiers ... Jews, as major operators in
this enterprise, bear a monumental blame for slavery – and the
holocaust.'

After some bibliographic references, Taguieff continues with the
following passage: 'This essentialist criminalization thus only targeted the West and Israel, i.e. the two figures of Satan, too many
in a world of Others populated by pious believers, pure revo-
lutionaries, generous humanists – in brief, angels and archangels
made men' (pp. 141–2). The quotations offered the reader in the
note just quoted (n. 232) and interposed between the two passages
cited above, thus have the function of illustrating an 'essentialist
criminalization' aimed at 'the West and Israel'. Our analyst's procedure consists once again, therefore, in confusing what should
be distinguished. In actual fact, the contentions of the work he
cites in this note are anti-Semitic, or Judeophobic, in so far as
the trade in black slaves was not a fact of Jewish history, but a
fact in 'the history of the West'. Consequently, what should be
noted and challenged here is the identification of Jews as 'major
operators in this enterprise' – this 'enterprise' having its effects
not just on North American society, but also on the bourgeoisie of the western coastal cities of France (in particular, Nantes
and Bordeaux), yet hardly in Israel or among Jewish communities – or at least, not essentially. To conclude from the argument of
Farrakhan or his disciples that 'the criminalization of Israel went
together with that of the West as a whole' thus means judging
that Westerners were not, any more than Jews, 'major operators
in this enterprise' – or at least that if they both were, this does not
justify such an 'essentialist criminalization'. (Arabs, Black Africans
themselves, Japanese, etc. were also 'major operators' in historical
enterprises of this kind.)

In other words, the procedure of Taguieff's argument has the
effect, and the purpose, of positing a strict equivalence between the

two following statements – the first from Farrakhan, the second being the historiographical consensus – in the sense that they are both the expressions of an 'essentialist criminalization': (a) 'Jews, as major operators in this enterprise, bear a monumental blame for slavery'; (b) 'Westerners, as major operators in this enterprise, bear a monumental blame for slavery'. In fact, the question of knowing whether the triangular trade was an event in Jewish history or in 'the history of the West' makes no more sense for Taguieff than it does for Farrakhan, given that the difference between statement (a) and statement (b) disappears in Taguieff's writing just as it does in Farrakhan's mind; hence the strange mirror – or repetition – effect.[3]

In his *Histoire d'antisémitisme*, Léon Poliakov relates an incident involving a Jew named Mendès, the owner of two 'black' slaves, the two slaves themselves, and the legal system of the ancien régime in Paris. The point of this story is to illustrate the social condition of the Jews under the ancien régime, and it closes a chapter devoted to 'militant anti-Semitism', which Poliakov presents as 'essentially a bourgeois Christian phenomenon'. Here is the passage:

> Let us conclude with an insight into the social condition of Jews in Paris in the latter days of the ancien régime. This is taken from a court case that the Bordeaux Jew Mendès brought in 1776 against the Blacks Gabriel Pampy and Amynte Julienne. (These two were slaves whom Mendès had brought back from the West Indies. In Paris, they had run away from their master, who applied to the court to make them return.) During the hearing, the Jew and the Blacks exchanged, via the speeches of their lawyers, the unflattering views that Europe held about each side. One side accused the sons of Ham of all being 'cheats and liars', the other responded that 'they could make the same charge about the Jewish nation, and the parallel might well not be favourable to them'. They accused Mendès of cruelty, citing several examples; but the most frightful torment they experienced was that 'their master prevented them from fulfilling the duties of the Catholic religion, in which they had the fortune to have been raised'. But

why did Mendès come and settle in Paris? According to the lawyer for Pampy and Julienne, 'the capital seemed to him the most favourable place to stay. All ranks here were much mixed up, and if a wealthy Jew did not enjoy the flattering attention that is the greatest need of a well-born man, he could at least enjoy all the pleasures that could be obtained for gold … If his stay in this city promised many pleasures for Mendès, it was fatal for his Black servants. For the Jew, far from letting them experience the kindness that characterizes the French, on the contrary caused them to regret the heavy work in which they had been employed in the colonies …' The court found in favour of Pampy and Julienne.[4]

The interest of this story, for our present purpose, is clearly that it can be taken to serve three contrary interpretations, depending on whether one adopts the standpoint of Farrakhan, of Taguieff or of Poliakov. In Farrakhan's perspective, this document is evidence that Jews were 'major operators' of slavery, since the slave-owner here was Jewish (and what is more, from Bordeaux). In Taguieff's perspective, it demonstrates that the 'criminalizing argument' of Farrakhan (or his disciples) against the West is unfounded, since this ancien régime court freed the slaves: the West is thus a universal benefactor and the victim of ingratitude. In Poliakov's perspective, the document shows that Jews, while not being blacks, were also not Christians – and sometimes seen as even less than the blacks who themselves, according to Montesquieu, were not viewed as men: 'It is impossible for us to suppose these creatures to be men, because, allowing them to be men, a suspicion would follow that we ourselves are not Christians.'[5] But would this not be, under cover of a scathing irony characteristic of the French classic tradition, a 'criminalizing argument'?

FRANCOPHOBIA AND JUDEOPHOBIA

On page 177 of *La Nouvelle judéophobie*, Taguieff describes the way in which, after 1989, 'neo-revolutionaries' substituted for the figure of the proletarian that of the disinherited or excluded, spelling out that in France 'it is recent immigrants and young people of Maghrebian and African descent who have been the object of this reinvention of the proletariat'. A study of the following extract will enable us to trace the course of Taguieff's thinking, and analyze the way in which, in his perspective, 'Francophobia and Judeophobia go together'.[6]

Francophobia and Judeophobia go together. The Islamophilia of these milieus crowns their hierarchical vision of ethno-social categories: the superior race-class is the pure 'multicultural'; the inferior one is the pure 'French' of European origin (neither Italian nor Spanish descent can rescue the 'French' from their innate horror). As for the 'Zionist entity' and its representatives in the diaspora, who are 'everywhere', this is beyond any category, off the scale: neither above nor below, but facing us as the embodiment of diabolic causality. The aesthetic-leftist theme of 'multicultural' beauty and the celebration of this in advertising is now joined, in the imaginary of certain activist elites, with an a priori sympathy for those people perceived en bloc as victimized 'foreigners' or 'immigrants', i.e. the irregular or 'clandestine', celebrated by the new right-minded as *'sans papiers'*. The individuals essentialized as victims or excluded are fictionalized as privileged bearers of a subversive potential that is lacking in others. Criminals, for example, and terrorists in their wake, whether or not they 'come from elsewhere' (or are imagined to) are transformed into 'rebels', 'resisters', and sometimes lauded as such. The Intifada can be replayed on French soil, the Algerian war likewise. To the question 'What does Palestine represent for you?', young people from Maghrebian immigrant background replied, for example, in the context of a survey conducted in 1997–98, 'It's a country fighting like the Algerians during the war there. They're courageous, because Israel is very powerful, they have weapons and money from the Americans'; 'Palestine is like Algeria when the French were there'; 'It's a country stolen from the Arabs by the colonialists, who put the Jews there to get rid of them'; 'Palestine is a banner for all Arabs who want to have justice and stand upright' (statements cited by Jacques Tarnero, 'Les territoires occupés de l'imagination beur', *Observatoire du monde juif*, November 2001). (pp. 178–9).

The objective reality of many of these individuals of foreign origin who are 'fictionalized as privileged bearers of a subversive potential that is lacking in others' is thus described by the author in the ominous formula: 'criminals, and terrorists in their wake'. In fact, the terms 'criminals' and 'terrorists' appear in his text without quote marks, signalling that this is indeed an objective representation, not the production of 'the imaginary of certain activist elites', whereas 'rebels' and 'resisters' are placed in quotes, signalling the contrary. And with the help of this 'aesthetic-leftist theme', 'young people from Maghrebian immigrant background' naturally come to identify with the Palestinians or the Algerians. In other words, once the criminal is fictionalized as a 'rebel', the national territory becomes the theatre of a sad comedy: 'The Intifada can be replayed in France, the Algerian war likewise.' Such a production should precisely lead the analyst of the 'new Judeophobia' to the following remark. The history of Maghrebian and also, to a large extent, African immigration – i.e. the history of these populations who are 'essentialized as victims and excluded', but whose objective reality seems more in Taguieff's view to indicate crime, terrorism or anti-Semitism – is bound up with the colonial question, and thus with a history told by Maghrebian or African parents, and in the case of Algeria, with the history of a war long denied as such in the official discourse of the French Republic, which referred to it rather by the disturbing euphemism of 'maintaining order'. Zionism, on the other hand, has not impinged on these immigrant populations in France. What should really be analyzed, and then deconstructed, is therefore this identification between the Algerian War and the Israeli–Palestinian conflict, with a view to unravelling the 'new Judeophobia' of these young people of Maghrebian origin who, when questioned by Jacques Tarnero, would seem susceptible to confusing, in their enthusiasm of their 'rebellion', representatives of the established order – the police as particular exemplar – and a lone individual wearing a Jewish kepi. This would mean forgetting, however, that in Taguieff's eyes, replaying the Intifada in France by attacking the Jewish minority, and replaying the Algerian war in France by attacking the French police, indicate precisely one and the same phobia. On page 180, in fact, Taguieff evokes violence aimed at 'Jews or "French", the latter being perceived by these "young people" as "native French"'. He goes on to spell out, on page 204, that in the mythology of the 'new Judeophobia: the *"feuj"* is the enemy, perceived either as too French (too assimilated) or as too foreign ("Zionist")'.* And once it is maintained that phobia about Jews is equally phobia about 'native French', Taguieff proposes to deepen this equivalence by resort to an analytical reading of the words of the 'young people from the *banlieues*': 'He [the victimized youth from the *banlieues*] can innocently use the words "Jew" ("*feuj*") or "French" as terms of abuse, hate the police ("*keufs*") and treat them as enemies to be ambushed.' We now have as objects of the 'new Judeophobia' observable in France today: the Jew, the 'native French' and the police. For attacking a policeman and attacking a Jew, according to Taguieff, is strictly one and the same thing in analytic terms: the very homophony between *'feuj'* and *'feuk'* proves it. In other words, Taguieff's reformulation of the psychoanalytic hypothesis of the authors of *L'Univers contestationnaire* would be that the real *'feuj'* is the *'feuk'*.

The reader can now understand that the point is in no way to refute the identification between the Israeli–Palestinian conflict and the Algerian War, since, on the contrary, the 'defence of Zionism' and the 'struggle against anti-Semitism', as Taguieff understands them, are precisely identified by these 'young people

---

★ *'Feuj'* is *'Juif'* in the popular youth slang known as *Verlan*, where syllables are inverted. In *Verlan*, a cop or *'flic'* is a *'keuf'*. However, the syllables are sometimes inverted once again – as below, in this paragraph – and so *'keuf'* becomes *'feuk'*.

from Maghrebian immigrant background', who share with him the same interpretative grid (if without sharing his value system), i.e. 'Palestine is Algeria when the French were there'.[7] And it is in the light of this axiom that we should understand his condemnation of Roger Garaudy,* when he cites, in notes 201 and 202 (pp. 124–5) appended to Garaudy's name and the title of his book, *Les Mythes fondateurs de la politique israélienne*, the conclusion of another book of Garaudy's, *L'Affaire Israël*, which is supposed to illustrate the 'demonization of Israel': 'The Zionist state of Israel has no legitimacy in the place it was implanted: neither historical, nor biblical, nor legal' (p. 124 n. 201). Garaudy's conclusion is thus identical to the words of these 'young people from Maghrebian immigrant background' who assert, on the subject of Palestine: 'It's a country stolen from the Arabs by the colonialists, who put the Jews there to get rid of them', this being why 'Palestine is like Algeria when the French were there'. Yet there is a significant difference between Garaudy's writings and the words of these young people: whereas Garaudy's books present Zionism as the work of a Jewish plot, the assertions of these young people of Maghrebian immigrant background present it as an effect of colonialism, and equally as the effect of specifically European anti-Semitism, since Zionism became one of the historical modalities for excluding Jews from Europe: an exclusion for which the Arabs had to pay ('a country stolen from the Arabs by the colonialists') – a plot, indeed, but certainly not a *Jewish* one (the question remains as to what the Arabs for their part intend to do with the Jews). Yet against all good sense, Taguieff presents the words of these young people as illustrating the thesis of a Jewish plot, introducing their statements with the remark: 'As for the "Zionist entity" and its representatives

---

* Roger Garaudy: born in Marseille in 1913. Elected to the PCF's Central Committee in 1945, Garaudy was the Party's official philosopher for much of the postwar period, until he became a dissident in the late 1960s and was expelled in 1970. After a return to his Christian roots, he converted to Islam and became a militant anti-Zionist, slipping from the mid-1990s onwards into Holocaust negationist positions, for which he has been condemned in court. Author of a very large number of books from 1945 onwards.

in the diaspora, who are "everywhere", this is beyond any category, off the scale: neither above nor below, but facing us as the embodiment of diabolic causality.' The quotations that are supposed to attest that the Jews 'are everywhere' thus appear, in the event, as highly inapposite, since, in the light of the statements gathered by Tarnero and cited by Taguieff, these young people interpret the Israeli–Palestinian conflict after the paradigm of a colonial war, and not that of a world Jewish plot, since if there is a plot it is rather that of the West – 'to get rid of them', i.e. the Jews. But here again the question of the analyst's silences arises, silences that, as we have seen, structure his line of argument and are anchored in an assumption, even a foundational myth, that Taguieff shares with these young people from Maghrebian immigrant background – that 'Palestine is like Algeria when the French were there' – but on which subject he draws strictly opposite conclusions. 'Defending Zionism', 'the struggle against anti-Semitism' and re-conquering the 'lost territories of the French Republic' are in fact precisely the same thing now as defending Israel, they are defending what Israel *signifies* – i.e. the West '(including Israel)', and consequently '*Algérie française*': its methods, its fantasies, its mystique. All that is needed is to reveal its gospel.

QUESTIONS OF METHOD

Following on from the text cited above, Taguieff mentions 'the figure of Khaled Kelkal', the presumed author of the terrorist attack at Saint-Michel station in Paris in 1995:

> We recall the way in which the figure of Khaled Kelkal, this 'youth' from Vaulx-en-Velin who seemed not to have any 'baggage' [*histoires*] – in fact, a petty criminal who had moved on to Islamism – was heroized after his directly filmed death (29 September 1995): the sorry end of a pathetic criminal-terrorist (connected to the GIA) was transfigured into the death in combat, arms in hand, of a courageous rebel, a hero and martyr

of the cause. The eternal hallucinatory return of Che Guevara; contemporary new-leftism has lived since 1989 off these ersatz avenging heroes. (p. 180)

According to this 'aesthetic-leftist' transfiguration, Khaled Kelkal was a youth from Vaulx-en-Velin who 'died in combat, arms in hand', i.e. a symbol of innocence, just cause and sacrifice. But Taguieff opposes this mystification with the true story of Kelkal, reminding his reader or informant that 'this "youth" from Vaulx-en-Velin who seemed not to have any "baggage"' only appeared that way in the eyes of the new leftists in desperate need of a new hero. Hence the scare quotes around 'baggage', which aim at demystifying the purely subjective gaze of the leftist aesthete, the gaze of a doting mother owl to which Taguieff opposes the lucid, severe and trenchant objectivity of the eagle: 'in fact, a petty criminal who had moved on to Islamism'. Kelkal was a petty criminal known to the police, which made it possible to identify his fingerprints on the debris of the bomb that exploded at Saint-Michel. And in the eyes of Taguieff, this criminal past shatters the myth of a youth with 'no baggage', since there is no break in continuity between the petty criminality of a Maghrebian youth and Islamist terrorism; such a person moves on naturally from one to the other, as Kelkal himself 'moved on to Islamism', i.e. to terrorism. The substantivized form of the 'criminal-terrorist' thus inscribes in grammatical terms the objective reality that is in question here, i.e. that for a youth of Maghrebian origin from Vaulx-en-Velin, petty criminality equals terrorism, the only question remaining whether it is terrorism that boils down to a form of petty criminality or vice versa, while appropriate legal and police treatment depend on the answer given.

To reply to this question, we need to look at notes 309 and 310 that are appended respectively to the heroizing of Kelkal and to the figure of 'courageous rebel' he represents. In note 309, Taguieff cites a communiqué from the GIA evoking 'the martyrdom of brother Kelkal, killed by an army of Christian soldiers', and goes on to propose an illustration of 'interpretation in terms of "anti-racist" victim', in fact the 'statements of young *"beurs"* cited by Jacques Tarnero': 'Khaled Kelkal wasn't given a chance, not at school and not in life, he was killed like a dog. Why?' 'It's always young Arabs who are shot in the back. Why?' The mythic narrative here originates with the communiqué of the GIA terrorists, this then being taken up in the words of the 'young *"beurs"*', words that undoubtedly maintain the tale of innocence and injustice, but substitute for the figure of 'martyr' that of the petty criminal who is 'killed like a dog'. As against the heroic or epic style of the GIA communiqué, the words of the 'young *"beurs"*' assert a far more prosaic reality, that of an inequality of opportunity 'at school' and 'in life'. But according to Taguieff, this 'victim' interpretation continues that of the 'martyr' and vice versa, just as the figure of terrorist continues that of the criminal, both interpretations being – according to him – aspects of one and the same political and social reality: the 'criminal-terrorist'.

Note 310 then concludes Taguieff's historico-critical analysis of the mythic account, by revealing the sociological illusions at work, whether deliberately or not, in the 'heroizing' of this criminal:

> This heroizing was facilitated by the publication in *Le Monde*, on 7 October 1995, of a long empathetic interview conducted in 1992 by the German sociologist Dietmar Loch, in the course of a study of young people from immigrant background in a Lyon *banlieue*. The young Islamic terrorist appears here as a victim of republican France, which was unable to integrate him, instead 'excluding' him and thus driving him to despair and revolt. The essential point is here: it is not the terrorist who should be viewed as responsible for his acts, but an exclusionary and discriminatory French society that led a good lad of Maghrebian origin to become a terrorist and commit attacks or murders.

Taguieff thus reveals the myth's inner workings: by publishing, soon after his directly filmed death, 'a long empathetic interview' with Kelkal, *Le Monde* allegedly accredited and conveyed the mythical account given by the German sociologist Dietmar Loch, thus serving as the media relay for a methodological, political and moral imposture, since the 'criminal-terrorist' (Kelkal) becomes the victim, while the victim (the republican order) becomes the guilty party: 'the essential point is here'.

The interview published in *Le Monde* is an extraordinary coincidence for sociology, since this monograph on a youth from the *banlieues* with an immigrant background proved to be a unique document on the experience, words and history of Khaled Kelkal, one youth of Maghrebian origin among so many others, three years before his involvement in terrorism and what turned out to be his 'exemplary' fate – in the sense of one from which a lesson should be drawn. This interview shows the existential difficulties of a young *lycée* student from the 'estates' who reached the *terminale* class, completing therefore a regular education that promised integration both at work and in social life, but a person who found it hard to cope with his school environment, and particularly the fact of being isolated because of his ethno-cultural and social origins. 'In my *lycée* class there were rich kids', Kelkal says for example in this interview, which Taguieff mentions but does not quote. Or again:

> At the end of the *troisième* class, top of the class in science! I did my biology dissertation for La Martinière, La Duchère.* They saw my essay. There was a girl in my class who had done the same thing. She was not as good as me, but she was French. They accepted her but not me. That already shattered me.

Likewise:

> Really, the law doesn't like Arabs. It's a two-tier system. The guy from Vaux-en-Velin who gets caught is sure to get a year and a half more than the others, that's certain. As far as I'm concerned, there's no justice. What they call justice is injustice.

---

* Lyon has three of the prestigious La Martinière colleges, one of these being La Martinière Duchère.

This isolation also attests to the fact that fellow students from the estates were rare in his *terminale* class, which emphasizes the singularity of his itinerary, since before moving on from criminality to terrorism he was a *terminale* student aspiring to La Martinière Duchère. In Taguieff's eyes, however, the 'essential point' is that by publishing such an interview on 7 October 1995, *Le Monde* was complicit in a mystification that aimed at making Kelkal into the 'victim' of an 'exclusionary and discriminatory' French society, whereas it is Kelkal's life – and not this myth – that should be investigated if the rules of good sociological method are to be satisfied.

The interview by Dietmar Loch is conducted according to the rules of a certain method (let us say, Durkheimian, which is also the method of the sociologists Beaud and Pialoux – who are victims, according to Brenner, of a 'sociological illusion'). That is to say, Loch's piece exhibits (a) determination of a field of research (young people from immigrant background in a Lyon *banlieue*); (b) elaboration of a working hypothesis (for example, that these young people are 'impervious to the norms of republican integration', or in an alternative hypothesis, slightly different from that of Brenner and Taguieff,[8] that the norms in question are first of all economic, social and ethno-cultural before being republican, hence the imperviousness of these young people); and finally, (c) objective recording of documents (unobtrusiveness of the analyst during the interview), in order to permit the sociologist to validate or invalidate his working hypotheses. This methodical interview, therefore, becomes for Taguieff 'a long empathetic interview', i.e. something conducted without a genuine method, uncontrolled and betraying a flagrant ideological sympathy with the purpose, as we have seen, of substituting a collective responsibility (that of the republican state) for an individual one (that of Kelkal).

These methodological considerations on the subject of Dietmar Loch's interview with Khaled Kelkal are also echoed by several others in Taguieff's book, their theme being a critique of empathy in the social sciences. Thus in note 362 devoted to a book by the Islamologist François Burgat, *L'Islamisme au Maghreb. La voix du Sud*,[9] Taguieff lambastes the 'radical cultural relativism' of the author and his method, summing this up in the following terms:

> The principle is simple, and can be formulated as follows: 'Everyone has their own modernity'. And any interference in the internal affairs of another 'modernity', including the Islamist (sic) one in the course of construction, is misplaced, illustrating the sins of ethnocentrism and imperialism. Do not judge, the 'Islamologophiles' accordingly advise, rest content with observing and understanding, with the requisite methodological empathy. It remains the case that this empathy itself frequently moves on from a methodological one to a political one, and the cool distance of the scientist gives way to the passion of the acknowledged defender or authorized celebrator. Hatred of Western modernity can thus lead to justifying the worst forms of savagery. (p. 212)

We can immediately understand that Durkheim and Lévi-Strauss are the implicit references of this methodological obscurantism with which Taguieff charges both the German sociologist and the Islamologist cited here, and from which, as a Galileo of the social sciences, his ambition is to deliver us. To follow him, in fact, 'observing and understanding' would be the principle of a pseudo-scientific methodology that, once inscribed in the public space, particularly that of journalism, turns out to 'lead to justifying the worst forms of savagery', and all in the name of a 'hatred of Western modernity'. We can therefore conclude that the Taguieff method consists in *judging* rather than 'observing and understanding'.[10] And this method would seem to apply to the whole field of the social sciences, which Taguieff seeks to put on a new basis. In fact, whether we are dealing with sociology, ethnography or history, the lesson is the same, as he reminds us in this note on a certain Israeli historian who is equally guilty of the same 'methodological empathy' (p. 99 n. 156):

This group of historians lives from its pro-Palestinian commitment at least as much as from its historiographical activities, which are largely reduced to seeking confirmation, by recourse to new archives, of the Palestinian claims about Israeli history. Moreover, as is to be expected, the majority of these 'new historians' are to be found on the far left, and may be seen as Communist activists … Ilan Pappé, a member of Hadah, the Front for Peace and Equality (of Communist allegiance), does not hide his real sources of inspiration (translated back into working hypotheses!), and candidly states: 'It is from them (Palestinian intellectuals) that I learned the Palestinian version of the events of 1948. Later, I sought evidence of their grievances in the archives. And this work succeeded in establishing the legitimacy of some of these grievances.'[11]

However, 'observing and understanding' means proceeding to a methodical analysis of empirical data, whereas *judging*, in this perspective, means concluding, something that both Pappé and Burgat indeed do, in so far as these conclusions do not imply (at least ideally – i.e. a 'regulative idea' in the Kantian sense of the term, a concept that Taguieff moreover cites and accepts) any other requirements than those of method, research hypotheses and analytical tools that are openly displayed. Thus to take the example of the candid Ilan Pappé, his methodological fault is not immediately clear, since taking either Palestinian or Israeli positions as working hypotheses in no way influences the method applied, the question being that of rigorous and objective use of archives, which presupposes that the researcher submits both his working hypotheses and his ideological orientations to the test of facts in the one case, and of criticism in the other. Now Taguieff in no way contests the content of Pappé's work, nor his ability to submit his personal convictions to objective discipline (although, like any research, this objectivity is imperfect and incomplete, but not necessarily partisan, which would invalidate any objective claim). And such a questioning of the critical objectivity of Pappé's work can in no way be considered self-evident simply because of his choice of 'Palestinian positions' as working hypotheses, even if this is where we find the weighty exclamation mark of methodological insinuation ('translated back into working hypotheses!'), and for two reasons. (1) Pappé, as cited by Taguieff, states that his work 'succeeded in establishing the legitimacy of some of their grievances', which means equally that Pappé's work contributed to (if not 'succeeded in') establishing the lack of legitimacy of other such grievances, the conclusion being that this is a work of criticism and not methodological obscurantism; (2) the choice of the Israeli positions as working hypotheses was also that of the 'new historians' concerned to put the collective memory of the Israeli nation to the test of history as an objective research discipline, basing themselves on the opening of Israeli military archives (an opening that lay at the origin of this current of 'new historians'), and ending up, here too, by validating certain aspects of Israeli collective memory and invalidating others.

We should therefore conclude that the 'methodological empathy' of which *Le Monde*, Loch, Burgat and Pappé are guilty boils down to the two following alleged faults: (1) failure to discriminate between what should be made public and what should not, such as the testimony of Khaled Kelkal (Dietmar Loch, backed by *Le Monde*), or the Palestinian collective memory of the Israeli–Arab wars (Ilan Pappé); and (2) failure to condemn the object of their research, in this case Kelkal (for Dietmar Loch, backed by *Le Monde*), Islamism (for François Burgat), or Palestinian collective memory (for Ilan Pappé). But these methodological faults, which Taguieff presents as errant paths in the social sciences, imply a counter-method that remains for its part quite obscure, in the sense that Taguieff does not in any way enlighten us about its ultimate principle. Yet – and this is the whole issue at stake in Taguieff's reestablishment of the social sciences – this principle is not a principle of scientific objectivity, but a moral principle, a knowledge of good and evil. Hence the question that confronts any social-science researcher worthy of the name, who has not yet been converted by the Taguieff critique of 'methodological empathy': how is this knowledge acquired? While waiting for a future work by this author that will tackle the question and explain his rules for the guidance of healthy minds, let us assume by way of hypothesis that his discourse on method would be critical of a text by the Israeli historian Zeev Sternhell, an intellectual who has a threefold interest for us here, in that he belongs to a generation of Israelis who won their country's national independence by force of arms; he is located in this current of Israeli 'new historians', in so far as this means questioning official or state memory and submitting it to the test of criticism; and finally, he has devoted the greater part of his work as a historian to the study of the French far right. Sternhell writes:

> For others, for example the children and grandchildren of the pioneer elite, whose ideas and decisions are still studied, or again for all those who set themselves up as jealous guardians of national glories, of the portrait of the group of founding fathers or their statues – in short, for these descendants and these would-be guarantors of correct memory, the historian who brings disagreeable truths to light, challenges myth or indeed shatters it, the historian who puts forward a somewhat nonconformist interpretation is perceived as a spoilsport, even a national enemy. This is not a particular phenomenon of Israeli society, it is very well known in France. In France, too, the emotional memories of some people, and a certain apologetic historiography, continue to try and falsify the perception of a past still present.[12]

But there is still a further difficulty. In fact, there is evidently a weighty distinction between the irresponsible 'methodological empathy' that the German sociologist Dietmar Loch displays, and that of François Burgat, Ilan Pappé or indeed *Le Monde*, which facilitated the heroizing of Kelkal by publishing Loch's 'long empathic interview'. This distinction is that while Burgat, Pappé and *Le Monde* wrote or published after the event (Islamism, the Israeli–Palestinian war, the attack at the Saint-Michel station), the German sociologist, as Taguieff reminds us, interviewed Kelkal in

1992, three years before the 1995 attacks. And so Loch did not interview a criminal, or an assumed criminal, but rather someone who was still just a 'youth from the *banlieues*', of Maghrebian immigrant parentage, even if a (former) delinquent. A more attentive reading of Taguieff's text, however, will enable us to resolve this difficulty. The denunciation ('a long empathic interview') of the German sociologist's method is justified here in these terms: 'The young Islamist terrorist appears here as a victim of republican France.' And by describing Kelkal here as a 'young Islamist terrorist', the common assumption shared by the German sociologist and *Le Monde* is thus deconstructed, an assumption that consists in presenting Kelkal as a youth of Maghrebian origin confronted by the weight of ideology (over a century of colonialism), economics (the 'thirty glorious years' followed by mass unemployment) and town planning (the shanty-towns followed by the 'dormitory estates'), in a society that was 'exclusionary and discriminatory', whereas the objective reality that that the myth transfigures was simply that of a 'young Islamist terrorist'. But as far as Dietmar Loch was concerned, when he interviewed Kelkal in 1992, how could he know that Kelkal was a 'young Islamist terrorist' and accordingly abstain from such 'empathy'? Let us suggest the following response: perhaps Taguieff is denouncing here the lack of philosophical formation of German sociologists, which would have enabled Loch to grasp the 'terrorist' essence of the young Kelkal back in 1992? But this is only mere conjecture, as we do not yet know anything about the perception of essences in the Taguieff metaphysic, a subject on which the author says nothing. (Perhaps he is keeping the explanation of his metaphysics for a future work, or even for a narrow circle of disciples?) The case remains that, if we do not have a reply to this question, we can be sure an inspired – or informed – prefect of police will certainly find one.

AN INTRODUCTION TO TAGUIEFF'S METAPHYSICS: THE HOLY FAMILY

Herr Dühring will keep the unchallenged glory of having constructed his original sin … with two men.
— Frederick Engels, *Anti-Dühring*

Tariq Ramadan's article criticizing the (new) communitarian intellectuals provoked a large number of reactions, including ones from the intellectuals he mentioned.[13] Taguieff's reply to Ramadan particularly deserves our attention, for three reasons: (1) He was the first person cited by Ramadan in his article. (2) His reply is at least consistent, as Taguieff had devoted some fifty pages to the 'Tariq Ramadan case' in the book that serves as his summa, *Prêcheurs de la haine. Traversée de la judéophobie planétaire*, which continues the analyses he developed in *La Nouvelle judéophobie* over nearly a thousand pages. The second part of a three-part 'epilogue' in *Prêcheurs de la haine* is titled 'Islamism and New-Leftism: The Tariq Ramadan Case or the Preacher Unveiled', and takes up pages 890 to 936 of this book. And finally, (3) Taguieff is apparently considered, both by those who share his ideological choices and by those who oppose them, as an 'authentic intellectual'.[14] Analysis of these fifty pages devoted to the 'Tariq Ramadan case' will enable us first of all to grasp, on the basis of a 'case study', what is essential in Taguieff's methodological orientations, and subsequently to clarify the metaphysical argument in this polemical dialogue.

Three rules for the direction of the mind

In concluding this case study, Taguieff writes that 'a new spirit of totalitarianism is on the rise', as beyond the 'Tariq Ramadan case' there is a current of thought or an ideology that has to be analyzed — or in the author's words, 'unveiled' — and this is to be done by whatever means an authentic intellectual has at his disposal, since Taguieff is a philosopher, political scientist, historian of ideas, director of research at the CNRS and teacher at the Institut d'Études Politiques de Paris, as noted on the back cover of his publications. The analysis he offers of the 'Tariq Ramadan case', moreover, is as extensive as it could possibly be – evidence of a profound research that satisfies all the criteria of scientificity (apparatus of bibliographic and critical notes, scholarly concepts, etc.). Taguieff, in fact, traces a methodical portrait of the Swiss intellectual, from his family ties through to his legal record, including the circumstances in which he obtained his doctoral degree. The reader not only learns that Tariq Ramadan failed to obtain the mention 'very praiseworthy' for his doctoral thesis (Taguieff even cites on p. 928 the 'official opinion of the man who was his professor and supervisor', presenting this as 'devastating for the clever impostor'), but also that several shadows hover over Ramadan's genuine university status and that an inquiry was opened on the subject of his supposed links with Islamist terrorism. On page 932, Taguieff mentions 'a disturbed individual by the name of Ramadan, whose connections with Islamist terrorist networks, and al-Qaeda in particular, have been for many years the object of investigation in both Europe and the United States'. And previously (p. 896 n. 9), Taguieff had informed his readers that as far back as 1995, Tariq Ramadan had been banned from visiting France by the then minister of the interior, Charles Pasqua: 'The French secret services suspected the Islamic Centre in Geneva of being a cover for the Algerian GIA'. Being so well informed about the 'Tariq Ramadan case', Taguieff can then maintain that Ramadan is 'questionable on the basis of a bundle of converging signs', so that all that remains is to unveil the man who, 'in the face of such accusations, no matter how well founded', seeks 'to hide behind the shield of the rhetoric of victimhood' (pp. 933–4). But what surprises the reader, beyond the confusion of genres that considerations of this kind are bound to introduce when coming from the pen of a social-science researcher, is the lack of the least analysis, the least commentary, the least quotation from any actual work by Ramadan, throughout these fifty pages devoted to a study of his 'case'. In September 2004, however, the object of this study was already the author of more than a dozen books, either alone or in collaboration, as well as of several dozen articles available on the internet. His texts are therefore well within reach for anyone who proposes to 'unveil' what the author in question thinks, writes and publishes, so that the conclusion any reader must inevitably reach at the end of this study of the 'Tariq Ramadan case' is that no such quotation or analysis of his published works appeared suitable to help denounce this 'clever impostor' whose doctoral thesis did not even obtain the mention 'very praiseworthy'. Taguieff, in fact, only cites from Ramadan's copious bibliography a few odd phrases taken from interviews published in the press (or on television); as well as the title of one of his books, *Aux sources du renouveau musulman (D'al-Agghani à Hassan al-Banna, un siècle de réformisme islamique*, 1998), which Taguieff accuses of being a 'deceptive' presentation of 'the anti-modern, anti-Western and fundamentalist doctrine of Hassan al-Banna'; and finally statements made by others on the subject of Ramadan's books, Ramadan himself, or again his real or supposed connections. As for actual texts by Ramadan, Taguieff gives us only two: first, an article published in *Le Monde* on 24 December 2001, titled 'Existe-t-il un antisémitisme islamique?', and second, the famous 'Critique des (nouveaux) intellectuels communautaires'. Before we come to the analyses that Taguieff proposes of Ramadan's texts, which take up all of three pages, we can thus already assert in advance the three rules for the direction of the mind that orient his investigation of the 'Tariq Ramadan case': (1) don't pay too close attention to Ramadan's written and published work;[15] (2) do, however, look very closely at the various police reports that mention the author in question, including the 'considered opinion' of a man who was his supervisor at university and refused to support his work on the grounds that it was 'purely ideological, lacking any scientific aspect' (cited by Taguieff on p. 928); and finally, (3) conclude that 'a new spirit of totalitarianism is on the rise'.

What is a 'racializing inference'?

On the subject of the first article mentioned, Taguieff writes, on pages 907–10 of his magnum opus:

> In a much remarked article published by *Le Monde* on 24 December 2001 under the title 'Existe-il un antisémitisme islamique?', Tariq Ramadan maintained in a reassuring manner what *Le Monde* readers wanted to hear, i.e. that 'nothing in Islam can legitimize xenophobia' and that 'anti-Semitism is unacceptable and indefensible' – he could certainly have added 'absolutely to be condemned', but this is his theological style.

The acute attention that Taguieff pays to words and concepts is very well illustrated here: Ramadan wrote 'unacceptable and indefensible', but not 'absolutely to be condemned'. And once the implicit has thus been brought to light, Taguieff can reasonably cast doubt on the sincerity of Ramadan's explicit statement:

> The clever preacher went so far as to recognize the reality of an 'anti-Semitic discourse that … is not solely the act of unemployed youngsters', but 'is also conveyed by intellectuals and imams who … see the manipulating hand of the Jewish lobby behind every setback'. For candid minds, who never imagine that language serves also to conceal and to lie, this article revealed the existence of a particularly enlightened Islamic intellectual, who was very courageous in his denunciation of the tendencies or excesses of members of his own religious community.

In other words, this article of Ramadan's was the work of a 'clever preacher' whose aim was to mystify 'candid' readers of a newspaper that specialized in mystification. But Taguieff, for his part, is not one of these, having already noted the 'theological style' of the 'preacher' well before the latter unveiled himself in a second article in October 2003. 'Scarcely two years later, the false revelation was replaced by the true one', Taguieff immediately adds, commenting as follows on the article in question:

the fine spirits of the left were stupefied to discover that their favourite Islamic preacher had drawn up a list of suspect Jews, intellectuals denounced as 'communitarian' and as unconditional supporters of Israeli policy, an operation of delation that amounted, in a context marked by the unleashed passions around the Middle East, to a call to hatred and violence against the intellectuals indicated

(Not to mention here the fact that this was also 'a call to hatred against my own person, as against any supposed member of the "Jewish community"', Taguieff goes on to spell out on page 911.) And after emphasizing the threatening character of this article and the procedure to which it resorts – that of a 'list of suspect Jews' – Taguieff formulates the essential point in his critical analysis as follows:

Being myself Jewish neither on my father's nor my mother's side, should I assume that I am 'Jewified' [*enjuivé*], in the term regularly used in France before 1945? At all events, the far from scrupulous Ramadan reduces my analyses of academics and my own intellectual position to the expression of my supposed ethnic origins, a form of reasoning that is customarily and correctly denounced as 'racist' – a particular form of biological determinism. We know its principle: 'culture follows race', or 'mentality follows race'. This is the racializing inference, which consists in deducing the opinions or positions of an individual from his ethno-racial origins, and thus in reducing all thinking to the expression of an origin or allegiance. Its schema runs as follows: 'Such and such an origin (or allegiance), therefore a corresponding opinion, political position, and worldview'. The Ramadan version of this short reasoning consists in reversing the inference: 'Such and such a political position, therefore a corresponding origin.'

These lines constitute the essential point in the critical analysis that Taguieff offers of a text written and signed by Tariq Ramadan, the remainder of his argument being more akin to a police investigation or a family portrait.

A 'schema' that Ramadan likewise resorts to in the accused article is also presented, one that Taguieff describes as 'racist' and on the basis of which it becomes legitimate to question the honesty of someone who previously maintained, in *Le Monde*, that anti-Semitism was 'unacceptable and indefensible' (though not 'absolutely to be condemned', as Taguieff has already remarked). This is why he concludes that Ramadan's profession of faith against anti-Semitism is simply 'one of those writings designed to be read by naïve minds and "useful idiots"' (p. 914 n. 45), which Taguieff is certainly not … apart from the fact that, once informed of the 'racializing inference' that underlies the article in question, the reader cannot fail to question the manifest and strange reappearance of such an 'inference'.

On pages 919–20, Taguieff writes that 'Tariq Ramadan's accusations against me are false and mendacious, seriously damage my reputation and my honour, and in reality apply to the unscrupulous accuser himself', evidently meaning not that Ramadan is Jewish, but rather that *he* is the 'communitarian' thinker, whereas Taguieff is a republican thinker. Thus, mentioning Ramadan's 'unconditional support' of the Palestinian cause, Taguieff asks: 'What could be more "communitarian" than this system of preferences dictated by both ethnic origin and religious allegiance?' And he adds:

> The fact that this fundamentalist Muslim of Egyptian origin, inevitably 'anti-Zionist', has a sympathetic dialogue with an ex-Communist of Egyptian origin by the name of [Alain] Gresh, a professional 'anti-Zionist' propagandist, constitutes a further sign of spontaneous 'communitarian' posture: it's only natural that a scion of the Muslim Brotherhood and an activist inspired by Middle Eastern Communism should understand one another.

This 'ex-Communist of Egyptian origin by the name of Gresh', had already been presented to Taguieff's readers as 'the biological son of the Egyptian Communist Henri Curiel' who 'seeks to present himself as his father's legitimate political heir', and described in particular as an 'Islamophilic militant' (p. 826 n. 17).[16] Henri Curiel was in fact, according to Taguieff, the 'originator' of 'the revolutionary left's pro-Islamic turn, as this can be observed with the Trotskyists or neo-Communists of *Le Monde Diplomatique*, going as far in certain cases as an Islamic–Communist alliance' (p. 825). The reader's difficulty is thus as follows: on pages 826–7, Taguieff explains that the 'originator' of the 'Islamo–Communist alliance' was 'the singular figure of the Egyptian Communist Henri Curiel'; then, analyzing a text by Ramadan on page 910, he denounces its 'racializing inference' as 'deducing an individual's positions or opinions from their ethno-racial origins', which amounts to 'reducing all thinking to the expression of an origin'; and finally, on page 920, he observes that 'it's only natural that a scion of the Muslim Brotherhood and an activist inspired by Middle Eastern Communism should understand one another', going on to denounce a 'spontaneously "communitarian" posture'. The reader will immediately conclude that the 'Islamo–Communist alliance' raging today on French territory has as its centre of gravity a 'communitarian' alliance between two disturbed characters 'of Egyptian origin', one being a 'scion of the Muslim Brotherhood', the other 'the biological son' of Henri Curiel. Does this mean that the formula of the Taguieff inference is not the 'Ramadan variant' – 'such and such political positions, therefore corresponding origins' – but rather: 'such an such an origin ... therefore a corresponding opinion, political position, and world-view'? It would seem so.[17]

Finally, Taguieff only needs to make clear that, if there is a victim of the denunciatory list drawn up by Tariq Ramadan, a genuine victim who lends this 'list of suspect Jews' its character as not merely 'indefensible' but 'absolutely to be condemned', since this is the republican style of the author, it is Pierre André Taguieff and no one else:

The problem is not that he cites Finkielkraut and Kouchner, but particularly that he tops the list with Pierre-André Taguieff, who is not Jewish. But since he fights anti-Semitism, Tariq Ramadan classifies him as Jewish; and this is anti-Semitic. Since Taguieff is on the wrong side, he cannot but be Jewish. Taguieff's presence at the head of Ramadan's list is not simply anodyne. He is first among the Jews, since as a non-Jew he supports the Jewish cause. This is the fall into anti-Semitism.

Those are the words of the journalist Philippe Val, who has 'demolished very well the preacher's insidious argument', as cited by Taguieff himself on page 910. A nice way to end the discussion.

SAINT PIERRE–ANDRÉ TAGUIEFF'S CONTRIBUTION TO THE HISTORIOGRAPHY OF THE SHOAH

With his January 2002 essay *La Nouvelle judéophobie*, published just a few months after the attacks of 11 September 2001, Taguieff suddenly became a 'communitarian' intellectual. And yet this essay was in no way an occasional text written in reaction to a national and international context marked by these attacks and the Second Intifada, let alone a mere 'polemic' [*pamphlet*] (as Tariq Ramadan put it), but precisely the culmination of a work of research that went back at least to November 1989, since it was then that Taguieff published in *Les Temps Modernes* (no. 520) an article with the title 'La nouvelle judéophobie'. Besides, it is only necessary to take a look at the bibliography of this prolific academic to recognize his longstanding concern to continue writing a history of anti-Semitism which had begun way back with Jules Isaac and Léon Poliakov, with the difference, however, that the Taguieff approach to certain dark periods in this history is rather singular, to say the least. Thus, in his imposing study on *Les Fins de l'antiracisme*, published in 1995, Taguieff devoted a chapter to the 'variations of Christian anti-racism', and in particular the attitude that the Catholic church displayed towards Nazism. The question for him was to analyze the way in which Christian universalism, as understood by the Vatican, was opposed to Nazi racism. On page 97, he cited a speech by Pius XI, given on 21 July 1938 to churchmen of the Italian Catholic Action, in which the pope reasserted the universality of Catholicism in these terms: 'Catholic means universal, not racist, nationalist or separatist; no, Catholic.' And Taguieff maintained that in this speech 'Pius XI did no more than summarize the central thesis of the letter signed by Ernesto Ruffini, secretary of the Congregation of Studies, Seminaries and Universities, which was dated 13 April 1938 and intended for wide distribution' (p. 98), this 'central thesis' being a vigorous denunciation of all racial ideology, without the least ambiguity. He adds, however, in referring to this letter, the remark:

> If he clearly spoke out against 'the severe persecution ... against the Catholic church in Germany', it is notable and surprising that he said not a word on the anti-Jewish persecutions, despite their being inherently connected with the firmly condemned Hitler regime.

The question Taguieff raises here is thus that of the silence of the Vatican on the Nazis' anti-Semitic policy from 1933 to 1945, a silence some people view as only (and then only partly) being broken by an encyclical from Pope John-Paul II in 1988.[18] But this is clearly not Taguieff's position, as immediately after raising this difficult question for Western Catholic consciences, he writes: 'It was not until Pope Pius XI's declaration of 6 September 1938, to a group of Belgian pilgrims, that the incompatibility between the Christian spirit and that of anti-Semitism was made decisively clear.' The reader learns, therefore, that on 6 September 1938 the Vatican broke its silence on Nazi anti-Semitic policy, and from the mouth of the pope himself. According to Taguieff, the question of the Vatican's silence on Nazi anti-Jewish persecution thus bears only on the period from 13 April 1938 to 6 September the same year, the few months of ambiguity that separate the letter from Ernesto Ruffini (denouncing the racial ideology of Nazism without mentioning anti-Semitism) from the 'decisive' statement of the pope on 'the incompatibility between the Christian spirit and that of anti-Semitism' – though this 'decisiveness' certainly escaped all those who saw fit to question the silence of the Vatican between 1933 and 1945, or even until 1998, and some would say later still. This 'decisive' statement given by Pope Pius XI on 6 September 1938 ran as follows, as cited in evidence by Taguieff himself:

> Mark well that in the Catholic Mass, Abraham is our Patriarch and forefather. Anti-Semitism is incompatible with the lofty thought which that fact expresses. It is a movement with which we Christians can have nothing to do. Anti-Semitism is inadmissible: spiritually, we are all Semites.

And so, in asserting on 6 September 1938 to 'a group of Belgian pilgrims' that 'anti-Semitism is inadmissible', Pius XI allegedly made a 'decisive' correction on the question of Nazi anti-Semitism.[19] And strengthened by this evidence of the anti-Nazi commitment of the Catholic church, Taguieff sets out to demonstrate further on an 'ideological reconfiguration' that already articulates the main distinctive features of what he called in 2002 the 'new Judeophobia':

> In its texts combating Nazism of 1937–9, the church was right to discern, behind anti-Semitism and anti-Christianism, a fundamental anti-Judeo-Christianism, inseparable from biological racism and from Germanic neo-paganism. This configuration disappeared along with Nazism ... In the most exclusionary ideological configuration today, that of Islamism, anti-Christianism and anti-Semitism are combined with an anti-racism that blends together with a radical anti-Westernism. It is urgent to take the measure of such changes, and draw the lessons needed to redefine 'anti-racism' in the broad sense. (p. 100)

In other words, the 'texts combating Nazism' from Pius XI were followed by those of Taguieff against 'Islamism' (or against the Islamo–Communist alliance). But as for the question of any 'texts combating Nazism' that the Vatican produced between 1939 and 1945, the author has nothing to say, no doubt deeming Pius XI's statement of September 1938 sufficiently 'decisive' that Pius XII, on succeeding him in 1939, had no need to return to the subject, and he can happily conclude this second section of his chapter on 'the anti-racist poetics of the church' with these words – which are not devoid, one must say, of a certain poetry:

> As long as the Hitlerite state endured, the objective of Christian anti-racism was clearly determinable, and perfectly congruent with the objective of evangelization: to contribute to the disappearance of a state racism, to struggle against a totalitarian regime that was both anti-Semitic and anti-Christian, the declared enemy of Christian civilization. Is it necessary to add that the Nazi monstrosity, by leading the church to take a clear position against anti-Semitism, triggered an extremely important turn by making possible the inauguration of a Judeo-Christian dialogue? The existence of an abominable common enemy made it possible to dissipate a number of misunderstandings and to close old wounds.

According to Taguieff, then, Pius XI's 'texts combating Nazism', which essentially means this address to a group of Belgian pilgrims dated 6 September 1938, made it possible 'to dissipate a number of misunderstandings and to close old wounds', on the basis of 'the existence of an abominable common enemy' that, according to the author, was equally opposed to both Christians and Jews. Besides, being 'spiritually Semite', were Christians – and the Holy See first and foremost – not themselves 'spiritually' victims of the Nazi genocide?

In relation to this historiography of the Vatican's anti-Nazi commitment, it seems appropriate to quote a few extracts from a text by Hannah Arendt from 1964, which gives an illuminating correction to the parenthesis opened here, but immediately closed, by Taguieff. Her text, titled '*The Deputy*: Guilt by Silence?',[20] was a review of Rolf Hochhuth's controversial play. Here is how Arendt summed up the message of this play: 'The play deals with the alleged failure of Pope Pius XII to make an unequivocal public statement on the massacre of European Jews during World War II, and concerns by implication Vatican policy toward the Third Reich.' In her review, Arendt also discussed the earlier period, from 1933 to 1939, including the attitude of Pius XI, predecessor of the wartime pontiff. After recalling that, while 'the German episcopate had condemned racism, neo-Paganism, and the rest of the Nazi ideology in 1930', it nonetheless rallied to the Nazi regime after the seizure of power in 1933 and continued to cooperate with it until its fall, even going so far as to afford 'the help of the churches ... in determining all persons of Jewish descent', including those within its own ranks. Arendt mentions the particular attitude of the Holy See under Pope Pius XI, as distinct from that of the national episcopates – German, French, Belgian or Dutch:

> The Holy See had its own policy with regard to the Third Reich, and up to the outbreak of the war this policy was even a shade friendlier than that of the German episcopate. Thus, Waldemar Gurian observed that prior to the Nazi seizure of power, when in 1930 the German bishops had condemned the National Socialist party, the Vatican newspaper, *L'Osservatore Romano*, 'pointed out that the condemnation of its religious and cultural program did not necessarily imply refusal to cooperate politically', while, on the other hand, neither the Dutch bishops' protestation against the deportation of Jews nor Galen's condemnation of euthanasia was ever backed by Rome. The Vatican, it will be remembered, signed a Concordat with the Hitler regime in the summer of 1933, and Pius XI, who even before had praised Hitler 'as the first statesman to join him in open disavowal of Bolshevism', thus became, in the words of the German bishops, 'the first foreign sovereign to extend to [Hitler] the handclasp of trust'. The Concordat was never terminated, either by Pius XI or by his successor [Pius XII]. Moreover, the excommunication of the *Action Française*, a French group of the extreme right whose teachings

of a *catholicisme cerebral* had been condemned in 1926 as a heresy, was withdrawn by Pius XII in July 1939 – that is, at a time when the group was no longer merely reactionary but outright fascist … The Nazi regime had started violating the provisions of the Concordat before the ink on it was dry, but all the time it was in force there had been only one strong protest against the Third Reich – Pius XI's encyclical *Mit brennender Sorge* (With Burning Care) of 1937. It condemned 'heathenism' and warned against elevating racist and national values to absolute priority, but the words 'Jew' or 'anti-Semitism' do not occur, and it is chiefly concerned with the anti-Catholic and especially the anti-clerical slander campaign of the Nazi party.

As for the attitude of Pius XII in the 1933–45 period, Arendt sums this up in the following terms at the start of her review:

> The facts themselves are not in dispute. No one has denied that the Pope was in possession of all pertinent information regarding the Nazi deportation and 'resettlement' of Jews. No one has denied that the Pope did not even raise his voice in protest when, during the German occupation of Rome, the Jews, including Catholic Jews (that is, Jews converted to Catholicism), were rounded up, right under the windows of the Vatican, to be included in the Final Solution.

According to Taguieff, however, this is to forget the 'decisive' statement that the Holy See delivered on 6 September 1938, when Pope Pius XI explained to a handful of Belgian pilgrims that 'anti-Semitism is inadmissible' – even if, we must recall, it was necessary to recognize anyone's 'right to defend himself, to take measures to protect himself against anything that threatens his legitimate interests'.[21]

By way of conclusion to *La Nouvelle judéophobie*, Taguieff writes: 'What remains specifically human in man is the wager in favour of a possible world in which hatred will not have the last word. Love remains our utopia, love combined with intelligence.' We can rest assured.[22]

4

Oriana Fallaci and 'The Jews':
An Ambivalent Resistance

How could a professional journalist, like some revisionist writer, fall into the lazy idea that the role of the Arabs in the invention of modern mathematics or the transmission of Greek philosophy to Europe is a centuries-old fraud? How dare she describe the 'sons of Allah' – the expression constantly recurs like an obsession – as abject and ridiculous creatures who 'spend their life with their backsides in the air praying five times a day' and 'breed like rats'? When, in a further fit of hatred and almost madness, she depicts Islamic immigrants as 'hordes of wild boar' who 'transform the glorious cities of Genoa and Turin into kasbahs', when she describes the alignment of 'sandals' and 'slippers' that 'sullies' the Piazza del Duomo in Florence, when she speaks of 'the sickly smells deposited at the entrance to an exquisite Romanesque church' or the 'disgusting traces of urine that profane the marble of a baptistery' – 'my God! These sons of Allah spurt a long way' – when, in a note specially added to the French edition, she dares to reply to Tahar Ban Jelloum that 'there is something in Arab men that repels women of good taste', then fear, stupor and sadness give way to nausea.

> – Bernard-Henri Lévy, *Le Point* (14 May 2002)

We discover here that Oriana Fallaci is not just an authentic free woman, atheist and progressive, independent and courageous, but that she is also a genuine writer. She writes in the

first person, yet with concern for the universal, she is dynamic
and rhythmical, violent in form and fundamentally inspired by
a burning love: that of truth in the service of freedom.
                    – Robert Misrahi, *Charlie Hebdo* (23 October 2002)

The main contention of the 'communitarian' intellectuals is
the strict equivalence between anti-Semitism and anti-Zionism.
Starting from this equivalence, they set out to measure the 'struggle against anti-Semitism' in terms of support for the state of
Israel, or the 'defence of Zionism'. But the fundamental point
of their thesis is something else: it lies in claiming that the 'defence
of Zionism' and the 'struggle against anti-Semitism' are only
legitimate on condition of being inscribed under the slogan of a
defence of the West – '(including Israel)', in Pierre André Taguieff's
neat formula. The support that Taguieff and Alain Finkielkraut
gave the writer Renaud Camus is indicative in this respect of
the 'communitarian' orientations of these intellectuals.[1] On page
200 of *La Nouvelle judéophobie*, Taguieff speaks of 'those who frenetically campaigned for several weeks in spring 2000 against the
"anti-Semitic statements" supposedly made by the writer Renaud
Camus in his journal for 1994', thus questioning whether this
campaign was justified. And he immediately goes on to spell out
his thinking on this point by devoting a note to it (pp. 200–1
n. 348), in which he writes:

> Unless we ascribe to this writer deep and concealed anti-Jewish
> intentions, his supposed 'anti-Semitism' is hard to demonstrate
> just on the basis of the fragments of text attacked by his accus-
> ers. Certainly, this text includes passages in which prejudices and
> stereotypes from the anti-Semitic tradition are repeated with sur-
> prising naivety, yet this is in a context where there is no call to
> hatred or violence.

It appears, accordingly, that in Taguieff's eyes, 'prejudices and
stereotypes from the anti-Semitic tradition' have a different significance depending on whether they appear from the pen of

Renaud Camus or of Tariq Ramadan, since nothing distinguishes the 'prejudices' and 'stereotypes' aired by these writers in their respective work. What is involved, in both cases, is questioning the Jewish origin of a certain number of intellectual or media figures who publicly express their point of view on questions of society or international politics. Concerning the article by Ramadan, however, Taguieff finds 'an appeal to hatred against my person as well as against any supposed member of the "Jewish community"' (*Prêcheurs de la haine*, p. 911), hence raising the question: what is it that distinguishes these two 'cases'? The continuation of the note that Taguieff devotes to the Renaud Camus case will permit us to confirm the response already sketched. In fact, after maintaining that those worried by 'discovering on all sides traces of "Pétainism", for example in [their] contemporary Renaud Camus', still find nothing to say about the 'anti-Jewish cries of certain "youths"', Taguieff proposes to enlighten his readers as to the origin of this kind of arbitrariness in indignation: 'It is true that, while they may not be readers of Céline's precious pamphlets, these dear little ones also despise France and the French in their own way.' In other words, what makes the anti-Semitic prejudices of Renaud Camus incommensurable with those of Tariq Ramadan is that the first not only embodies 'that identity known as "France"' (Shmuel Trigano), but defends it, whereas the second not only does not embody it, but despises it or attacks it – just like those who campaigned frenetically against Renaud Camus, or 'these dear little ones' who, on the evening of 6 October 2001 at the Stade de France, did not all display tricolour flags.[2] In *L'Imparfait du présent* (2002), Finkielkraut devotes some of the most deeply felt pages of his book to the 'Renaud Camus affair', introducing his argument with the words:

> For more than fifteen years I have been a 'Jewish collaborator' on France Culture ... Being the son of a deportee, a second-generation French citizen and a permanent resident, I could only feel attacked by the exclusivism of this declaration of love, by

the door that it seemed to slam in my face by confining me to a point of view that, though legitimate, was *external*. And yet, when the scandal broke, I did not find myself in the expected camp. (pp. 54–5, original emphasis)

Going on to cite Durkheim, who on the subject of the Dreyfus affair referred to those intellectuals who, by virtue of their 'practice of scientific method', 'were less ready to give way to the pull of the crowd and the prestige of authority', Finkielkraut calls for an attentive reading of the complete works of Renaud Camus, and denounces the fact that, in this case, 'the trial was concluded before even being held' (pp. 55–7). But Finkielkraut, for his part, has read Renaud Camus, and particularly the lines of Camus' *Discours de Flaran* that he cites on pages 58–9 of *L'Imparfait du présent*:

If poetry is unacceptable after the death camps, or can appear so, it is because all speech passed through the mouths of the executioners … It is because the same mentality that constructed the camps, built the railways towards them, found the deadly formula for the gas and justified the unjustifiable, during this time also composed poems, wrote operas, organized art exhibitions. It is because all meaning is compromised, every image is sullied and all beauty is tarnished, that human beings are ashamed to reveal themselves.

These lines from Renaud Camus are commented on by Finkielkraut as follows:

In such a climate of thought, Renaud Camus' reflections on the degrees of national allegiance, his refusal to misconstrue the share of heritage in identity, his staunch attachment to the little that remains of 'knowledge through time', take on a different sense from the essentialist, racist, criminal sense that people have hastened to see in them.

To follow this author, then, it would appear that the 'essentialist, racist and criminal' sense of anti-Semitic prejudice depends on the 'climate of thought' in which it is expressed, and that the attention paid 'to the death camps' is highly significant of this 'climate of thought', since it is the lines Renaud Camus devoted to the memory of the camps that seem to have earned him Finkielkraut's profound esteem and ardent defence. We intend, therefore, to investigate Finkielkraut's homage – and that of other intellectuals along with him, including Daniel Sibony – to a book that is singularly vulgar, violently xenophobic, and racist pure and simple: Oriana Fallaci's *The Rage and The Pride*. For if certain texts by Renaud Camus demand an expert exegesis before an 'essentialist, racist and criminal' meaning (that they do not have) can be conferred on them, this is not the case with this book by Oriana Fallaci, in whose eyes Muslims 'breed like rats'.

ORIANA FALLACI, A 'COMMUNITARIAN' JOURNALIST?

A few weeks after the attacks of 11 September 2001, the Italian journalist Oriana Fallaci published a long article that was subsequently published in book form as *The Rage and the Pride*.* Then, in response both to the hostility that this book aroused, and to the tremendous sales that required successive reprints, particularly in France and Italy (where 800,000 copies had already been sold by May 2002), a new edition appeared along with a preface that was eventually transformed into a second book, *The Force of Reason*, reasserting and developing the essential point of her original work against her contradictors, or, as she put it, her censors. Finally, a third book closed what became her testamentary trilogy, *Interview with Myself* followed by *The Apocalypse*, published in France after

---

* *La Rage et l'orgeuil* (Paris: Plon, 2002) contains certain amendments and additions to the original Italian text, which Fallaci again revised for the American edition, *The Rage and the Pride* (New York: Rizzoli, 2002). I have indicated below where passages cited by Segré cannot be found in the English text.

the author's premature death.* If *The Rage and the Pride* had been written in the emotion aroused by the 11 September attacks in the United States (the author was herself living in New York at the time), the two following books were a cool and calculated expansion of the original text, and the unity of both style and content throughout the trilogy is incontestable evidence that they all share the same inspiration. The essential point of her argument can be summed up as follows. Islamic terrorism is not an aberration of Islam, an obscurantist and criminal reaction to a series of social and political questions, but rather the culminating expression of a religion whose dogmatic content conveys a barbaric obscurantism right from its appearance in the sixth century CE. On page 125 of *The Rage and the Pride* she can therefore write: 'Ousama [sic] Bin Laden and his disciples, I shall never tire of repeating, are only the most recent manifestation of a reality to which the West has been stupidly or cynically shutting its eyes for centuries.' We should make clear, moreover, that the journalist maintains at several points that Islam is not a race but a religion, and consequently her invectives against Islam cannot be seen as racist – which, however, does not prevent her from speaking elsewhere of 'Eurabia' as the foreseeable culmination of Islamic conquest, after asserting, in *The Rage and the Pride*, 'I have never had any sentimental or sexual or friendly relationship with an Arab man. In my opinion there is something about his brothers in faith which repels women of good taste' (note to p. 179 in the French edition).†

Given the racist tendencies scattered throughout Fallaci's text, but also and above all, given the essential point of her argument – reducing Islam to all the stereotypes of a xenophobic imaginary, from the threat that Arab and Muslim otherness represents to the Italian journalist's 'civilization', through to immigrant populations both infested with disease and lusting for conquest – the phobic or pathological dimension of *The Rage and the Pride* seems hard to challenge; hence the question, what is it in France or Italy today

---

* Neither of these essays has appeared in English.
† Absent from the English edition.

that determines the degree of tolerance for such racist lines of argument? The response to this question, as I see it, is simply the greater or lesser degree of permeability to the slogan of a 'defence of the West', in the theologico-pagan form that was provoked in reaction to the traumatism of '11 September'. But since such a defence of the West against Arab and Muslim barbarism is today presented as solidarity with the state of Israel – according to the Taguieff formula, '(including Israel)' – the 'communitarian' intellectuals engaged in the 'defence of Zionism' and the 'struggle against anti-Semitism' immediately recognized *The Rage and the Pride* as an expression in pamphlet form of their own theses on 'the new Judeophobia'. As witness the point of view of Taguieff himself, expressed in the weekly *Actualité juive* on 20 June 2002, that the Italian journalist 'sees things correctly, even if certain of her formulations can shock', and ending his analysis of Fallaci's book: 'My critique would possibly bear on its rather pamphlet-like style, but not on the substance.' As for Finkielkraut, he wrote in the weekly *Le Point* (24 May 2002) that 'Oriana Fallaci has the stellar merit of not letting herself be intimidated by the virtuous lie', while regretting that 'she did not resist the temptation to confine those whom she calls the sons of Allah to their evil essence'. Yet this reservation has no other purpose, from Finkielkraut's pen, than to undermine the arguments of the book's detractors in an ironical and acerbic manner: 'This will enable virtue to regain the upper hand, and enable *Télérama* to denounce the LePenization of minds in a Europe contaminated by the populist "virus".' And a few weeks later he repeated his analysis of the book, this time in *Actualité juive*, following his compeer Taguieff in a complete agreement on fundamentals despite reservations on certain extreme formulations. For his part, Finkielkraut particularly noted, as an example of 'racism', the statement by the author of *The Rage and the Pride* that 'Muslims tend to breed like rats'. (The exact quote is simply: 'they breed like rats'.) But despite this reservation, he adds once again: 'It's a pity, all the more so in that Oriana Fallaci's attitude enables the virtuous lie to take the high ground and condemn any criticism of Islam as racist', even venturing to say that 'there is a certain truth in her exaggeration', after noting the literary force of the book: 'I was struck right away, even captivated, by the vigour of her style and the force of her thinking.' As against this, we might note the analysis of this same book by Gilles Kepel, whom it would be hard to suspect of Islamism. When questioned by the weekly *Le Point*, he wrote that the only interest of Fallaci's book, albeit a real one, was its value as evidence, more precisely as a symptom, in the sense that

> 11 September was an immense catalyst: this horror made it possible to name the Other, the enemy, the threat, to give it a face in the icon of Bin Laden, reducing the *banlieue* gangs and the illegal immigrants of Ponte Vecchio to this in a general confusion of feeling.

And he concluded: 'What opinion polls puzzle to perceive in crowd psychology, literature – bad literature above all – prompts us to decipher.'[3] Drawing inspiration from his analysis, we shall seek to decipher the way in which the writings of Oriana Fallaci published after 11 September 2001 show how Israel and the Jews are 'included' in the defence of the West. One detail of the Italian journalist's text, however, immediately attracted our attention: the insistent absence of the name Auschwitz, just where this seemed necessary.

AN AMBIGUITY IN FALLACI'S TEXT

Oriana Fallaci's statements on the subject of Israel and the Jews are not without a certain ambiguity, once their headline effects are discounted. For instance, the lines on pages 177–8 of *The Rage and the Pride* in which, after having posited an equivalence between Nazism and Islam, she suggests that indulgence or understanding towards Islam, or the Palestinians, is related to a rampant anti-Semitism:

The fad or rather the fraudulent mockery that in the name of Humanitarianism (sic) reveres the invaders and slanders the defenders, absolves the delinquents and condemns the victims, weeps for the Taliban and curses the Americans, forgives the Palestinians for every wrong and the Israelis for nothing. And which basically would like to see the Jews once more exterminated in Dachau and Mauthausen.*

At first reading, Fallaci is repeating here, from her own point of view, the equivalence between anti-Zionism, or vehement criticism of the Israelis, and anti-Semitism. And yet a more attentive reading of this passage immediately displays some ambiguities that may be highly significant, hence the interest in dwelling on them. Fallaci thus denounces 'Humanitarianism (sic)' because it 'absolves the delinquents and condemns the victims', introducing us here to the analogy: criminal/victim = Taliban/American = Palestinian/Israeli (which indicates the ideological perspective of the Italian journalist that a 'delinquent', if of Arab and Muslim origin, is more or less an Islamic terrorist). It is therefore deceptive humanism, according to Fallaci, to absolve the guilty and condemn the innocent, precisely corresponding to the fact that such people 'weep for the Taliban and curse the Americans' – the verbs 'absolve' and 'condemn' radicalizing their emotional charge here into 'weeping' and 'cursing', thus giving extra emphasis to the abject turn of culpability into innocence and vice versa. (Hence the 'sic' attached to 'Humanitarianism'.) On the other hand, once the third couple in this analogical relationship is introduced, 'Palestinians' and 'Israelis', a significant nuance interrupts the monotonous course of her argument. In fact, it is no longer a question now of a 'guilty' party for whom one 'weeps' and an 'innocent' whom one curses, but rather of two guilty parties – one who is 'forgiven everything', the other who is 'forgiven nothing'. And it is no longer possible now to equate the attacks against

---

* The final sentence of this passage, which Segré cites from page 186 of the French edition, does not appear in the English.

America of 11 September with those targeting Israeli civilians in
Tel Aviv or Jerusalem, given that the America that is 'condemned'
and 'cursed' is innocent, as distinct from Israel, which is guilty
but not 'forgiven' for anything. But of what then are the Israelis
guilty? Reacting disproportionately to terrorist attacks? This is
rather unlikely, given the deep homage Fallaci pays to 'Putin's
Russia' in her book. The second ambiguity in the text cited will
perhaps enable us, if not to resolve the enigma, at least to see a way
out. In fact, it seems highly unlikely that in 2002 Oriana Fallaci
had still heard no mention of Auschwitz, and the way in which
an extermination camp was different from a concentration camp,
yet she writes: 'And which basically would like to see the Jews
once more exterminated in Dachau and Mauthausen'. This kind
of confusion could not fail to draw the attention of an expert in
considerations of genocide,[4] given that Fallaci is someone well
versed in the history of anti-Semitism, and consequently in what
connects this history to negationism, and the latter in turn to
the slogan of 'defence of the West'. Let us therefore set out on
this path.

THE FORCE OF PREJUDICE

In *The Force of Reason*, Oriana Fallaci writes that 'The list of abuses
[that she suffered following the publication of *The Rage and the
Pride*] also includes the trial celebrated against me in Paris. A trial
promoted for religious racism, xenophobia, blasphemy, instiga-
tion to hatred of Islam.' And she adds: 'A trial undertaken, I still
cannot believe it, with the contribution of the leftist Jewish association "LICRA". (Apparently unmindful of the manifesto I had
just written against the resurgence of anti-Semitism in Europe.)'
(p. 24). This 'apparently unmindful' Jewish association is mentioned again on page 64:

> As for the trial, it was triggered not only by the complaint filed
> by the Muslims of the 'MRAP' (Mouvement contre le Racisme

et pour l'Amitié entre les Peuples), but also by the complaint filed by the Jews of the 'LICRA' (Ligue Internationale contre le Racisme et l'Antisémitisme).

If the prosecution brought by the 'Muslims of the MRAP' followed a logic that was denounced by the author in the accused book, i.e. the conquering and inquisitorial logic of Islam, the association of the 'Jews of the LICRA' with the 'Muslims of the MRAP' struck her as incomprehensible, given her own commitment 'against the resurgence of anti-Semitism'. This is why she adds, after explaining to her readers that she was saved from prison by a 'procedural technicality': 'But this did not delete the fact that the leftist Jews of "LICRA" had aligned against me with the Muslims of "MRAP". A senseless wickedness which at that time I did not understand. Now, on the contrary, I do.'

This manifesto against anti-Semitism to which she refers her readers seems to be her article 'Sull'antisemitismo', published by the Italian newspaper *Panorama* on 18 April 2002, in which she wrote, in particular: 'I find it shameful that national television channels lend themselves to the renaissance of anti-Semitism by weeping over the Palestinian dead while playing down the Israeli dead with neutral commentaries.' Praising this article in his contribution to the book *Les Habits neufs de l'antisémitisme en Europe*, Sergio Minerbi presents it as one of those 'other voices' in Italy that have opposed the criminalization of Israel, writing that it is 'one of her most famous articles', and in an appended note giving a bibliographic reference, he adds: 'See also her book *The Rage and the Pride.*' By referring the reader to both sources, Minerbi is thus identifying them as joint examples of the courage of an Italian journalist who did not hesitate to take up a clear position against the 'new anti-Semitism'. But it was Fallaci herself who first associated these two texts, presenting them in *The Force of Reason* by referring in the French edition to Émile Zola's *J'accuse* – on the one hand *The Rage and the Pride*, this '*J'accuse* that engulfed him as *The Armillary Sphere* engulfed Mastro Secco', and on the other her article 'Sull'antisemitismo', as her '*J'accuse* against anti-Semitism'. On this basis, she had only to conclude, on the subject of the 'Jews of LICRA':

> I do [understand] because, even if your grandparents died at Dachau or Mauthausen, it is not easy to be brave in a country where there are around ten million Muslims and more than three thousand mosques. Where Islamic racism and hatred for infidel-dogs prevails but is never brought to trial, never condemned. (p. 65)

We find once again here this reference to the camps of Dachau and Mauthausen, which is particularly surprising, unless we assume that, apart from the concentration camps of Dachau and Mauthausen, Fallaci had no reliable information on the existence of extermination camps at Auschwitz, Chelmno, Belzec, Sobibor or Treblinka.

There follows a long list of misdeeds that the Arab–Muslims have committed with full impunity, from the construction of mosques to the transformation of Marseille into a 'Maghrebian city', where the Bellevue Pyat quarter has become 'a slum of filth and delin-quency, a Kasbah where on Fridays you cannot even walk in the streets because the great mosque does not have enough room and many pray in the open air' (p. 67). And at the end of this descrip-tion of an entity known as 'France' that has now been invaded by Islam, the author concludes:

> Yes, now I do understand those ungrateful Jews of 'LICRA'. Now I do. Collaborationism is always born of fear. Yet their case reminds me of the German Jewish bankers who, hoping to save themselves, in the Thirties lent money to Hitler. And who, despite this, ended up in the ovens. (p. 68)

The association between the 'Jews of LICRA' and the 'Muslims of MRAP' thus evokes for the Italian journalist a historical paral-lel with Germany in the 1930s: 'the Muslims of MRAP' are the

Nazis, Fallaci is the resister to Nazism, and the 'Jews of LICRA' are 'the German Jewish bankers who … lent money to Hitler'. It remains that the 'ovens' of Dachau and Mauthausen were not those of Auschwitz, and there is still more ambiguity to be found in Fallaci's text. We are on the track of something.

Fallaci's account of the prosecutions brought against *The Rage and the Pride* begins by mentioning the hearing opened by the Federal Office of Justice in Berne on the basis of articles 261 and 261b of the Swiss penal code, potentially leading to a judgement for contumacy – a risk of finding herself in prison if the hearing took place without her knowledge and, if found guilty, she subsequently visited 'the country of watches, and banks beloved of tyrants, sheiks and emirs, the Bin Ladens, Arafats and their like'.*
And after spelling out the prosecution against her in Switzerland, the author adds the following remark:

> Article 261b has already made so many victims. One is the animal rights activist Erwin Kessler who, like Brigitte Bardot, cannot abide the Muslims practice of butchering the lambs like Dracula – that is, slowly drawing their blood. For criticizing this practice, he got two months in prison and no suspension of sentence. Another is the eighty-year-old historian Gaston Armand Amaudruz who used to print a revisionist monthly (revising history, refusing its official version, is by now forbidden) and because of that was sentenced by the Court of Lausanne to one year in prison plus a heavy fine. Another is the French historian Robert Faurisson who was prosecuted in 2001 by the Court of Fribourg and sentenced to a month's imprisonment. The reason: an article he had published in France, and then given to a Swiss magazine. (Despite his late age, he too was denied suspension of sentence.) Anyway, Switzerland is not the only country where I risk ending up behind bars. (p. 27)

---

* Page 26 in the French edition, absent in the English.

In this pantheon of victims of the Swiss Penal Code's articles 261 and 261b, i.e. the victims of ignorance and bigotry, Fallaci's name is thus inscribed alongside those of Kessler, Bardot, Amaudruz and Faurisson. The ambiguity that an association of this kind displays is striking, to say the least.

The denunciation of halal ritual slaughter by the 'defenders of animals' is equally aimed at Jewish ritual slaughter, as Fallaci recalls elsewhere. In fact, on the subject of 'poor Brigitte', guilty of having denounced 'barbaric halal slaughter', she makes clear in a parenthesis her personal point of view on this question:

> [Halal butchery is barbaric] to the same extent as *schechitah* or kosher butchery. I mean the Jewish practice of slitting the animals' throats without stunning them and then letting them die little by little, drained of their blood, drop by drop. So when all the blood has flown down, the meat is 'pure'. Nice and white, pure. (p. 63)

If these lambs and calves arouse the sympathy of the Italian writer, so does 'poor Brigitte', who was condemned for having said or written:

> That the Muslims have stolen her homeland. That even in the remotest villages French churches have been replaced by mosques and the Lord's Prayer by the muezzins' caterwauling. That even in democratic regimes there is a limit to tolerance, that halal butchery is barbaric. (p. 63)

So we know, on the other hand, that Muslims in her eyes are neither lambs nor calves. In *The Rage and the Pride*, in fact, Fallaci writes that Muslims 'breed like rats'. And in *The Force of Reason*, she returns to this formulation with a view to replying to her detractors and clarifying her meaning:

> (Among the charges moved against me at the trial in Paris there was the following sentence of mine: 'Ils se multiplient comme les rats.' They breed like rats. A little brutal, I agree, but indisputably

accurate.) The fact is that no trial, no liberticide law, will ever be able to negate what they themselves boast. In the last half-century Muslims have increased by 235 per cent. (Christians only by 47 per cent.) ... No judge will ever be able to dismiss the figures (supplied by the UN) which attribute to the Muslims a growth fluctuating between 4.60 and 6.40 per cent a year. (Christians, only 1.40 per cent.) (p. 53)

On reflection, therefore, the author qualifies her expression as 'brutal, but accurate', meaning that the brutality in question lies not so much in the fact itself as in the truthful expression of it. In other words, 'the earth turns', and Oriana Fallaci can do nothing about it: 'to the Muslims a growth fluctuating between 4.60 and 6.40 per cent a year. (Christians, only 1.40 per cent.)' She is therefore justified in concluding that 'Muslims breed like rats'. Consequently, therefore, the question raised is whether, in Fallaci's animal imaginary, Jews are more akin to the 'rat' or the 'lamb', particularly since, as far as ritual slaughter is concerned, nothing distinguishes Jews and Muslims, apart from the word '*schechitah*' being italicized in her original text, and thus differentiated graphically, whereas the word 'halal' is not, as if Hebrew were harsher on the delicate hearing of the Italian writer. As for Brigitte Bardot's other accusations against Muslims, the distinction between Jews and Muslims would seem only quantitative (Jews being less numerous than Muslims), but not qualitative – unless we suppose that Hebrew chants have a more agreeable resonance, to the ears of women of good taste, than the chants of the muezzin, which her italicizing of the word '*schechitah*' precisely seems to deny. The Jews at least have the benefit of their discreet numbers – at least, so long as they are not seen to be 'everywhere'.[5]

On the subject of the revisionism of Amaudruz and Faurisson, the reader learns that 'revising history, refusing its official version, is now forbidden' (p. 26). If the debate on judging crimes of opinion, particularly the question of revisionism or negationism (e.g. the *Loi Gayssot* in France), is certainly worth discussion, it is however ambiguous, to say the least, to praise Gaston Amaudruz and Robert Faurisson as champions of 'liberty' for challenging the 'official version' of history. In fact, this '80-year-old' (Amaudruz) and his compeer (Faurisson) (also of a 'late age') maintain, against the 'official version', that during the Second World War there were neither extermination camps (as distinct from concentration camps) nor homicidal gas chambers. In other words, if gas chambers did indeed exist, they were only for destroying lice, i.e. a rule of hygiene recognized by the defenders of animals themselves – just like gassing rats too, if need be. Is this simply 'revising history', 'refusing its official version'? Should we conclude that Fallaci displays great magnanimity, or simply a naïve ignorance of the historical issues involved in the revisionism of Amaudruz and Faurisson? Yet she has only tender words on the subject of those who challenge 'the official version of history'. For example, on the subject of a 'Seminar on the Means and Forms of Cooperation for the Dissemination of the Arabic Language and its Literary Civilization' held in Rome on 28–30 March 1977, she writes that 'the sad affair … concluded with a unanimous Resolution which called for "the diffusion of the Arabic language" as well as for "the *superiority* of Arab culture"'. From then on, 'all over Europe',

> whoever defined himself or herself as an 'intellectual' seemed to live in the obsession of demonstrating *la grandeur* of Islam, the *superiority* of Islam. And everything served the purpose. Falsehood, deceit, mendacity. More or less, what happens in Zamyatin's *We* and in Orwell's *1984* … That symposium where almost everyone apologized for the iniquities (Crusades, colonialism, etc.) that ungrateful Europeans had inflicted on the Beacon of Light. Where everyone expressed contempt for those who still nourished doubts or prejudices about Islam. (pp. 155–6)

This symposium, in Fallaci's view, as part of a 'cultural war' between Islam and the West, is evidence of genuine treason since its explicit object was to spread Arab and Muslim civilization in Europe. But the main interest of this text for us lies elsewhere, in her reference to 'falsehood, deceit, mendacity', which cast a new light on the meaning that the expression 'revising history' has for Fallaci. We already knew that for her Islam is neither a race nor a religion nor a culture, still less a civilization, but simply an enterprise of criminal banditry on a world scale born in the seventh century CE, while the Koran, from a literary point of view, can be summed up as a vast call for murder, relayed throughout the day by muezzins hurling their savage cries in the ears of Brigitte Bardot. We already suspected, moreover, that the 'Cultural Identity' of Europe and the West was the world's one and only 'Beacon of Light', an object of envy for Arabs and others. We believed, moreover, that revision-ism was the 'freedom' to tell history differently from the 'official version'. We now learn that it can also be a question of 'falsehood, deceit, mendacity'. 'Revising history', therefore, does not have the same meaning in these two cases. In other words, denying the existence of extermination camps (as distinct from concentra-tion camps), for the Italian journalist, or the use of homicidal gas chambers at Auschwitz, Treblinka, Chelmno, Belzec or Sobibor, is a legitimate freedom to propose a non-official version of history; whereas to imagine that Islam was at one time a 'Beacon of Light' for Europe – for example, in the heyday of Granada's fountains of light and philosophy, while Christian Europe was bathed in darkness[6] – is to rewrite, falsify and wipe out history. Hence the question: What actually distinguishes these two revisions of history, in Fallaci's view? Perhaps that the first brings truth (that of Amaudruz and Faurisson) in place of a lie (the 'official history'), whereas the second brings a lie (that of the Muslims and their col-laborators) in place of Fallaci's truth?

TRADUTTORE, TRADITORE

On page 180 of *The Force of Reason*, the author directly addresses herself to 'the present head of the Red Brigades', who maintained that 'in order to destroy American imperialism and Zionist entity the Red Brigades had to make a common front with Saddam Hussein and Bin Laden's fighters'. And Fallaci, involved in the anti-fascist Resistance from the age of fourteen, replies: 'Have you any idea of what Resistance meant for our fathers?! It meant hangings, firing-squads, crematory-ovens' (p. 181). This new occurrence of 'crematory-ovens' from the Italian journalist's pen is thus the fourth explicit reference to the Nazi death camps (or to the ovens used by the Nazis to reduce the bodies removed from the gas chambers to ashes). We have, first of all, (1) in *The Rage and the Pride*, where she speaks of the 'Humanitarianism (sic)' that 'basically would like to see the Jews once more exterminated in Dachau and Mauthausen';* then (2) on page 65 of *The Force of Reason*, on the subject of the 'Jews of LICRA', whose 'grandparents died at Dachau or Mauthausen'; next (3) on page 68 of the same book, where she speaks of 'German Jewish bankers who, hoping to save themselves, in the Thirties lent money to Hitler. And who, despite this, ended up in the ovens'; and finally, (4) at the place just cited, where she speaks in relation to the 'Resistance' of 'firing-squads' and 'crematory-ovens'. These four occurrences attest to a 'different way' of telling history which is not dissimilar from that of the leading French revisionist, Paul Rassinier, himself a former *résistant* and deportee, whose so-called revisionist thesis is that there were no extermination camps during the Second World War, but only concentration camps.[7] In other words, for Rassinier and his disciples such as Faurisson and Amaudruz, Auschwitz, Treblinka, Sobibor, Chelmno and Belzec are a myth of Jewish bankers. As far as Rassinier et al. are concerned, no *Judenvernichtungslager* or 'camp for the destruction of Jews' ever existed. Is this the view of history that Fallaci shares, hence the indulgence she shows for this pair of octogenarian victims of the Swiss inquisition (Faurisson and Amaudruz)? This is the real question.

In the article Fallaci published in the Italian newspaper *Panorama* on 18 April 2002, in which she vigorously denounced

---

    * As noted above, this phrase from page 186 of *La Rage et l'orgueil* does not appear in the later English edition.

the European position towards the Israeli–Palestinian conflict, deeming this pro-Palestinian and anti-Semitic, we can read the following passage:

> I feel ashamed that *Osservatore Romano*, which is the pope's newspaper – a pope who not so long ago left at the Wailing Wall a letter pardoning the Jews, accuses of extermination a people exterminated in millions by the Christians. And by the Europeans too.

The destruction of European Jews is thus for Oriana Fallaci an established historic fact, just as she accepts that the criminals involved here were not Muslims. Besides, in this article made up of twenty short paragraphs each introduced by the phrase 'I feel ashamed', the first paragraph explicitly mentions the extermination camps, since she writes about the Palestinian demonstrators 'dressed as kamikazes' that they 'would sell their mothers to a harem' in order to 'see the Jews back in the extermination camps' (*pur di rivedere gli ebrei nei campi di sterminio*). Finally, in this same article, she renders homage to her Jewish comrades in the antifascist Resistance, reminding the anti-Zionists on the Italian left of 'the contribution these very Jews made to the antifascist struggle'. How then can Oriana Fallaci be suspected of any kind of sympathy towards the revisionism of Paul Rassinier and his disciples? How can we fail to conclude that, no matter how surprising this might appear, she is simply unaware of the negationist arguments of Amaudruz and Faurrison when she writes that revisionism is nothing more than the 'freedom' to 'revise history', to 'tell it differently', while elsewhere she speaks of 'falsehood, deceit, mendacity'? And yet, taken as a whole, the only sentence in which she explicitly mentions the 'extermination camps' and the 'gas chambers' is once again ambiguous:

> *E che pur di rivedere gli ebrei nei campi di stermino, nelle camere a gas, nei forni crematori di Dachau e di Mauthausen e di Buchenwald e di Bergen-Belsen eccetera, vendereberro aun harem la propria madre.*

And who would sell their mothers to a harem in order to see
the Jews back in the extermination camps, in the gas chambers
and crematoria of Dachau and Mauthausen, Buchenwald and
Bergen-Belsen, etc.

The stubborn ambiguity of her expression is clearly the common
point between Dachau, Mauthausen, Buchenwald and Bergen-
Belsen, that all four of these were concentration camps – as
distinct from extermination camps, and particularly from the four
camps that were designed for extermination pure and simple,
Sobibor, Treblinka, Belzec and Chelmno. In these camps alone
nearly two million Polish Jews – men and women, the elderly and
children – were gassed almost as soon as they got off the train,
without any selection, and for a very clear reason: the only object
there was destruction, the work of annihilation. But Fallaci's
list also, and above all, stands distinct from the best known and
most deadly extermination camp of all, that of Auschwitz, where
nearly a million Jews died. And who would dare to say, at the
start of the twenty-first century, that they have never heard of
Auschwitz? How then are we to interpret this Italian journalist's
resistance to uttering the name of Auschwitz in place of Dachau,
Mauthausen, Buchenwald and Bergen-Belsen? This difficulty in
Fallaci's text, moreover, did not escape her French translator Claire
Benveniste, who offered a French translation of this article on the
internet site 'Réponses-Israel'.[8] Her translation, in fact, comes up
against precisely the difficulty that the text presents here, and runs
as follows: 'And who would sell their mothers in order to see
the Jews back in the *concentration* camps, in the gas chambers and
crematoria of Dachau and Mauthausen, Buchenwald and Bergen-
Belsen.' Thus, leaving aside the small point that Benveniste omits
the word 'harem', she makes a 'correction' that is certainly significant by substituting 'concentration' (*campi di concentramento*) where
Fallaci's original text had 'extermination' (*campi di sterminio*). In
other words, Claire Benveniste, the 'Réponses-Israel' site's translator, knows very well that Dachau, Mauthausen, Buchenwald and

Bergen-Belsen were concentration camps and not extermination camps – and so, in all innocence, she offers a correction.

What then does this inability to name Auschwitz, Sobibor, Treblinka, Chelmno and Belzec – except by way of her lapidary expression '*eccetera*', which at least leaves open the question of their existence – say about the 'resistance' of the Italian writer?

THE LAST WORD

April 2007 saw the French publication of the final volume in the Fallaci's trilogy – *Entretien avec moi-même*, followed by *L'Apocalypse* (the original Italian edition had appeared in 2004).* In this last book, Fallaci continued the same line of argument as in the two previous ones, as analyzed above. But did she finally utter the name Auschwitz, thus recognizing that Auschwitz was not Dachau – an extermination camp was not a concentration camp – and that this point is essential if we are to remember what Nazism was? Or did her final volume confirm the Italian journalist's sympathies for Amaudruz and Faurrison, those poor octogenarians persecuted by the Swiss Gestapo?

Once again, in her self-interview, defence of Israel is the token of Fallaci's philo-Semitism, conferring on her defence of the Christian West against Islamic tyranny the aura of universalism. She thus asserts, on page 192, 'My dear friend, there is only one democracy outside the West, and that's the government of Israel.' This is the argument of philo-Semitic reaction: the defence of the West ('including Israel', which is otherwise outside the West), a thesis that is developed most fully on page 135 of Fallaci's last text: 'Do I have to repeat it? Where there's anti-Americanism, there's anti-Westernism. Where there's anti-Westernism, there's pro-Islamism. And where there's pro-Islamism, there's anti-

---

* No English translation of this volume, *Oriana Fallaci intervista sé sessa – L'Apocalisse* (Milan: Rizzoli, 2004) or of either of its texts, 'Interview with Myself' and 'The Apocalpyse', has been published.

Semitism'; hence the strict equivalence between anti-Westernism and anti-Semitism. But the author also reminds us of her attachment to the memory of the Jewish victims of Nazism, which was not anti-Western, particularly relating on pages 49–50 a childhood memory of *Kristallnacht*:

> Then Daddy explained to me that they hadn't been breaking glasses. They'd been breaking the windows of shops belonging to Jews, burning their books, arresting them. I felt my legs give way under me. My teacher, Elene Rubicek, was Jewish. What if they'd arrested her? Well, she really was arrested. In 1944, under the Saló republic. Along with her mother who was eighty years old. Both ended up at Dachau. In an oven.

Once again, therefore, there is no mention in this final book of the crematoria of Auschwitz, simply those of 'Dachau'. And after all, is it Oriana Fallaci's fault if her teacher was deported to Dachau, and not to Auschwitz? Besides, what is the meaning of our own stubborn insistence on examining her text from this angle, looking for the name Auschwitz as if that of Dachau were not enough? Is it not wanting to make the Jews into the sole and unique victims of Nazism, to the detriment of others? And, all things said and done, is it not to try to 'falsify history', as the Communists did by claiming to have been the only resisters to fascism? This may well be the case, if we are to judge by what Fallaci says about this subject in *Entretien avec moi-même*:

> I'm annoyed. Yes, I'm annoyed. Because for half a century the Communists tried to monopolize the Resistance, to have people believe that they were the only ones involved ... It's not just an insult to history, it's an insult to other people's dead. (pp. 82–3)

We may wonder, therefore, whether it is not against a similar appropriation by the Jews of the memory of the camps that the Italian journalist defends herself, hence her reluctance to mention the name of Auschwitz, or to recognize any difference between an extermination camp (Auschwitz, but also Treblinka, Sobibor, Chelmno, Belzec) and a concentration camp (Dachau, Bergen-Belsen, Mauthausen or Buchenwald). And we may also wonder whether this is her reason for mentioning, in full knowledge of the case, the names of Faurisson and Amaudruz alongside her own in the pantheon of victims of a scandalous Swiss law, as victims of an inquisition – victims of 'hypocrisy', 'lies' and 'bigotry'. Might it not be that the name of Auschwitz has become 'an insult to history', and worse still, 'an insult to other people's dead' – hence the moral necessity of passing over it in silence, in favour of the names of Dachau, Mauthausen, Buchenwald or Bergen-Belsen? In seeking to answer this question, we have to continue the text just cited through to its conclusion:

> Exactly like some Communists tried to do, and are still trying to do, in Italy. It's not just an insult to history, it's an insult to other people's dead. It's like pretending that it was only Jews who were killed in the German concentration camps, which amounts to saying that other prisoners – Polish Catholics, Russian prisoners, Gypsies, homosexuals, antifascists of various nationalities and religions, including Princess Mafalda and Nenni's daughter who died in Dachau – were staying there on holiday.

And in fact, in Dachau or 'the German concentration camps' it was *not* just Jews who were killed, and with good reason: Jews were essentially deported to Auschwitz, Treblinka, Sobibor, Belzec and Chelmno, which were not concentration camps but camps for the extermination of Jews, *Judenvernichtungslager*. It is saying this, then, that represents in the eyes of Fallaci, Rassinier, Faurisson or Amaudruz 'not just an insult to history', but 'an insult to other people's dead' – and particularly, to the dead of Dachau. And we must then conclude that, if Auschwitz fails to make an appearance anywhere in Fallaci's 'war against the resurgence of anti-Semitism', this is not out of ignorance or amnesia, but for the simple reason that this name is unutterable: an 'insult' or an obscenity. And for this reason, the texts of Oriana Fallaci published after 11 September 2001 require from us the two following clarifications:

1) There was a Nazi camp by the name of Auschwitz to which close to 1,300,000 individuals were deported, including 1,100,000 Jews, these last being systematically put to death because they were Jewish: 960,000 Jews died there.[9] There were camps by the name of Sobibor, Belzec, Treblinka and Chelmno, completely isolated from the outside world – even the world of concentration camps – in which 2,000,000 Polish Jews perished.[10] This type of camp was what the Nazis called a *Judenvernichtungslager*, a camp for the destruction of Jews. Dachau, Mauthausen, Buchenwald and Bergen-Belsen, for their part, were concentration camps. According to Pierre Serge Choumoff, 'the minimum number of detainees at Mauthausen and Guzen who were killed by gassing in those two camps and at Hartheim is thus in any case more than 10,200, i.e. nearly a tenth of the total of those who died at Mauthausen and its annex camps'.[11] (Mauthausen had close to 200,000 detainees, of whom nearly 100,000 perished.) The figure for deaths by gas in the Buchenwald camp is 18,685.[12] (There was also a gas chamber at Dachau, but apparently not at Bergen-Belsen.) However criminal they were, the concentration camps were not extermination camps. The Nazis' idea of them was different, and they put their ideas into practice, as the fearful statistics reveal: one person in two died in Mauthausen, whereas more than nine Jews out of ten died in Auschwitz; there were 100,000 deaths at Mauthausen, 1,000,000 at Auschwitz. Neither Mauthausen nor Dachau nor Buchenwald nor Bergen-Belsen was a *Judenvernichtungslager*; their purpose was to work to death individuals who were ideologically resistant to the dictates of Nazi policy, rather than to exterminate a people perceived and defined as an obstacle to Nazi plans. This distinction in no way reduces either the horror of the concentration camps or the heroism of anti-Nazi resisters; it is simply a fact.

2) The Renaissance is neither an emblem of Arab–Muslim civilization nor of Oriana Fallaci's 'cultural identity'; it was an attribute of truths, those eternal truths that the philosopher Alain Badiou tells us he likes to compare with the wandering Jew: 'I love this comparison of eternal truths, advancing and being reborn in becoming, with the wandering Jew.'[13]

CONCLUSION: WHAT IS THE 'NEW ANTI-SEMITISM'?

In *The Force of Reason*, Oriana Fallaci addresses herself to the Italian deputy prime minister, writing to him: 'You go to Jerusalem, you weep crocodile tears at Yad Vashem with a kepi on your head, then you fornicate in the most terrifying manner with the sons of Allah.'* The Italian journalist goes on to lambaste the minister's hypocrisy – on the one hand he salutes the memory of the victims of Nazi genocide, on the other he 'fornicates' with Muslims. In her view, in fact, there is a glaring contradiction between the two actions, since, following the equivalence between Nazism and Islam that governs her whole text, this amounts to weeping over the victims only to immediately ally himself with their executioners; hence the mask of emotion and symbol ('Jerusalem', the 'kepi', 'Yad Vashem') only hides 'crocodile tears'. The nature of this 'fornication' with the 'sons of Allah' remains to be investigated. Is it a question of support for the negationist ideas that are current in the Arab–Muslim world? Or rather, support for the terrorist movements that seek the destruction of Israel and the murder of Jews wherever they are to be found? Or again a military, even nuclear, support for states that openly threaten to 'wipe Israel off the map'? Not at all. This 'fornication', for Fallaci, is still more abject, as she explains: 'the Deputy Prime Minister ... declared that "giving immigrants the vote is legitimate because immigrants pay their taxes and want to integrate"' (p. 95). This then is the

---

   * This passage, from page 82 in the French edition, is omitted in the English.

glaring proof of the minister's hypocrisy, his 'crocodile tears' at Yad Vashem: he wants to 'give the vote' to immigrants who are in large part Muslim. The Italian journalist has thus drawn the full consequences of the thesis of a 'new anti-Semitism' – in other words an anti-Semitism of immigrant, proletarian and swarthy origin calling for a police response with a clearly essentialist, racist and criminal flavour. The remark of a certain far-right group in France on the subject of the beneficial effects of this thesis (as noted by Cécilia Gabizon and Johan Weisz) then acquires its full meaning, going far beyond mere anecdote:

> A text distributed by the Cercle Européen d'Aquitaine, a 'new right' club, asks whether, 'thanks to the re-launch of the Intifada, a kind of holy alliance might well be possible' between the 'white man' and the 'enemy within', of a kind that 'would make it possible to undo the mechanism that assimilated us systematically to Nazism'.[14]

This 'undoing' is apparent in the texts published after 11 September 2001 by a woman who was a great journalist, and a courageous adolescent, before succumbing to the 'malady of death'.[15]

Appendix: Mass Culture and 'The Jews'

It is evident, therefore, that the so-called upper class among the western Jews, and particularly in France, is in a highly advanced state of decomposition. It is no longer Jewish, yet it is not Christian, and it is incapable of substituting a philosophy, still less a free morality, for the creed that it no longer has. While the Christian bourgeoisie still stands thanks to the corset of its dogmas, traditions, morality and conventional principles, the Jewish bourgeoisie, deprived of these longstanding stays, poisons the Jewish nation with its putrescence. It will poison other nations too, if it does not decide – as we most fervently desire – to adhere to the Christianity of the ruling classes, and to rid Judaism of a burden.

> – Bernard Lazare, *Le Nationalisme juif*

For the way in which it falls to Jews, in the West, to assume a 'sacral function' – or, to put it differently, the way in which Israel is 'included' in the defence of the West, we propose to submit to the reader's judgement two illustrations drawn from mass culture, which we thereby distinguish from popular culture – the former being subject to the requirements of capital, the second to those of oral transmission.

We are not Israelis!

On 12 September 2001 United States cinemas began screening *Swordfish*, a film by Dominic Sena. This was thus conceived and completed before the attacks of the previous day. It was shown on French television on 13 March 2005 (at peak viewing time on France 2). John Travolta plays Gabriel, an ambiguous character, attractive and repugnant at the same time, but at all events fascinating. He is a kind of bad angel ready for anything to achieve his goals, and particularly ready to kill the innocent. The film's opening sequence shows the heist of the century, which is his work. Explosive belts are tied to the hostages' waists. Following a failed initiative on the part of a policeman, one of the belts explodes, leading to the others erupting in a chain reaction. There are dozens of deaths. (The film is constructed as a narration of what leads up to this spectacular drama, then, once the heist and the explosion are reached – the start of the film – the narrative continues where it left off. The narrative thread thus informs us now about what preceded.) To succeed in his heist, Gabriel needs the involvement of the best hacker in the United States, an individual who is able to break through banks' computer firewalls in a matter of minutes. A ravishing female lets this hacker – the film's hero, a handsome young man who is short of cash – know that Gabriel needs him. She also gives him a sum of money sufficiently large for him not to be able to refuse the invitation. Once arrived in the bandit's hideout – a kind of discotheque presented as a haven of debauchery with a riot of drugs, alcohol and sex – the hacker meets Gabriel, who makes him an offer of work in return for an enormous sum of money (and sex).[16] At first, the hacker refuses. But, being divorced, he needs money to pay a lawyer and thereby obtain custody of his daughter – who is currently in the charge of her mother, an alcoholic remarried to a producer of West Coast porn films. Gabriel reminds him that he has no choice. In order to free his little girl from the hands of the devil (alcohol and porn films), he has to agree to put his genius to work for Gabriel. But who is Gabriel? As the story proceeds, the character is revealed: a man who is trying to save Western societies from Islamic terrorism, i.e. from what threatens them with complete destruction. And in this cause, he is ready for anything. If millions of dollars are needed to finance this life-and-death struggle against terrorism, then he will find this money by whatever means necessary. Only the end matters, i.e. the survival of Western societies. But the hacker questions Gabriel: do we have the right to kill innocent people and resort to terrorism ourselves in order to save Western societies from terrorism? Yes, Gabriel replies, we have the right to kill a thousand innocents in order to save ten thousand. That is his belief. At the climax of the film, the heist succeeds and Gabriel disappears with the help of his conjuring skills, taking millions of dollars with him and leaving behind dozens of innocent victims (the explosion at the beginning). He has pulled off the heist of the century thanks to the combination of two geniuses, himself and the hacker (who was constrained and forced, initially to save his daughter, but in the course of the heist to save innocent people from the death to which Gabriel condemned them if the hacker did not comply with his orders and break the banks' firewalls). The film's final sequence resolves the enigma posed by the character of Gabriel: a white yacht sailing on the Mediterranean suddenly explodes. It belongs to an Arab emir suspected of connections with terrorism. At the same moment, FBI agents finally discover on their computer files the mysterious identity of Gabriel: this counter-terrorist terrorist, this bad angel of puritanical America, is a man impossible to pin down, who takes over the identity of dead persons. Gabriel, his current identity during the film's action, was a Mossad agent. The allusion is transparent: America's bad angel could only be a Mossad agent.

The habit doesn't make the monk

On 15 April 2004 a documentary titled *Antisémitisme. La parole
liberée* was shown on France 2. Directed by Élie Chouraqui and
Yves Azéroual, the documentary's theme was as follows: Chouraqui
and Azéroual filmed and questioned young people from the Paris
banlieue of Montreuil on the subject of the Jews and, given the
statements they collected, concluded that anti-Semitic speech was
'liberated' in France today. Yet the 'France' that these directors
filmed, questioned and surveyed throughout their documentary was entirely that of immigrant populations – Arabs, blacks,
Muslims or other '*banlieue* youth'. As a result, the spectator could
conclude that anti-Semitic speech in France today is immigrant
speech, in the literal sense of the term: speech that does not come
from French society but from elsewhere, from abroad, from the
other. The procedure the directors of this documentary used was
remarkably effective: it assumed that installing a camera by a tea
table in a gilded salon in the sixteenth arrondissement of Paris,
among respectable people, would in no way allow the conclusion of a 'liberated' anti-Semitism. Chouraqui and Azéroual's
documentary should therefore be set against the currency of
anti-Jewish prejudice in non-immigrant French society, which is
precisely what a television presenter later did.

The story of this is as follows. During a broadcast of the programme *Tout le monde en parle*, Thierry Ardisson hosted Éli
Chouraqui, one of the two directors of *Antisémitisme. La parole
liberée*. They were then joined on the set by Dominique Lapierre
and Jerry Collins, who were invited to promote their latest novel
Is New York Burning?, published in April 2004.[17] Thierry Ardisson
explained the novel's plot: al-Qaida terrorists had managed to
plant a nuclear bomb in the heart of New York, demanding that
within five days the Israeli prime minister Ariel Sharon evacuate
all Jewish colonies from Gaza and the West Bank, otherwise New
York would be totally destroyed by nuclear explosion. Sharon
refused any evacuation, and by way of reprisal proposed a nuclear

attack on Pakistan, which was suspected of having supplied the terrorists' bomb. But President George W. Bush opposed this, unwilling to have innocent people pay the price of the terrorists' evil plans. He also refused to intervene militarily against Israel, where religious fundamentalists were threatening New York by their intransigence. Having faith in America, Bush decided to entrust the New York police with the task: We've got five days to find the bomb! And finally, thanks to their patriotism, courage and self-denial, the New York police – supported by the whole of America, from its president down to New York ordinary folk – managed to find the bomb and dismantle it before the ultimatum expired. New York saved New York – but also, in passing, Pakistan and Israel, so that the spectator could conclude that New York had finally saved humanity. Turning to Élie Chouraqui, Thierry Ardisson asked the director: 'Wouldn't that make a good film for you, adapting the novel for the cinema?'

Banlieue *youth and mass culture*

What then distinguishes the anti-Jewish prejudices of the young-sters from the Montreuil *banlieue* questioned by Chouraqui and Azéroual on the subject of 'the Jews' – with their replies that 'the Jews have money', 'we don't like Yids', etc. – from the anti-Jewish prejudices conveyed by the entertainment industry in America and Europe? The initial answer is that young people in Montreuil do not have the same means of distribution at their disposal, whether we are talking of the Hollywood industry that produced the film *Swordfish*, shown in France on a national TV channel in the guise of a 'Sunday evening film', or the publishing industry that Dominique Lapierre and Jerry Collins have avail-able to them, selling millions of copies across Europe and the United States. We would then conclude that the latter influence the former, rather than the other way round – given it is they who control the image-producing machinery. But another answer is that Chouraqui and Azéroual got the Montreuil youth to speak for themselves, whereas there is none of this for the creators of mass culture: no one comes round to ask them what they think of 'the Jews' or of Israel; they tell us spontaneously. And what do they say?

According to the film *Swordfish*, the state of Israel (here Gabriel), as portrayed by John Travolta, the sensual and impulsive Hollywood actor, is the shadow side of Christian, Western, white America – its evil genius, its tempting angel. The hacker is the good spirit, defender of widows and orphans, a kind of 'born again' type. The alliance between Israel (the Mossad agent) and America (the hacker) is undoubtedly based on a common need to combat terrorism, but it remains structurally asymmetrical, an alliance between the wolf and the lamb. Gabriel, in fact, is a hero without faith or law, a man ready for anything who knows no distinction between good and evil: he is the wolf, for whom the only law is that of the stronger. It is the hacker who is put to the test, forced into an alliance with Gabriel, the bad angel, in order to save his daughter from hell (an alcoholic mother and a stepfather who produces porn films): he is the lamb, for whom the law exists to protect the weak. The objective alliance between wolf and lamb in the war against terrorism thus displays a basic asymmetry: it is Gabriel who kills, steals, debauches and enslaves, while the hacker is the one who saves. Or to put it another way: there is on the one hand the tempting, sinuous and fleshy animal of raw power, and on the other hand the 'born again'. As for the Islamic or Arab terrorist, the 'alien' enemy, this is a white yacht that sails on the sea and disappears: something imaginary, in the end.

According to *Is New York Burning?*, Israel, by its intransigence, is the cause of evil, and in particular the cause of Islamist terrorism. The Jewish fundamentalists, in fact, and along with them Israeli prime minister Sharon, are ready to sacrifice New York. Better still, Sharon is ready to immediately launch nuclear weapons against Pakistan (implying that the use of atomic weapons is an Israeli ethno-cultural specificity), preferring to massacre millions of Pakistanis rather than give in to the terrorists' legitimate demands for the evacuation of Jewish settlements in the occupied territories. But President Bush is not prepared to destroy the lives of hundreds of thousands of innocent people, even Pakistanis, and so it is without recourse to violence that the New York police finally save their city from the holocaust to which Israeli intransigence condemns it. As for the Arab or Islamist terrorists, they demand the withdrawal of the settlers from Gaza and the West Bank, and promise in exchange to disappear (by removing the bomb without exploding it), confirming by this act that American policy is intrinsically innocent, and that, if America is the victim of terrorism, this is the fault of Israel.[18]

In conclusion, we should note that the currency of anti-Semitic prejudices and stereotypes in the discourse of American TV evangelism is precisely what Rony Brauman reminds us of at the end of an interview with the magazine *Mouvements*:

> Anti-Zionism is as old as Zionism, and was originally a Jewish movement. If all the Jews who opposed Zionism before the Second World War are accused of anti-Semitism, this would include the majority of Jewish intellectuals. We cannot stop there, however, as, since the creation of Israel, it is true that anti-Zionism is also in some cases a convenient mask for anti-Semitism. But once this has been said, we need also consider that Zionism itself can equally serve as a mask for anti-Semitism. We see this very clearly in the United States. Mel Gibson is a traditionalist Catholic of a sort that is very close, in fact, to evangelicals in this regard. The latter are pervaded by a theological anti-Judaism, and it is this theological anti-Judaism that has led them to align themselves with radical Zionists in the name of the prophecy that the gathering of Jews in Palestine will be the prelude to the fulfilment of the messianic promise. The next step, however, is the disappearance of the Jews – something that the supporters of Bush curiously overlook. More generally, a consistent anti-Semite believes that the place of Jews is elsewhere. There are three ways of getting rid of the Jews: either massacring them, or

reducing them to silence, or dispatching them to a land of their own. There is thus an anti-Semitic anti-Zionism, an anti-Semitic pro-Zionism, and of course a non-anti-Semitic anti-Zionism. (Nos. 33/34, July–August 2004, p. 131)

Analysis of the 'anti-Semitic pro-Zionism' of the American tele-evangelists is in fact a research programme that opens up a whole field of American mass culture. As witness an article by Henri Tinq published in *Le Monde* on 20 October 2004, explaining the commercial success of evangelical literature in the United States:

> *Survivors of the Apocalypse* is a pulp fiction series devoured by evangelical America. Since 1995, eleven volumes have appeared in the bookstores (60 million copies sold). The latest, in 2003, was titled *Armageddon*. This bestseller is the work of pastor Tim LaHaye, one of the champions of the American religious and Zionist right, trained at the Bob Jones fundamentalist university … For the 'Christian Zionists', no doubt is permissible: it is in Israel that the Messiah will return after gathering the Jewish people. It is in Israel that the final battle will take place, as proclaimed in the [biblical] *Apocalypse*, between God and the forces of Evil, on the plain of Armageddon, which has spawned so many books and films. The Messiah will not return before all Jews have returned to Israel. They will convert to Christianity on pain of perishing in a holocaust when Armageddon comes.

We can understand, then, the rallying of 'communitarian' intellectuals to the slogan of 'defence of the West', and their lack of insistence on claiming a Jewish particularism – which is determined to 'perish in a holocaust when Armageddon comes'.

Epilogue

Perhaps it was something still unknown: Theodora Kats, a new
silence of writing, that of women and Jews.
　　　　　　　　　　　　　　– Marguerite Duras, *Yann Andrea Steiner*

On Saturday, 13 January 2007, in the context of a radio programme
on France Culture, Jean-Claude Milner put forward a 'thesis'[1] on
the subject of Pierre Bourdieu and Jean-Claude Passeron's study
The Inheritors (1979; first published, 1964): 'I believe this is an
anti-Semitic book.' A brief exchange between Milner and Alain
Finkielkraut immediately followed:

> A.F: Really? Well indeed! Listen, since you've put this so very
> sharply, and perhaps we should have another programme on this
> question … that question. You're plunging into a kind of …
> J.-C.M: I'll leave that point aside, but …
> A.F: Yes, leave it aside.

I see the main interest of this short dialogue as lying not so much
in Milner's 'thesis', however 'provocative' this was,[2] but rather in
Finkielkraut's surprise, if not perturbation, despite being himself
an intellectual who had in the years after 2001 put forward a large
number of 'theses' of a highly 'Well indeed!' type. The question
is thus to reintroduce the mediations, with a view to grasping the
thread leading from Bourdieu and Passeron's sociological study

to this 'new anti-Semitism' that Alain Finkielkraut has constantly fought with such extreme vigilance.

In *L'Imparfait du présent* (2002), Finkielkraut invited his readers 'to move to and fro between two loyalties: contingency and concept'. What this involves, in fact, is 'extracting what is memorable from the flow of actuality', which requires 'holding details in high esteem'. Commenting the major or minor items of news in the course of 2001, this author sought to regard these facts not just with attention, but with vigilance, looking for words that were, if unperceived by ordinary mortals, indicative to the alert observer. Thus, under the title 'A Nike Cap for an Old Dictionary', Finkielkraut noted on 10 January 2001 that the *Petit Robert* dictionary 'advertises its new edition by presenting key examples of new words':

> For example, '*boulot*', illustrated by a sentence from [the comedian] Coluche: 'As for work [*boulot*], there's not a lot of it around. Better leave it to those who like that kind of thing.' Or '*plomb*', removed from inert matter and given life by this quotation from Izzo: 'Tango, nostalgia: it was better to stop. It would make me blow a fuse [*péter les plombs*], and I needed all my head.' Or again, in a more poetic and gentle register, the word '*arabe*', which Daniel Pennac appropriates for today's good cause: 'Who says that Arabic is a guttural language, the dry voice of the desert, hoarse with sand and scrub? Arabic is also the murmur of a dove, the distant promise of fountains.'

And Finkielkraut comments:

> No disorder in this exhilarating bouquet, but rather the message: 'Don't be afraid, kids! You were terrorized by unknown words, sadistically confronted by the inextinguishable novelty of something older than you, you were called on to honour language and revere its spirit ... But as your new dictionary, I tell you that this nightmare is over: it's now up to language to take note of your speech and fall in line. My role is not to train you or correct

you, but simply to listen. I'm not normative, I'm switched on. I no longer dictate, I take dictation. I don't prescribe anything, I transcribe. And rather than obstinately defending my territory, I welcome the stranger with open arms. Beneath my austere air lies a heart that beats for all victims of exclusion. Purism isn't my cup of tea, as I know no good usage other than usage itself, no value other than movement, no law other than that of hospitality. A model, me? No, a reflection. Society moves, I move with it. The world changes, I shift and dance with it. My pages are up to date, and when I appeal to literature, it's not to mortify you or chain you to the rancid words of the classics; it's rather, as you see, to stamp the seal of approval on your multiracial and rebel reality. So, if you please, a bit of disrespect: stop confusing me with the old buffers of the Institut de France! I'm on the side of life. My flag is the flag of difference. My camp is with the adolescents: I've chosen liberty and given words human rights.' To show that it's not prudish, and has finally abandoned the old folks' home with its proper protocol, the *Petit Robert* boldly includes in its advert the word '*niquer*', illustrated by this fragment from a novel by Philippe Jaenada: 'I started inviting girls to a restaurant with the hope of shagging them [*les niquer*].' Cool.

Let us also try to extract what is memorable from the flow of actuality, and accordingly hold details in high esteem.

Finkielkraut's argument is that the introduction into the dictionary of slang or vulgar words or expressions ('*boulot*', '*péter les plombs*', '*niquer*') sanctions the abandonment or even betrayal of a demand that is constitutive of education: teaching pupils to 'speak properly'. In fact, 'speaking properly' is not natural, but requires apprenticeship. And how can it be taught except by 'training', 'correcting', 'prescribing' and 'dictating'? In its advert, the *Petit Robert* thus attests to a dereliction on the part of the very people whose function it is to impose correction in language – and thereby also in behaviour. For it's a short step from speaking badly to acting badly, and in the eyes of an alert observer, the latest edition of the *Petit Robert* is significant of the threat to French society today: putting 'a Nike cap on an old dictionary'. But this threat is no more than a school prank. Unless we should interpret this as a rather earlier 'ostentatious sign' of the kind that would subsequently offend the old schoolteacher, and conclude that he is succumbing here to a fit of primal anti-Americanism – hence the threatening Anglicism at the end? A hypothesis that cannot be immediately dismissed … particularly with a view to what Daniel Bensaïd describes as a certain 'France, suffering from seeing its "rank" in the world hierarchy threatened, and unable to complete its task of colonial mourning'.[3]

These reflections on apprenticeship in the French language, or more exactly in 'speaking properly', always lead us back to the debates that preceded and followed May 1968 and, in the particular field of linguistics, opposed linguists to grammarians. Thus, in his *Clés pour la langue française* (1975), Georges Mounin wrote:

The ordinary grammarian attitude is a normative one. It teaches what should be said, and still more forcefully what should not be said. It sometimes says why, often with the wrong reasons, especially when it bases itself on considerations of logic or psychology. This bad pedagogy of the norm is further aggravated by purism, which could be approximately defined as the most demanding, most restrictive, most falsely reasoning norm, and on top of everything the most socially tyrannical. But teachers trained by teachers, grammarians, or even linguists who find it hard to free themselves from grammar, almost all those who govern the teaching of language, are still deeply influenced by purism. This situation is highly prejudicial to any improvement in language teaching, and continues to remain under the shadow of a perceptible conflict between purists and linguists. The former have long been irritated to find themselves challenged, on a ground that they viewed as their private property, by a young science whose approaches they reject; while the latter find it all too easy to denounce the excommunications of gossip columnists, the ineffective indignations of fine spirits whose only valid authority is very often sociological and not linguistic – or the ignorance, errors and misconceptions of the unmandated regents who, in the belief of defending their language, do it more harm than good by paralyzing, or even strangling, its users. (pp. 18–19)

But beyond the opponents of what Althusser called the 'ideological revolt' of May 1968, this portrait of the grammarian, or more precisely of the 'purist', as hair-splitting and 'socially tyrannical' pedant, clearly recalls Molière's comic doctor. And the resemblance is all the more striking in that, by opposing norm to usage, the 'purist' seeks to de-legitimize a popular usage of language based on orality. In fact, the exclusive authority of writing – the *auctoritas*, in the Latinized Aristotelianism of Molière's doctor, a trifle sadistic – has always been concerned to exclude popular practice from the canons of 'proper speech' and 'proper action'. This is why, against precisely this tyranny, Malherbe's recourse to the idiom of market porters to determine good usage of language here and now, Molière's revisiting popular farce, and Mounin's recalling that human beings naturally learn to speak, were all political practices and theories of language – so many resistances to a norm that was 'sociological and not linguistic', police-like and not educational, deadening and not enlivening. Conceiving the sociological (i.e. bourgeois) nature of the norm, however – its inegalitarian nature and its role in reproducing social inequalities, in and through school – is precisely the subject of Bourdieu's *The Inheritors*. And Alain Finkielkraut is not mistaken about this – witness his sharp condemnation of this book, on the same radio programme of Saturday, 14 January 2007 on France Culture. Hunting down 'the inheritors' is what these sociologists are about.

What should we say, then, once this historical, ideological and theatrical background to Finkielkraut's reflections on the teaching of French is sketched out, about the introduction of the word '*boulot*' into the dictionary, and its illustration by a sentence from

Coluche: 'As for work [*boulot*], there's not a lot of it around. Better leave it to people who like that kind of thing.'

For some people, adept at dictation, training and correction under the authority of the written word, this is a real attack on the norm of 'speaking properly', since '*boulot*' is a slang term, and Coluche a comedian with roots in popular culture, his language being completely an oral one – a spoken language, as distinct from written language. Besides, this praise of idleness, no matter how ironic, questions the virtue of labour. For others, however, this means noting the importance and legitimacy of popular culture, in particular the way that it scoffs at bourgeois prejudices on the subject of 'speaking properly', 'acting properly' and 'thinking properly' – the normality of which is, as we know, beneath its worldly veneer, nothing less than obscene. Like that 'story of a bloke on the Pont de l'Alma: a normal bloke, you know … not a Jew'.

But if '*boulot*' and '*péter les plombs*' are slang words or expressions, and if '*niquer*' is not just slang but vulgar into the bargain, what should we say, on the other hand, of the word '*arabe*' and the quotation from Daniel Pennac that illustrates it? At first sight here, after all, and clearly distinct from the previous examples, there is nothing here either slang or vulgar, not even a hint of spoken language as distinct from written language, since the illustration given by the dictionary is precisely poetic: 'hoarse with sand and scrub', 'language of doves', 'promise of fountains'. But this would be forgetting that 'the word "*arabe*" [is] deliberately appropriated by Daniel Pennac for today's good cause'. But what is 'today's good cause', if not 'the foreigner' who is welcomed 'with open arms', 'the victims of exclusion', the 'law of hospitality' or indeed 'the multicultural and rebel present'? This then is what an alert observer finds between the lines of a poetic illustration of the word '*arabe*': the introduction of 'today's good cause' instead and in place of the norm. But what, according to Finkielkraut, should govern the good usage of the word '*arabe*' in a dictionary worthy of the name? To answer this question, let us consult the 'old dictionary' of the French language that the author of this gossip column implies: *arabe* = foreigner who doesn't want to work, unless he takes the *boulot* of the French, who *pètent les plombs* at the least opposition, and only has one thing in mind, namely, *niquer* our girls and our classics. 'There are too many Arabs in France', as a well-informed father named Moustache once said …

By writing *Ahmed le subtil. Farce en trois actes* (1994), Alain Badiou revisited *Scapin's Deceits* by Molière, bringing the characters up to date: the deceitful valet, who helps sons free themselves from the normative tutelage of their fathers, is Ahmed, in other words an Arab; one of the fathers is Monsieur Moustache, who waxes nostalgic for Algérie Française, the other an official in the 'PQCF';* the action takes place today in the *banlieue* of a big city. In this way, Badiou reconnects with the creation process of Molière's farce, which drew its characters, plot, stage business and language from popular culture – the culture of the faubourgs, as well as from the *commedia dell'arte*, from ancient carnival and the comedy of Plautus. In a word: precisely all that the church set itself to repress, according to Nietzsche, so that instead and in place of the actor, armed with cunning and a stick, there comes the 'priest', the man of the Book over which he keeps jealous guard – the indulgence in one hand, the instrument of torture in the other. But above all, by naming Scapin's character 'Ahmed', Badiou takes issue with 'the rancid word of the classics we're accustomed to', and by this invasion attests to the '*arabe*' signifier and its recent academizing by the dictionary. For Badiou, on the other hand, this means reasserting that the classics are 'ours' – they belong to a 'we' who are attached to the reality of popular emancipation. As for the purist, he is the figure that Monsieur Moustache assumes once he moves from the *banlieue* into the city, from farce to legitimate theatre, or to sum it up, from the populist orality of a racist slogan to the policed writing of a gossip columnist.

★   ★   ★

★ Alain Badiou's invention: the Parti de la Qualité Communiste Française.

The de-legitimization of orality goes back a long way. Historically, it was expressed in the form of a biblical sect, the Sadducees, who stood for a literalist approach to the law of Moses and rejected Jewish oral tradition, the tradition of the rabbis of Israel, for whom the law of Moses had two sides, a written and an oral reception, just as the human being is born of both man and woman. By way of example, the Sadducees supported a literal reading of the *lex talionis*, as opposed to the rabbis of Israel, who understood Moses' teaching as an explicit rejection of this law. Two quite contrary relationships to orality, generating two quite contrary relationships to writing. Which is why the Sadducees were, historically, the first anti-Semites, whereas 'all poets are Yids'.[4]

In his book of interviews with Rony Brauman, *La Discorde. Israël-Palestine, les Juifs, la France* (2006), Alain Finkielkraut is questioned by Elisabeth Lévy in these terms: 'Alain, your dialogues with Benny Lévy show that your connection with Judaism is not easily defined' (p. 94). To which he replies:

> What I bear in mind from Rony Brauman's statements [Brauman had presented himself as 'ignorant' on questions of 'Jewish study': p. 93], is the word 'ignorance', which is very interesting. I am sure that we would not have been described as ignorant in the days of our early study and contestation. We were emancipated. As militants, and as students, we were children of the Enlightenment, we saw ourselves as being above all forms of religious obser-vance. And then we saw the world invaded by screens, chasing out books and stupefying their users, young and old alike. In the face of a technology that makes everything available, and a demo-cratic process that makes everything equal, I understood for my part that secular culture and Judaism of study ('Being Jewish is a matter of study', Jean-Michel Salanskis rightly said) belonged to the same admirable and perishable culture. (p. 94)

'Being Jewish is a matter of study', Jean-Michel Salanskis 'rightly' said, as quoted by Finkielkraut. And Jean-Claude Milner seems to conclude from this that *The Inheritors* is 'an anti-Semitic book'. But Finkielkraut does not agree with this. Such short cuts are not permissible. One has to remain moderate, intelligible … For our own part, we observe that the reaction whose zealous servers these people are resembles the reaction of the Sadducees to the point of being indistinguishable: repression of Jewish orality in favour of a literalist reading of a teaching that has become Book, the capital letter being evidence that the apprenticeship of speech is now inegalitarian and socially tyrannical. The sadism of the Letter. *The malady of death.*

To conclude his book, *Fragments mécréants*, Daniel Bensaïd wrote: 'What connects the singular fragment with the form of the whole. Perhaps this is the meaning of internationalism.' Perhaps Jewish history is nothing else than this.

The world is threatened by the greatest catastrophe of all time: in less than a month, the entire planet will be submerged by an immense tidal wave. There will probably be no survivors. Every government, equally impotent, appeals to the intermediaries of God. 'It only remains to pray,' says the pope, 'to prepare our way to eternity.' 'For once, I agree with the papists,' says the archbishop of Canterbury. 'Let the will of Allah, the merciful, be done,' says the Grand Mufti of Jerusalem. While the chief rabbi of Israel goes to the Knesset with a solemn declaration: 'We have thirty days to learn to live under water.'[5]

Notes

'ANTI-SEMITISM EVERYWHERE' IN FRANCE TODAY

1. Alain Finkielkraut, *Au nom de l'autre. Réflexions sur l'antisémitisme qui vient*, Paris: Gallimard, 2003, p. 9.
2. Nicolas Weill, *La République et les antisémites*, Paris: Grasset, 2004, p. 15.
3. Referring of course to the *Kristallnacht* of 1938, when hundreds of Jews were killed by the Nazis.
4. These actions had been preceded by those against genuine fascists and negationists (e.g. Roger Garaudy and Bernard Antony), brought most often by the anti-racist organizations the Ligue Internationale Contre le Racisme et l'Antisémitisme (LICRA) and the Mouvement Contre le Racisme et pour l'Amitié entre les Peuples (MRAP), which led to a certain jurisprudence being established. In the last decade, however, with the change of target, the MRAP withdrew from this kind of action.
5. Emmanuel Brenner (ed.), *Les Territoires perdus de la République. Antisémitisme, racisme et sexisme en milieu scolaire*, Paris: Mille et Une Nuits, 2002, pp. 17–18.
6. *La République et les antisémites*, p. 33.
7. Pierre-André Taguieff, *Prêcheurs de haine. Traversée de la judéophobie planétaire*, Paris: Mille et Une Nuits, 2004, p. 192.
8. Bernard-Henri Lévy, *Récidives*, Paris: Grasset, 2004, p. 873 (our emphasis).
9. Alain Badiou, *The Meaning of Sarkozy*, trans. David Fernbach, London: Verso, 2009, p. 35ff.

10. *La République des livres,* 28 November 2007.
11. See *The Meaning of Sarkozy,* p. 5.
12. *LQR. La propagande du quotidien,* Paris: Raisons d'Agir, 2006, p. 39.
13. Pierre Péan, *Le Monde selon K,* Paris: Fayard, 2009.
14. Shlomo Sand, *The Invention of the Jewish People,* trans. Yael Lotan, London: Verso, 2010.
15. *Circonstances 3, portée du mot 'juif',* Paris: Lignes, 2005. Published in English in the collection by Alain Badiou, *Polemics,* trans. Steve Corcoran, London: Verso, 2006.
16. 'Racisme, une passion d'en haut', a contribution to the meeting of 11 September 2010 at Montreuil on 'Les Roms, et qui d'autre?', text available in English on the Verso website.

THE PHILO-SEMITIC REACTION

1. Julien Benda, *La Trahison des Clercs,* Paris: Grasset, 1927, pp. 225–6.

I. THE 'COMMUNITARIAN' IDEOLOGY

2. Ramadan oddly appears to forget that Saddam Hussein's Iraq, secular and nationalist, was supported and armed by the Western democracies, from the time he launched his war of aggression against the ayatollahs of Iran until his impulsive invasion of Kuwait, and that the American turn against him was due in particular to the need to maintain a military presence in the Gulf, once a certain desire to end this surfaced in Saudi Arabia. The argument from Israeli security, however, if undoubtedly pertinent, had always been so – Hussein's Iraq having inscribed in its constitution the legal duty to put an end to the Israeli state. It is thus hard to use this argument to explain the turn of the Western democracies against their ally Hussein from the time of the First Gulf War, a turn that moreover remained partial until the Second Gulf War. Conversely, this casts light on the independence of American strategic interests, at least until the rise of Paul Wolfowitz.
3. I should recall that use of the adjective 'communitarian' to refer to this current of thought was not Ramadan's invention. As witness: the interview with Alain Finkielkraut by Aude Lancelin, a

journalist with *Le Nouvel Observateur*, on the TV programme 'Cultures et Dépendances':

> Monsieur Finkielkraut, as someone who has battled so vigorously ... against communitarianism, with an established place as a republican, universalist and public figure, with a position at the Polytechnique and on France Culture, do you consider it possible to question whether this is compatible with an activity, even an activism, as communitarian commentator on a radio station?

The station in question was a Jewish 'communitarian' one, on whose airwaves Finkielkraut had a weekly programme, and the implication was therefore that this 'activism' displayed a 'communitarian' orientation which was incompatible with his 'position as a republican thinker'. Finkielkraut, moreover, did not deny this, as he replied to the journalist: 'We are no longer in an age when Fabre-Luce could criticize Jews for falling into a dual loyalty.'

4. Extract from an interview with Nadine Vasseur, in *Israël Autrement. Des écrivains et des artistes témoignent*, second edition, Paris: Actes Sud-Babel, 2004, pp. 38–9.

5. See the recent edition of Karl Marx's essay on the Jewish question, *Sur la question juive*, trans. Jean-François Poirier, Paris: La Fabrique, 2006. Marx's text here is introduced and commented upon by Daniel Bensaïd.

6. But the spectrum of Israeli military activities, according to Adler, also includes other alliances. Thus, apropos of the conflict between Putin's Russia and the Chechen separatists, he stresses that 'the natural sympathy that the Israelis feel for the Russians in this affair' seems only natural to him (p. 225) and, in connection with the hostages taken in the Dubrovka theatre in October 2002 and the massacre that followed, does not hesitate to put forward a thesis that strangely relativizes the responsibility of the Russian authorities in this drama: 'It is even said that the Israelis unfortunately supplied the so-called soporific gas that had unexpected and deadly effects, since they were not yet sufficiently familiar with its use' (p. 226). Note here the candour with which the author echoes the same 'it is said' that circulates about the Israelis ('it is said', as well, that they were behind the American war in Iraq – and many other wars, starting with the Second World War), and we may question the effect that similar candour would have from the pen of other authors, for example

Tariq Ramadan, if he chanced to write, inspired by Alexandre Adler's book: 'It is said (Zionists themselves say) that the Israelis supplied the so-called soporific gas that had unexpected and deadly effects, since they were not yet sufficiently familiar with its use, hence their desire to experiment on human guinea pigs, in the event the Chechen hostage-takers and their Russian hostages.'

7. Marie Syrkin, *Golda Méir*, cited by Maxime Rodinson in *Peuple juif ou problème juif?*, second edition, Paris: La Découverte, 1997, p. 216.

8. Cited by Eric Hazan in *LQR. La Propagande du quotidien*, Paris: Raisons d'Agir, 2006, p. 95.

9. Alain Finkielkraut tackles the advent of Nazism elsewhere, in writing of an *'Amérique indemne'*. *Au nom de l'Autre*, Paris: Gallimard, 2003.

10. In his 'Reply to John Lewis', Althusser wrote:

> A good deal of water has flowed under the bridge of history since 1960. The Workers' Movement has lived through many important events: the heroic and victorious resistance of the Vietnamese people against the most powerful imperialism in the world: the Proletarian Cultural Revolution in China (1966–69); the greatest workers' strike in world history (ten million workers on strike for a month) in May 1968 in France – a strike which was 'preceded' and 'accompanied' by a deep ideological revolt among French students and petty-bourgeois intellectuals; the occupation of Czechoslovakia by the other armies of the Warsaw Pact; the war in Ireland, etc. (*Essays in Self-Criticism*, London: New Left Books, 1976, pp. 35–6)

11. In his *History of Zionism: From the French Revolution to the Establishment of the State of Israel* (New York: Schocken, 2003), Walter Laqueur relates that the main opposition Chaim Weizmann encountered in London when he tried to obtain the famous declaration from Lord Balfour, came from notables of the English Jewish community; see chapter 8, 'Zionism and its Critics'.

12. See in particular chapter 9, 'A New Racism', and chapter 15, 'Leftism and Fascism', which set out to analyze the ancestry of the leftism of May 1968 and the fascism of the 1930s, as well as chapter 14, 'The Final Identification with the Sadistic-Anal Mother', which purports to explain the analytic origin.

13. See *Le Meurtre du Pasteur*, Paris: Grasset, 2002. On the subject of Freud's *Moses and Monotheism*, Lévy writes:

The father, God, the Jewish God, the Jew, had to die in order for the Christian truth of Darwin to be fulfilled. Examining the Jewish text, however, Freud could not find the least trace of this murder: the first murder was a murder between brothers, and it is clear that the first book of the Bible exclusively relates the Father, the life of fathers, the Father as living. (p. 299)

14. In his book *Mai 1968, l'héritage impossible* (Paris: La Découverte, 2002), the historian Jean-Pierre Le Goff recalls that the counter-demonstration of 30 May was above all a response to the ideological revolt of the time:

> The chauvinist and xenophobic slogans, such as 'France for the French', were aimed less at immigrant workers than at the 'agitators' and 'professional revolutionaries' who had supposedly come to sow disorder in the country and take part in an 'international plot'. Daniel Cohn-Bendit was directly targeted. Shouts of 'Cohn-Bendit to Berlin' and 'The redhead to Beijing' met with more response than the occasionally heard 'Cohn-Bendit to Dachau'. (p. 101)

It remains true that 'occasionally' the intimacy between the reaction and the '*univers concentrationnaire*' conferred on the slogan 'We are all German Jews', an unchallengeable pertinence, without any need to resort to the analytic concept of denegation.

15. Since the May 1968 students' chant 'We are all German Jews' is an obstacle to the anti-progressive argument that contesting a reactionary ideology leads logically to anti-Semitism, analysis of this famous slogan has become an essential exercise for the theorists of the 'new anti-Semitism'. Witness Jean-Claude Milner's demonstration in his own book on the May events:

> The demonstrators did not say 'We are all Jews'; they said 'We are all German Jews'; one poster even said 'We are all Jews and Germans'. The two last formulae are not equivalent, but they have one feature in common, the presence of a classic national label: *Germans*. The national reference comes from Georges Marchais [General Secretary of the PCF], indeed; but as far as the emergence of the name Jew is concerned, one that Marchais did not employ, this fulfils a quite specific function. It serves to compensate for the risk of subjective fracture that the name Jew still carries. It brings

the question onto the terrain of passports; it whitewashes the slogan by projecting it into the sphere of a facile universal and its most slender embodiment, the state. Let us even accept that the name German was still the bearer of an ugly connotation, from memory of the War; after all, this is what Georges Marchais assumed. By taking it up, however, the demonstrators proclaimed, once again and in a different form, that 1945 belonged to the past. The most forgotten past, since it was still close, not yet made into history. The name German did not open any wound in them. Better, it asepticized the possible wound that the name Jew might revive. (*L'Arrogance du présent. Regards sur une décennie. 1965-1975*, Paris: Grasset, 2009, pp. 174–5)

The demonstration here is far more subtle, but the thesis is the same; the ultimate object is denegation, a way of rejecting what 'the name Jew might revive'. And however subtle, it displays the same acrobatics. In effect, when Marchais described Cohn-Bendit as a 'German anarchist' in *L'Humanité* on 3 May, and when the government subsequently banned this 'agitator' from French territory on the 21st, taking advantage of his having left on a visit to Berlin, the values that the PCF shared with the government were clearly apparent. In the eyes of the students, however, this political consensus was evidently a function of the xenophobic France of Vichy, or what Alain Badiou calls the 'Pétainist transcendental' (see *The Meaning of Sarkozy*). The inevitable response, then, is to identify ourselves precisely with those whom the right-minded, reactionary national consensus of the state rejects; we identify precisely with the object of your refusal, which is why 'We are all German Jews'. In his contribution to the seminar series 'Marx au XXIe siècle' at the Sorbonne, devoted to 'History and Event in Alain Badiou', Quentin Meillassoux cited Kubrick's film *Spartacus* and its dénouement:

> When the slaves are defeated, each of the rebels replied to the Roman legionnaire's demand as to which of them is Spartacus: 'I am Spartacus'. He appropriates for the present − a present that has become eternal − a proper name that has become the generic name of every struggling slave.

The slogan of the May 1968 students was in this sense nothing else than a way of responding, to every French policeman who asked, 'I am Daniel Cohn-Bendit'. But above all, by substituting 'German

Jew' for the individual name 'Cohn-Bendit', the students were highlighting the irony of history about the 'German anarchist', in other words the obscenity of the expulsion decree, besides reminding the 'father' of what he had not said to the French police under Vichy, this past 'most forgotten because it was close, not yet made into history'. Milner's argument is certainly subtle, but it is still just as servile.

16. In *La Nouvelle judéophobie* (Paris: Mille et Une Nuits, 2002), a book I shall examine here in detail, Pierre-André Taguieff likewise explains that the attacks of 11 September 2001 were 'anti-American attacks (no less than symbolically anti-Jewish)' (p. 124 n. 202). Since however the World Trade Center and the Pentagon are not, until some new dispensation, Jewish symbols, but rather what Vladimir Illich Ramirez Sanchez, aka 'Carlos', calls (as quoted by Taguieff on p. 71 of his book) 'command centres of Yankee imperialist aggression against the peoples of the world: military command at the Pentagon and financial speculation in New York', it is necessary to conclude that they are in Taguieff's view symbols of the father – and that in this sense, the 11 September attacks were indeed 'symbolically anti-Jewish'.

17. Trigano's position vis-à-vis Turkey in this book is particularly significant as to the 'psychology' of the 'communitarian' intellectual. Discussing the way in which France's 'dereliction of identity' is more widely a European one, he writes:

> We have seen an illustration of this very recently with the question of the entry [into the European Union] of Turkey, which has become politically Islamist. The logic of elites and government (favourable to this) is apparent here, in complete opposition to public opinion in its great majority, as opinion polls show. (p. 103)

And the author immediately takes the side of 'public opinion' against 'the logic of elites and government', in the name of a necessary reconciliation of Europe with its own identity. For, according to him, Turkey's entry into the European Union would mean that 'European unity paradoxically makes Europe a political entity now entering the cultural, political and religious sphere of the Islamic world.' 'Dar el Islam?' he asks, only to answer immediately: 'What a pathetic phenomenon, to see a powerful civilization obliterate itself, dissolved in its own contradictions!' (pp. 103–104). Trigano's nightmare vision of a Europe conquered culturally, politically and religiously by Islam seems to have been inspired by Bat Yeor's study of the Euro-Arab dialogue, cited on two occasions (pp. 105, 106), and his concept of 'Eurabia'; hence the author's contribution to the 'renewal of the pact' of European identity:

> The French dereliction of identity, which we have deplored, is extended as we can see by a European equivalent. The issue is thus very far-reaching. Fundamentally, it is the Christian nations that this concerns. This is the failure of an entire civilization. The attitude of the Vatican and the Christian nations – particularly France as 'protector of the Holy Sites' and the Eastern Christians, precisely the Arab Christians – is in this respect symptomatic. It has completely abandoned them to Islamic threats in order to unite with the Arab world. (p. 104)

Reminding France of its role as 'protector of the Holy Sites' (echoing its vocation as 'eldest daughter of the Church'), and Europe as a whole of its Christian identity, the author thus delivers the final meaning of Turkish entry into the European Union: 'the failure of an entire civilization'. Yet Turkey is one of the states with a Muslim or Islamic majority most well-disposed towards Israel, and it goes without saying that Turkish membership of the European Union is a preliminary condition for Israeli membership of either this very Union or any other Mediterranean alliance that might include it, in the same way that Turkish membership of the Union would be the birth certificate for a citizen-based conception of Europe instead of a Christian identity-based conception that is deliberately closed. In fact, those people in France who are hostile to Turkish entry into the European Union are equally hostile to that of Israel, with the qualification that on the subject of Israel the 'logic of elites' and 'public opinion' appear to coincide, as André Glucksmann remarks in his *Discours de la haine*:

> When Silvio Berlusconi suddenly proposed to extend Europe to Russia, Turkey and Israel, the reply from the French side was: 'Why Israel?', that 'There is no geographical connection' (which is true) and 'no historical or cultural tie between Israel and Europe' (which is a pinnacle of deliberate illiteracy). (p. 81)

By writing, on the subject of the countries of the European Union, that 'fundamentally it is the Christian nations this concerns', Trigano makes himself the herald of an identitarian conception of Europe and of France as 'protector of the Holy Sites', which, if it suggests some kind of supervisory mandate over Palestine, does not on the other hand favour Israeli entry into the European Union. Yet Israel is interested in such an 'entry', as evidence this note that appeared in the *Jerusalem Post* (French edition) for 29 January/4 February 2008:

> The Netherlands Minister of Foreign Affairs, Maxime Verhagen, has committed himself to working towards Israeli membership of the European Union. Verhagen, who met with president Shimon Peres on Tuesday [in the context of his diplomatic visit to Israel], declared that Israeli membership was important for him, since Israel has succeeded in maintaining democracy, stability and liberty in extreme conditions.

This is attested to by Israel's isolation on the international scene, an isolation to which Trigano likewise declares himself sensitive. We may then conclude that 'communitarian' sensibility respects the strict limit of 'public opinion', something of which Alain Finkielkraut also offers us an illustration. In his article 'Les vicissitudes du juif charnel' (published in issue 6 of *Cahiers d'études lévinassiennes*, an issue devoted to the theme of universality), he brings up the question of Turkish entry into Europe. Along with Trigano, Finkielkraut sees this as a symptom of Europe's dereliction of identity, a symptom whose origin he detects, like Trigano himself, with Habermas and his disciples, in particular the German sociologist Ulrich Beck, whom he cites as maintaining that 'only an image of man and culture that is non-anthropological, anti-ontological, radically open, deserves to be called European' (p. 228). On which Finkielkraut comments:

> It is inspired by this duty of memory, this religion of humanity, this definition, or rather lack of definition, that the champions of Turkey's joining the European Union have accused their opponents, with ostensible disgust, of seeing Europe as a 'Christian club'. Why do they not want to have Turkey join the European Union? Because Turkey has a different history and a different majority religion. This then means that, for you, Europe is a Christian club – and it is enough to use these terms to reject the argument. (pp. 228–9)

But the 'argument' in question has lost nothing of its opaque nature, unless we believe that only a country whose 'majority religion' is Christianity has the right to join the European Union – in which case, if it is not exactly a 'club', it would be none the less an exclusively Christian Union. Hence the question arises as to who a European is, according to the author of such an argument? Hence, too, the famous response of Groucho Marx: 'I don't care to belong to any club that accepts people like me as members.' After all, why not maintain instead that Finkielkraut's work is no more than a vast, unlikely and superb provocation? This hypothesis seems all the more consistent in that, with the *Cahiers d'études lévinassiennes* having been founded by Benny Lévy, there would seem to be a certain contradiction in its having become the tribune of this polemicist – at least, if it were not a deliberate farce. In fact, surveying the trajectories of former militants of the Gauche Prolétarienne in his review of Jean-Claude Milner's book on the 1965–76 decade, *L'Arrogance du présent*, Éric Aeschimann wrote in *Libération* (12 February 2009):

> While Benny Lévy applies himself to Hebrew, Christian Jambet and Guy Lardreau have embarked on their own paths towards the 'spiritual': the former becoming a specialist in Shiite thought, the latter focusing on eastern Christianity ... When, at Benny Lévy's request, another former Gauche Prolétarienne stalwart, Gérard Bobillier, founded Éditions Verdier, Christian Jambet edited a series titled 'Islam spirituel'. In the mid 1980s, Milner also re-encountered Benny Lévy, and these four individuals constantly crossed paths – until the final schism. During the summer vacation, Éditions Verdier organizes its Banquet de Lagrasse in the Aude. They would meet up and discuss. It turned out that each of them had become the representative of 'his' monotheism. But one evening in 1998, Benny Lévy decreed that Judaism was no longer negotiable. 'Now that Jambet and Lardreau were defending Christianity, he saw them as having chosen the camp of anti-Judaism', one witness recalls. Milner, as a committed atheist, pressed for separation: for him, Judaism, as a religion of the letter, has everything to lose from a convergence with Christianity, a religion of the spirit. An altercation took place between Benny Lévy and Jambet. It was 'firm', according to some people, 'violent' according to others. The 'Islam spirituel' series was abandoned.

(Aeschimann's article can be consulted on the website of Éditions Verdier, which thereby vouches for its content.) Since it would be far too incoherent to dismiss the Oriental spiritualism of Jambet and Lardreau only to welcome a political argument exalting the Christian identity of Europe, if not significant of a certain political vision of the world, we have to venture not just a hypothesis but a Pascalian wager: Alain Finkielkraut is a brilliant and misunderstood Jewish humorist.

2. ON ETHNO-CULTURAL SOCIOLOGY

1. Brenner was in fact the university historian Georges Bensoussan, as pointed out by Thomas Deltombe in *L'Islam imaginaire. La construction de l'islamophobie en France, 1975–2005* (Paris: La Découverte, 2005), referring in a footnote on page 302 to the website of the publisher Fayard, which had let the cat out of the bag. The author had good reason for resorting to a pseudonym.

2. In his introduction to the collection of testimonies that make up the collective work *Les Territoires perdus de la République*, Brenner speaks of the courage that teachers needed in order to

   > express themselves on a subject that might seem shameful to them, agreeing to break the stranglehold of an intellectual terrorism which sees mentioning the ethno-cultural origin of an aggressor or a thug who creates anti-Semitic disturbances … as 'playing into the hands of the Front National'. (p. 22)

   Ethno-cultural sociology was born.

3. Our study is based on the first edition of the book, dated 2002, as it was this that 'turned around the debate on secularism'.

4. This can be consulted on the haaretz.com website.

5. It is worth noting that Finkielkraut refers to Brenner's book in an interview with *Le Monde* that precisely covers the scandal created by his interview with *Haaretz*: 'And we have to start by rehabilitating education. If the French language does not re-conquer this lost territory of the *banlieues*, then, yes, discrimination in employment and housing will get worse' (*Le Monde*, 27–28 November 2005).

6. The second edition of this book (2004) again has 'dirty Jew' in the masculine (p. 148), indicating that this was not a typographic mistake but indeed what was written in the workbook.

7. We may note here that the choice of Jorge Semprun's book, if it was a question of informing the assistant about the 'Jewish genocide' and consequently the singularity of the extermination camps, indicates a certain confusion in the mind of the teacher, despite the claim that she had done work 'on the mechanisms of negationist discourse' (according to her colleague Barbara Lefebvre). Semprun was in fact imprisoned in the Buchenwald concentration camp. It would have been useful therefore to add to this loan of books also Primo Levi's *If This Is a Man*, Elie Wiesel's *Night* or the Vrba–Wezler report, as well as Semprun's fine book. But let this be.

8. In a comment published in *Le Figaro* on 29 September 2006, Robert Redeker, philosophy teacher at the Lycée Pierre-Paul-Riquet in Saint-Orens de Gameville, raised the following question:

> How should we explain the ban on thongs at Paris-Plages this summer? The official argument was odd: 'disturbance to public order'. Does this mean that gangs of frustrated young men risked turning violent at the display of beauty? Or is it a fear of Islamist demonstrations, 'virtue brigades' on the shores of Paris-Plages? And yet the failure to ban the veil in the street, despite the criticism that this sign of women's oppression arouses, would seem more likely to 'disturb public order' than the thong. It is not fanciful to think that the ban on thongs expresses an Islamization of minds in France, a more or less conscious submission to the dictates of Islam.

If Redeker had found himself in Marie Zeitbeger's staff room, it seems he would have concluded, in a display of resistance to the Islamization of French society: 'I prefer our girls to come to school wearing thongs rather than veiled.' We can recognize the courage and attraction of this idea: who would dare go further? So, let us conclude with him: 'Female citizens, students and pupils, Islam will not pass: on with your thongs!'

9. Stigmatizing pupils of Maghrebian origin and reviving the slogans of French colonialism, as a way of combatting the far right, is not the least paradoxical aspect of ethno-cultural sociology. But still more paradoxical is 'communitarian' activism against the Islamic veil. Thus Yves-Charles Zarka writes, in a supplement to the periodical *Cités* that he edits:

> To give even an inch on the refusal of the veil in public space would be interpreted as a victory of Islam over the impure and

corrupt West, against the values on which French society is based … The veil is both a religious sign and a mark of discrimination, it is the symbol of the establishment of a society of virtual apartheid that opposes men and women as citizens of different class, and grants men possession and control of the body, liberty and even life of women. (*Droit de Cités*, no. 1)

The obligation of a woman to cover her hair, however, was originally an ancient rabbinical instruction before being taken over by Islam, with the nuance that in Jewish tradition this concerns only a married woman and not an adolescent (not to mention that in many interpretations, particularly Ashkenazi, it is met perfectly well by covering the hair with a wig, even a blond and silky one). It remains the case that, apart from this nuance – decisive in conceptual terms, but this is another question – Zarka's ethno-cultural exegesis applies just as well to the Muslim tradition as to the Jewish. And as far as the 'public space' goes, observant Jews have the same trouble in meeting his requirement, all the more so as this parallel between Muslim and Jewish tradition is precisely what Shmuel Trigano brings to light in a highly revealing manner. In his book *L'Exclu: Entre Juifs et Chrétiens* (Paris: Denoël, 2003), he offers a critical reading of the philosopher Alain Badiou, particularly his *Saint Paul: The Foundation of Universalism* (trans. Ray Brassier, Stanford: Stanford University Press, 2003), writing, against that philosopher's Paulinism:

It is surprising to note how readily Alain Badiou, with a libertarian and leftist reputation, takes on board Paul's whole doctrine, even his sexist theory about the status of women. Defending the veiling of women that Paul recommended, as sign of 'an acceptance of the difference between the sexes' (p. 105), he believes that the meaning of this is 'that it should be manifest that the universality of this declaration includes women who accept to be women'.

In Paul's ethno-cultural context, the question raised was that of the attitude to adopt towards rabbinical Judaism; and according to Badiou, Paul's doctrinal singularity, particularly in contrast to that of the apostle John, was that he was concerned not to abolish Jewish ethno-cultural practices, but rather to make these a matter of indifference in relation to Christian universalism. ('It is John who, by turning the logos into a principle, will synthetically inscribe Christianity within the space of the Greek logos, thereby subordinating it to anti-Judaism': p. 43.) The 'communitarian' intellectual, for his part, thus precisely criticizes in 'Paul's doctrine' – and consequently in the philosopher who defends it – his laxity in relation to an ancient Jewish practice, calling it a 'sexist theory', so that, criticizing Badiou's Paulinism from a supposedly Jewish point of view, Trigano finds himself alongside the apostle John who, according to Badiou, was precisely the originator of an anti-rabbinical Judaism that aimed at *abolishing* rabbinical Judaism! But even more paradoxical is the dialogue between Benny Lévy and Alain Finkielkraut on the 'question of universalism'. During a debate on secularism (held on 22 July 2003 in Paris, and published in a book of interviews with Benny Lévy by Alain Finkielkraut, *Le Livre et les livres*, Paris: Verdier, 2006, pp. 83–97), Lévy introduces his thesis on the essential significance of clothing in Jewish tradition with the words:

> In preparing for this debate I wanted to pick up on what is said in France on the question of the Islamic veil ... I believe that the main anti-Jewish philosopher in France, whose name (but this doesn't matter, we can forget his name) is Alain Badiou, said on the question of the veil – given that he is for the Islamic veil in schools: 'After all, *this is only* a question of clothing.' And for me that is the key point. He didn't understand the importance of what he was saying there. For the question of clothing is the very question of the universal.

In fact clothing as signifier, according to Lévy, is 'the very question of the universal' in the sense that nothing less is at stake than the question of 'being-Jewish':

> ... if we are in a period when the power of the Gentiles is beginning to persecute us – mark my words – then, even if it is only a question of altering a simple suit ... you have to sacrifice your life! ... because it is the whole *yaadout*, the whole being-Jewish that is at stake ... because this little item of clothing, the little kepi, stands here for everything else. (Ibid., pp. 87–8)

Referring to the teaching of the leading French philosopher on the question of the Islamic veil, therefore, Lévy cannot ignore how, according to Badiou, the Islamic veil and the Jewish kepi are rigorously equal, since they are both ethno-cultural particularisms that are intrinsically, absolutely *indifferent* in relation to the question of the universal, of truth or knowledge – in short, in relation to secular teaching. This is why Badiou is equally in favour of the Jewish kepi in school. It is certainly possible to discuss his doctrine, one can even oppose it and – why not? – see in it a conception of the universal that is contrary to rabbinical teaching, inasmuch as this clothing is not absolutely indifferent, but possibly essential to the construction of a singular universal, at least when 'the power of the Gentiles is beginning to persecute us'; on the other hand, it is outrageous to make out that this is the argument of 'the main anti-Jewish philosopher in France'!

And more than an outrage, it is a contradiction, when Finkielkraut, as Lévy's interviewer here and co-founder of the Institut d'Études Lévinassiennes, in this same debate stands for the banning of the Islamic veil and Jewish kepi, on the grounds that, according to him, it is necessary first of all to take a distance from 'opponents of any repressive measure', who defend 'the secularism of "yes" to various modalities of present-day life: the veil, the kepi, the turned-back cap, piercing, mobile phones, baggy trousers and bare midriff' (*Le Livre et les livres*, p. 91). Apart from the fact that Finkielkraut avoids the essential point here – that this law is perhaps not as innocent as it seems, particularly in that the ban in question precisely *does not* oppose piercing, mobile phones, baggy trousers or bare midriff, but rather the Islamic veil and the Jewish kepi, the scarf and the skullcap (whether turned-back or not), only these being targeted as items of clothing by the secular law (and leaving aside the fact that Finkielkraut does not mention other religious signs in his list, but only the Jewish and Muslim) – any reader even minimally informed about Aristotle's teaching on the principle of non-contradiction cannot fail to raise the following question: If Badiou is 'the leading anti-Jewish philosopher in France', what then is Finkielkraut? A humourist?

But the best is still to come: Éric Marty, in his book *Une querelle avec Alain Badiou, philosophe* (Paris: Gallimard, 2007), is worried about the 'public support' Badiou gave to the 'right to wear the Islamic veil in schools and colleges' (p. 37), and adds in a note: 'See on this point the deeper defence of wearing the Islamic veil in schools that Badiou gives in his book on Saint Paul' (p. 38 n. 1). The 'public support' in question is in fact the philosopher's article in the 22–23 February 2004 edition of *Le Monde*, and reprinted in *Polemics*, in which he says in particular:

Imagine the principal of a *lycée*, followed by a squad of inspectors armed with measuring rules, scissors and law books, to check at the school gates whether the scarves, kepis and other head-covers are 'ostentatious'. A postage-stamp-sized veil on top of a hairpiece? A kepi the size of a two-euro coin? Very dodgy, indeed. (p. 100)

So not only is Badiou's public support for the 'right to wear the Islamic veil' very explicitly a public support for the right equally to wear the Jewish kepi, but on top of this, Marty wants to make us believe, by referring us to 'the deeper defence of wearing the Islamic veil in schools that Badiou gives in his book on Saint Paul', that Paul's laxity towards this 'sexist theory' – as Trigano calls it – concerns the 'Islamic veil', more than five hundred years before the appearance of Islam! But perhaps he believes this himself. Perhaps Éric Marty will, before long, publish a book taking issue with historians.

10. The Sofres inquiry cited by Brenner was published as an appendix to the book *Les Antifeujs. Le livre blanc des violences antisémites en France depuis septembre 2000* (Paris: Éditions Calmann-Lévy, 2002, pp. 201–29). The 'technical note' accompanying this reads as follows:

This poll was carried out by Taylor Nelson Sofres between 28 January and 1 February 2002. It was done by phone call with a national sample of 400 individuals representative of the population resident in France aged between 15 and 24. It opted to apply a quota method (sex, age, activity) and a stratification by region and urban category. The results for each question are presented initially in global terms, then divided according to a number of criteria: the sex of the individual questioned, their age category, occupational situation, social origin, favoured political party, parents' geographical origin, level of religious practice and educational level. Before examining the full results of this unprecedented poll on young people's image of Jews, it is indispensable to remember that the results by category have to be considered with extreme caution, given the small samples in some categories.

11. A recent survey commissioned by the Anti-Defamation League and conducted in seven European countries relativizes still more any Maghrebian ethno-cultural specificity on these questions. In the summary of the results of this survey published in the weekly *Actualité Juive* for 19 February 2009, the statistical data appear as follows: On economics, 41 per cent of Europeans questioned continue to believe

that 'Jews have too much power in the world of business'. Hungarians (67 per cent) cling most strongly to this idea, followed by Spaniards (56 per cent) and Poles (55 per cent). In France, 'only' 33 per cent believe this, though this still represents 5 per cent more than in 2007. Besides, Jews are accused of having 'too much power over international financial markets' by 74 per cent of Spaniards, 59 per cent of Hungarians and 54 per cent of Poles, but by only 27 per cent of French people and 15 per cent of British. This opens a whole new perspective of research for ethno-cultural sociology.

12. To be completely accurate, there is also a third reference, once again concerning perception of the Shoah, but this time without any difference coming to light between young people of Maghrebian origin and the others, Brenner's argument here emphasizing 'the advance of relativism' among young people of all ethno-cultural groups: 'We need only emphasize the advance of relativism. A survey conducted in January 2002 [the Sofres survey] showed that 51 per cent of French people between fifteen and twenty-four believed that freedom of expression meant that negationists should not be prosecuted' (p. 69). This remark is thus marginal to his ethno-cultural thesis.

3. ANTI–TAGUIEFF

1. Taguieff writes, with a skilful formula: 'The Islamists are not alone in their enterprise of terror and destruction aimed at the West and the pluralist democracies (including Israel)' (*La Nouvelle judéophobie*, p. 228).

2. If Taguieff describes the myth of the world Jewish plot as 'grotesque', and its momentary champion as the 'supreme leader of the Taliban', he can still write, in his comment on Roy's text:

> All the same, we must resist the call to hatred, to hatred of hatred, we must refuse to join the vicious circle of mimetic hatreds. Neither succumb to the 'pathos of the victim', nor concede to the 'anger of the avenger'. This is one of lessons I have learned from *If This Is a Man*, Primo Levi's great book ... (p. 231)

The transition from 'grotesque' to 'temptation of hated' signals a break in the order of discourse, i.e. precisely what distinguishes Roy's text from the mythical imaginary of Mullah Omar and his 'grotesque' obsession with a 'Jewish cause behind every event'. The appeal to

Primo Levi, however, intends to identify Roy's line of argument with a Nazi one, which is why it shows such strength of character for Taguieff not to succumb to the 'pathos of the victim'. The contemporary avatar of Nazi discourse, in his view, is thus Roy's argument, which attests to this more than that of Mullah Omar; but what he presents as evidence of this is precisely what demands an explanation.

3. On the subject of the tenacity and origin of the prejudice attributing to Jews a silent slaving conspiracy, in relation to white slaves as well as black, see Edgar Morin's sociological classic *Rumour in Orléans* (New York: Pantheon, 1971).

4. Léon Poliakov, *Histoire de l'antisémitisme* (2 vols), vol. 1: *L'âge de la foi*, Paris: Éditions Calmann-Lévy, 1981, pp. 448–9.

5. Montesquieu, *The Spirit of the Laws*, book XV, chapter 5, 'On Negro Slavery'.

6. This is also the course of Alain Finkielkraut's thought. When he was asked by the weekly *Le Point* (12 May 2005) to put his signature to a text calling for a struggle against 'anti-White racism', he replied that 'it has taken courage and lucidity to take note of the unprecedented connection between Judeophobia and Francophobia'. This is in fact an axiom of so-called 'communitarian' thought, from Brenner via Taguieff to Finkielkraut.

7. Evidence of this, anecdotal and thus symptomatic, is Taguieff's statement about the 'supposedly right-minded Daniel Bensaïd', whom he cites among the *'porteurs de valise* of "Palestino-progressivism"' (*Prêcheurs de la haine*, p. 307 n. 13). There can be no doubt, in fact, that the author's invectives against these *'porteurs de valise'* are not aimed just at defenders of the Palestinian cause, but more widely at all those in France who campaigned for Algerian independence.

8. Taguieff actually spells out to his readers, in the introduction to the fourth and final section of his book, which is devoted to the 'silences on the new Judeophobia':

> We note a strange and disturbing blindness of political circles (particularly on the left), likewise of the French media, towards the new expressions of anti-Jewish hatred, especially when these are bound up with the Israeli–Palestinian conflict and are partly attributable to certain populations from Maghrebian and African immigrant background – in short, when they appear to be the act of 'youth from the *banlieues*', a good part of whom remain impervious to the norms of republican integration. (p. 173)

9. François Burgat, *L'Islamisme au Maghreb. La voix du Sud*, revised and expanded edition, Paris: Payot, 1995 (first edition, 1988).

10. All the more so in that 'methodological empathy' is sometimes the only attitude needed for understanding, whether in observing remote tribes in Amazonia or approaching Flaubert, on whom Sartre wrote in the preface to his study of the writer: 'My initial hostility then changed into *empathy*, the attitude necessarily required for understanding' (*L'Idiot de la famille*, Paris: Gallimard, 1971, vol. 1, p. 8; Sartre's emphasis). Taguieff's methodological considerations thus lead us more certainly in the steps of Emmanuel Brenner, Barbara Lefebvre and Sophie Ferhadjian than in those of Durkheim, Lévi-Strauss or Sartre.

11. See Ilan Pappé, *A History of Modern Palestine: One Land, Two People*, Cambridge: Cambridge University Press, 2004.

12. Zeev Sternhell, *Aux origines d'Israël. Entre nationalisme et socialisme*, Paris: Fayard, 1996, pp. 12–13 (Preface to the French edition).

13. In particular, Alexandre Adler in *Le Figaro*, Bernard-Henri Lévy in *Le Point* and André Glucksmann in *Le Nouvel Observateur*.

14. On the procedure of 'de-legitimizing the opponent', Joss Dray and Denis Sieffert observe: 'This is a constant in the bitter battle that Tarnero wages, and even an authentic intellectual previously better inspired such as Pierre-André Taguieff' (in *La Guerre israélienne de l'information*, Paris: La Découverte, 2002, p. 107); while Jacques Tarnero, for his part, notes 'the very talented book by Pierre-André Taguieff, one of the most perspicacious researchers on this question [i.e. the new Judeophobia]' ('Sionisme et antisionisme', in *Le Sionisme expliqué à mes potes*, p. 199). Whatever the partisan position adopted, there is thus a consensus on one point: Taguieff is an 'authentic intellectual', in particular contrast to Jacques Tarnero, deemed too 'communitarian', no doubt with regard to the republican objectivity of his colleague.

15. We should add that the unveiling of the 'impostor', if such an unveiling had to be based simply on the analysis of his works, would not be all that easy, given how 'clever' Ramadan is. As witness the attempt by Emmanuel Brenner, laborious to say the least, that proposes to give an example – the only example, in fact – of the way in which Ramadan is a 'past master of double language'.

In a radio dialogue with Nicolas Sarkozy on France 2, broadcast on 20 November 2003, Tariq Ramadan maintained that he had always denounced wife-beating. Yet in his book *Islam, le face-à-face des civilisations* (Tawhid, 2001), Ramadan explains that if all non-violent pressure of a husband on his wife has failed.

– there then follows a quotation from Ramadan's book by which Brenner seeks to reveal 'the past master of double language' –

'then, and only then, would "beating" be permitted … What is involved here is then … a blow symbolically expressed with the aid of the *siwak* branch … The message addressed to men could not be clearer: it is the path of dialogue and discussion with the wife that corresponds to the spirit manifest in the Revelation. The teaching does not stop with this verse and its interpretation: the example of the prophet, more than anything, was in a position to express the behavioural ideal.' (Tarique Ramadan, cited by Emmanuel Brenner, in *'France, prends garde de perdre ton âme'*, pp. 116–17 n. 81)

It is clear that the ethno-cultural sociologist sins here out of honesty, or lack of method, since the trick would have succeeded if he had only cited the essential point, i.e. that according to Tariq Ramadan, 'beating would be permitted'. However, once he ventures to point out the difference between what Ramadan asserts here, 'that he has always denounced wife-beating', and what he wrote elsewhere, that Islam counsels recourse to 'a symbolically expressed blow' after all other 'non-violent pressure' has failed, the effect is singularly comical. If this is all the threat that Islam and the double language of its unveiled preacher pose to Western women today, we should immediately alert the many associations for battered women in France, who might well then campaign for a radical Islamization of French society.

16. We should make clear here that this information on Alain Gresh's origin is not something Taguieff has from a police report, but was provided from Gresh himself. In his book *L'Islam, la République et le monde*, he presents himself first of all as born in Egypt, 'from a Coptic father and a Jewish mother' (p. 10), before going on to explain:

I landed in France as the Algerian war was coming to an end. I made the acquaintance of Henri Curiel – it was only later that I discovered he was my biological father – and his *'porteurs de valises'* friends. They were being released from prison. (p. 15)

17. In the same way, it seems that an order banning someone from French territory is equally appropriate for an Egyptian Communist, a German anarchist or a Swiss Islamist.

18. For a critical account of the Holy See's text of 1998, 'We Remember: A Reflection on the Shoah', see the book by Georges-Elia Sarfari, *Le Vatican et le Shoah ou comment l'Église s'absout de son passé*, (Paris: Éditions Berg International, 2000) and particularly the response from the International Jewish Committee on Interreligious Consultations appended to this book ('Response to Vatican Document "We Remember: A Reflection on the Shoah"').

19. The reader will remember here that Tariq Ramadan's statement was also that 'anti-Semitism is inadmissible', though not 'absolutely to be condemned', as Taguieff immediately notes. On the subject of Pius XI, however, he might well say that 'such is his theological style'.

20. See Hannah Arendt, '*The Deputy*: Guilt by Silence?', in Eric Bentley (ed.), *The Storm over the Deputy*, New York: Grove Press, 1964, p. 85ff.

21. As an epigraph to chapter 10 of his *Histoire générale du Bund* (Paris: Denoël, 1999), Henri Minczeles quotes the words of the Polish Colonel Adam Koc, head of the OZON, a government party, on 21 February 1937: 'We cannot approve of violence and brutal anti-Semitism. This undermines our national dignity and infringes our honour … We understand, however, our people's instincts of legitimate defence' (p. 271). No doubt this is one of the 'texts combating anti-Semitism' that should be studied in French secondary schools, along with those of the Vatican and Saint Pierre-André Taguieff.

22. The way in which the Christian utopia informs the convictions of so-called 'communitarian' intellectuals is certainly one of the most singular features of this current of thought. As witness the analysis that Alain Finkielkraut proposed of the urban violence of November 2005. On 6 November, during his weekly programme on Radio de la Communauté Juive, *Qui Vive*, he explained:

> I am horrified by the vandalism unleashed today across the whole of France, horrified but not surprised. This apocalypse was predictable, it was particularly heralded by the report of the minister of national education on signs and expressions of ethnic or religious allegiance in secondary schools in so-called difficult zones, a report of June 2004 presented by Jean-Pierre Aubin. This report particularly informs us that a number of pupils seek by their clothing to demarcate themselves from France, or from those, pupils or teachers,

who are referred to as 'French'. This report also reveals that certain authors, particularly the philosophers of the Enlightenment, are ever more frequently challenged: 'Rousseau is against my religion.' We also learn that the teaching of history is the object of a general accusation on the part of certain pupils and those who influence them: it is supposedly mendacious and partial throughout, conveying a distorted Judeo-Christian view of the world. There are several examples ... This challenge, the report also says, has become almost standard, and can be radicalized and politicized whenever more sensitive questions are tackled, in particular the Crusades, the Jewish genocide – frequent negationist assertions – the Algerian War, the Israeli–Arab wars and the Palestinian question.

Listeners to the Radio de la Communauté Juive thus learn that there is supposedly a 'style of clothing' specific to France or 'the French', and that if pupils in secondary schools in 'so-called difficult zones' seek to 'demarcate' themselves from this, that is a sign heralding a 'predictable apocalypse'. Listeners also learn that these same pupils challenge the teaching they receive, whether this bears on the thought of Enlightenment philosophers or on history, and that 'this challenge ... has become almost standard, and can be radicalized and politicized whenever more sensitive questions are tackled, in particular the Crusades, the Jewish genocide – frequent negationist assertions – the Algerian War, the Israeli–Arab wars and the Palestinian question'. And yet, if the 'challenging' by pupils of the 'Jewish genocide' is the main concern, and if it is easy to understand how 'the Israeli–Arab wars' or the 'Palestinian question' can be 'sensitive' questions, delicate to handle for a history teacher, one might inquire rather more closely on the subject of 'the Algerian War': What view of the Algerian war are these secondary school teachers offering, if history lessons covering this episode in the decolonization process are the object of 'challenge', particularly on the part of pupils who moreover ostensibly display an ethnic or religious origin that is not 'French'? As for the 'Crusades', which we know – or think we know – were a pretext for the massacre of Jews in Europe, notably in Worms and Mainz, before culminating in the massacre of the Jewish and Islamic population of Jerusalem when the Holy City was taken by the Crusaders, a spectacle sometimes described as a river of blood that rose to the knees of the Christian knights who slaughtered men and women, infants and old people, we can ask:

What view of history is the department of education conveying if teaching about the Crusades arouses radical and politicized challenge from secondary-school pupils in 'so-called difficult zones'? Finally, what common measure is there, in the mind of this analyst, or in the minds of the authors of this official report, between 'challenging' the Crusades and 'challenging' the genocide of Jews by the Nazis? Questions that Alain Finkielkraut's analysis of the riots of November 2005 answers as follows:

> Pétanque balls were thrown at police from tower blocks ... stones at the firemen, primary and secondary schools burned down, likewise gyms, buses full of passengers set on fire, shops and businesses pillaged, cars burned ... There is no connection of cause and effect between the increase in inequality, the wretchedness of the *banlieues*, unemployment, poverty and precarious jobs on the one hand, and acts of this kind on the other. No economic and social determinism can justify this pillage and this desire to kill. There is something irreducible here, the origin of those who commit them ... They are not social riots, not hunger riots or economic riots, they are ethnic riots directed against France ... Here again, we must resist any generalization, they are mostly Arabs and Blacks with an Islamic identity, if not religion – but this does not mean all Arabs and Blacks.

To believe Alain Finkielkraut, what is 'irreducible' is thus the 'origin' of the rioters, who 'mostly Arabs and Blacks with an Islamic identity' – which does not mean 'all' Arabs and blacks took part in the riots – the analyst goes on to make clear. But it remains the case that this is what is 'irreducible': 'they are ethnic riots directed against France'. In other words, the causes of the urban riots of November 2005 were in the last analysis ethno-cultural or ethno-religious, and not socio-economic. That is at least the conclusion of this 'communitarian' analyst, which he repeated a few days later, on 17 November, this time in an interview with journalists from the Israeli daily paper *Haaretz*: 'it is clear that this revolt has an ethnic and religious character'. The difficulty that his listeners have to face, however, is that urban riots, pillage and violence, whether spontaneous or organized, against the police, against people or property – just like drugs, gangs, weapons or even rap, etc. – are not the peculiarity of 'Arabs and Blacks with an Islamic identity'. The same phenomena occur in the big cities of the United States, as well as in Latin America, even though Arabs are few and far between there, as are blacks 'with an Islamic identity'. It is possible to reject the idea that the cause of these riots, pillage and violence is to be found in the socio-economic conditions of these populations, who are often from immigrant background, and to reject any 'economic and social determination'; but it is completely inconsistent to recognize in it some kind of Maghrebian, Arab or Muslim particularism. Besides, Finkielkraut himself acknowledges the inconsistent character of his analysis, since, after rejecting 'progressivism' and its 'logic of apology', which he describes as 'a kind of race to remove blame from the guilty parties, either by hiding their origin and saying "the youth", or, when they are forced to recognize and admit this, immediately denouncing their conditions of life and the stigmatization of which they are victims', and after concluding that 'what is happening in France today is a gigantic anti-republican pogrom', our analyst can add all the same:

> These young people from immigrant background are expressing the hatred of a section of the Arab–Muslim world against the West, and more particularly against the old colonial powers, including France; but there is in this hatred for the West a kind of disordered Westernism. Fundamentally, these young people are pressing to its ultimate conclusion the impatience of the democratic individual with any forms, mediations and institutions. They are pressing to its ultimate consequences the devouring passion for wellbeing. Their vocabulary is sometimes that of radical Islamism, but their world is one of absolute individualism, of 'everything right now', video games and pornography … Their ideal is one of availability: 'what I want, where I want, when I want'. And clearly school has no place in this ideal, since school means patience, school is a mediation.

Finkielkraut shows his real analytical ability here, since he now observes that the behaviour of the rioters, the culture inspiring them, the worldview that animates them, are in no way to be sought in an immigrant ethno-cultural origin – that of 'Arabs and Blacks with an Islamic identity' – but rather in the assertion of values that are, in the last analysis, those of 'absolute individualism, "everything right now", video games and pornography'. In other words, far from being a revolt against oppression, as the 'progressive' would like to describe it, idealizing it to the point of taking refuge in denial, the revolt of the 'youth from the *banlieues*' is rather an indication of a kind of voluntary slavery, in the sense that it conveys the very 'ideal' that oppresses them, even embodying its most radical version: 'Fundamentally, these young people are pressing to its ultimate conclusion the impatience of the democratic individual with any forms, mediations and institutions', or with 'school' which teaches 'patience'. So it is not after all reading the Koran, attending mosques or wearing the Islamic scarf that fuels 'the impatience of the democratic individual', but rather television, video games and pornographic films – which are rather unconvincing as Arab or Islamic ethno-cultural peculiarities, at least in France, or more widely, in the Western democracies. Finkielkraut also speaks, in a rather 'retro' if not anachronistic style, of a 'disordered Westernism'. And so, once it is established that the urban riots, the pillaging, the collective expressions of a savage nihilism, are not 'ethnic riots directed against France' but a rather unflattering mirror in which Western democratic societies are suddenly and violently forced to view themselves, what should we conclude? Finkielkraut, for his part, concludes as follows:

> I do not know how remedies can be found, but we have to look reality in the face, and at this moment, the only thing we can hope for is a severe education, strict and severe; but this is something that the institution does not want, and the bishops don't want it either. I was completely floored by their declaration ... This is what the archbishop of Bordeaux, chair of the French conference of bishops, Monseigneur Jean-Pierre Ricard, declared: 'Repression and incitement to collective fear are no adequate response to these dramatic tensions in our society. It is vital to open up to new generations, often lacking in hope, a future of liberty, dignity and respect for others.' It is absolutely shattering to see the French church completely abandon the Augustinian view of evil for this kind of whitewashed Rousseauism. It would seem that no one wants to speak a language of truth any longer, and so I believe we're heading for something worse.

It seems to follow, then, that for Alain Finkielkraut the only 'language of truth' worthwhile today is not that of Rousseau (which, moreover, seems to be 'contrary to [the] religion' of the 'communitarian' intellectual, at least in the interpretation of 'Rousseauism' proposed by Mgr Ricard, archbishop of Bordeaux), but rather 'severe education' backed up by the 'Augustinian view of evil'. Does this mean that 'evil' is a substantial and distinct reality, identifiable as such, with 'mainly Arabs and Blacks with an Islamic identity' being its incarnation in contemporary France? That the 'severe and strict education' needed in response to the urban riots of our day is a 'language of truth' that teaches secondary-school pupils in 'so-called difficult areas' that the Crusades were a heroic re-conquest, by the armies of Christ the King, of the lost territories of the West? And that evil must be stamped out? Does it mean, therefore, that the most backward, obscurantist and xenophobic Catholic fundamentalism has found its high priest in the 'communitarian' intellectual? Or should we rather conclude that this radio broadcast was a stunt inspired by Orson Welles, heralding the imminent arrival of alien invaders?

4. ORIANA FALLACI AND 'THE JEWS'

1. In his book *La Campagne de France. Journal* (Paris: Fayard, 2000), Renaud Camus questioned at several points the 'clear overrepresentation' of 'Jews or those of Jewish origin' among journalists and intellectuals on 'public service radio', whether it was a question of the integration of foreigners in France or more broadly of 'the French experience as lived for some fifteen centuries by the French people on the soil of France'. And on the subject of the radio programme *Panorama* on France Culture, he concluded:

> This programme and a large number of others are deeply biased by an exaggeratedly tendentious composition of the panel of participants. And I believe I have the right to say this. If I don't, then I take it anyway. I take it in the name of this ancient culture and this native French civilization that are my own, whose achievements over the centuries are more than honourable, and that I regret scarcely hearing any more in the very country that was theirs.

In the same vein, he states elsewhere in his *Journal*, again on the subject of this 'Jewish point of view' on questions of French society and culture: 'What I regret is not that it exists, not at all; but rather that it tends all too frequently to replace the old voice of French culture and to cover it.' Statements of this kind were at the origin of the 'Camus affair', leading to the withdrawal of his book in 2000, then to a republication purged of the culpable lines, which were replaced by blank spaces.

2. On page 182 of *La Nouvelle judéophobie*, Taguieff speaks of 'the expressions of Judeophobia, the existence of Francophobe attitudes in these same populations of foreign origin yet of French nationality', and to illustrate his claim, immediately reports incidents at the football championship between France and Algeria at the Stade de France on 6 October 2001, which he introduces with the words:

> Aggressive lack of good citizenship: booing the national anthem sung by the French team in a stadium, whistling at Zidane who was guilty of playing in the French team, waving an Algerian flag, crying the name of the new hero: 'Ousama! Ousama!', then violently interrupting the match, which was intended to symbolize a friendly understanding, as happened in the evening of 6 October 2001 at Saint-Denis, in the presence of several Socialist and Communist celebrities.

If (1) booing the French national anthem, (2) siding with a player for reasons outside the field of sport, (3) shouting the name of a Saudi terrorist suspected of being the instigator of a mass crime, and (4) interrupting the normal course of a sporting fixture, this 'match intended to symbolize a warm understanding', are all indications of a lack of good citizenship that can be qualified as 'aggressive' – 'waving the Algerian flag' in the stands, on the other hand, is not immediately recognizable as such. Until a new dispensation, in fact, the stands are designed for people to wave flags as a sign of peaceable support for the team of their choice. It seems unlikely, however, that in the eyes of this author *anyone* waving a flag in a football stadium other than that of the French team thereby gives proof of an 'aggressive lack of good citizenship', or at least displays extreme emotionality and knows nothing of the social rules that govern this type of sporting event. But 'waving the Algerian flag' at a France–Algeria football match 'intended to symbolize a friendly understanding' is supposedly the sign of an 'aggressive lack of good citizenship' – in the view of a French citizen coming back from the Stade de France on 6 October 2001.

3. We should also note the verdict of Rabbi René Samuel Sirat, who concluded in *Actualité juive* that 'it would be the worst victory for the extremists if we were contaminated by their methods and reactions'.

4. See in particular Alain Finkielkraut's book *L'Avenir d'une négation. Réflexions sur la question du génocide*, Paris: Gallimard, 1982; as well as my own critical analysis of this in *Qu'appelle-t-on penser Auschwitz?*, Paris: Lignes, 2009.

5. Besides, if Islam is more akin to barbarism than to religion, Judaism in Fallaci's eyes is also not a very respectable religion, as she indicates by her reflections on ritual slaughter and on the patriarchs. On page 191 of this second book, for example, she writes that 'before cancelling our identity, Islam aims to extinguish that irresistible provocation [i.e. Christianity]. That sensational bet. You know how? By its ideological robberies.' And she immediately grants, this time in concessionary vein, that this 'ideological pillage' does not concern only Christianity: 'They also aim to steal Judaism, we know. When they state that the first prophet of Allah was Abraham, as founder of Israel the poor Abraham goes belly-up' (p. 192). But she goes on to add a parenthesis designed to carefully distinguished between the 'ideological pillage' of Christianity and the 'ideological pillage' of Judaism: 'And useless to comment that, if I were Jewish, I wouldn't give a damn. Who wants a Founding Father who is ready to slit his own child's throat for the glory of some God?' Jews and Muslims thus have the key common feature of slaughtering innocence itself in their throes of delirious fanaticism, whether in the form of a child or a lamb.

6. On the subject of the Andalusian era of rabbinical Judaism, Éric Smilévitch, in the preface to his translation of *Lumière de l'éternel* by David Crescas (published by Verdier), notes: 'In its time Spanish Judaism was more than a culture, almost a whole civilization, of which those not involved in it understood very little. Their Christian contemporaries, for example, who did all they could to destroy it.' As for the Arab philosophical sources of Maimonides' *Guide for the Perplexed*, see René Lévy's study *La Divine insouciance. Études des doctrines de la providence d'après Maïmonides* (Paris: Verdier, 2009). The grandeur and singularity of Spanish Judaism were undeniably the fruit of its confrontation with Greek philosophy, particularly that of Aristotle, as transmitted, discussed and investigated by the subtle and profound thinkers of Islam. As always, xenophobia is necessarily uneducated; hence, no doubt, the expulsion of the Jews from Spain.

7. On the subject of Paul Rassinier's revisionism, Pierre Vidal-Naquet writes:

Rassinier's particular fame is that he was the first to explain systematically that there was no genocide, and to exonerate the Nazis from 'this terrible and infamous accusation' (*Drame*, p. 107). For 'the drama of the European Jews … is not that six million of them were exterminated as they claim, but simply that they make this claim'. (*Les Assassins de la mémoire*, p. 53)

Rassinier was the first French revisionist, and the *maître à penser* of those who followed, even if before Rassinier the initiator of this ideological current was Maurice Bardèche, for whom 'What happened at Auschwitz, Maidanek and other places had to do with the Slavs; our concern is with the West' (cited by Vidal-Naquet, in *Les Assassins de la mémoire*, Paris: La Découverte, 1987, p. 51; first edition Maspero, 1981).

8. See alephbeth.net/israel/Oriana_Fallaci.html.

9. E. Kogon, H. Langbein and A. Rückerl, in *Nazi Mass Murder: A Documentary History of the Use of Poison Gas* (New Haven: Yale University Press, 1993), give the following estimates: 1,334,700 died in the Auschwitz gas chambers. According to the historian Georges Wellers, 1,323,000 of these were Jews; while according to the historian of the Auschwitz camp, Franciszek Piper, there were a minimum of 1,300,000 deportees to Auschwitz, including 1,100,000 Jews, out of whom 960,000 died.

10. This is the figure given by Léon Poliakov in his introduction to a collection of texts and documents on the Auschwitz camp. See his *Auschwitz*, Paris: Éditions Julliard, 1964, p. 15.

11. See Germaine Tillon, *Ravensbrück*, Paris: Seuil, 1988 (first edition, 1973), p. 453. This specialist study of the Ravensbrück camp reproduces documents concerning the existence of gas chambers in the concentration camps. See in particular Annexe 3: 'Les exterminations par gaz à Mauthauen et Guzen', from which the Choumoff quotation given above is taken; Annexe 4: 'Le sabotage de la chambre à gaz de Buchenwald'; and Annexe 6: 'Le chambre à gaz de Dachau'. See also Kogon et al., *Nazi Mass Murder*.

12. See *Ravensbrück*, p. 467. This is the figure given in the SS 'protocol', 'discovered at Liberation and cited at the Nuremberg trial'.

13. Alain Badiou, *Logics of Worlds: Being and Event II*, trans. Albert Toscano, London: Continuum, 2009, p. 518. This comes after Badiou cites a text of Malraux in which the author conducts a fictional dialogue with Picasso.

14. Cécilia Gabizon and Johan Weisz, *OPA sur les Juifs de France. Enquête sur un exode programmé (2000–2005)*, Paris: Grasset, 2006, p. 83.
15. A reference to Marguerite Duras' brief, essential and absolute text, *The Malady of Death*, trans. Barbara Bray, New York: Grove Press, 1986. We should also make clear that, if the Italian journalist presents herself as a 'Christian atheist', the conception of atheism she propounds has a certain similarity with the paganism of the far right. In *The Force of Reason* she spells out its principles in the following terms:

> However, Plato is wrong when he says that war comes from human passions, that only man makes war. When a lion pursues a gazelle, sinks its teeth in its throat and rips its body to pieces, it commits an act of war. When a bird swoops down on a worm, grabs it in its beak and swallows it alive, it commits an act of war. When a fish eats another fish, an insect eats another insect, a gamete pursues another gamete, they commit an act of war. When weeds invade a cornfield, the same. Even an ivy that wraps itself around a tree commits an act of war. War is not a curse which characterizes human nature: it is a curse which characterizes Life. There is no way to avoid war because war is a part of Life. Repulsive, hideous? Of course. So hideous that my atheism stems mainly from it. That is, from my refusal to accept the idea of a Creator who invented a world where Life kills Life, where Life eats Life … I don't believe in the masochism of turning the other cheek, nevertheless. And if I am invaded by weeds, suffocated by ivy, poisoned by an insect, bitten by a dog, attacked by a human being, I fight. (p. 23)

The atheism of this 'Christian atheist' thus implies a world in which struggle for survival means war, conceived as the irreversible law of all existence – vegetable, animal and human, so that there is nothing to be done other than accept this law. Ivy and weeds, for their part, don't question it: they throttle and invade. This little 'life philosophy', however, which underpins 'the rage and the pride' of the Italian writer, is part of a whole ideological history, that of social Darwinism, based on the assertion of a continuity or isomorphism between the vegetable, animal and human worlds. In other words, what is true for the lion and the gazelle, the bird and the worm, the weeds and the crops, the ivy and the tree, etc., is true for man and his neighbour. And this is the alternative: either the crops or the weeds, either the tree or the ivy, either 'me' or 'him' – with the reservation that what is unsaid or merely implied at the root of this discourse is that the opposition between crop and weed, tree and ivy, lamb and rat, etc., does not refer to the anonymity of vegetable and animal existences, but rather to an *order of value* which is all the more evident since it is not and must not be questioned: 'me' or 'him'. Which is to say: 'me'. That is: 'me', Oriana Fallaci, the embodiment of innocence, the Western 'cultural identity' wounded in its flesh; and not 'him', the Muslim, the alien foreigner, the guilty party – guilty first of all for not being 'me'. If Christianity is naturalized in this way, mythologies of all kinds rush in, and with them a certain political use of the word 'West'; hence, perhaps, Fallaci's remark about 'women of good taste' and her haunting by the phantasm of 'Eurabia', to which she seems to oppose the slogan – brutal, no doubt, but exact – of 'de-ratting'.

In *Modernity and the Holocaust* (Cambridge: Polity, 1989), Zygmunt Bauman recalls how 'one of the earliest and principal ideologists of German National Socialism, R.W. Darré, took the practice of animal husbandry as the pattern of "population policy" to be implemented by the future *Völkisch* government', and cites by way of illustration a text of Nazi ideology drawn from Darré's 1930 book on *Marriage Laws and Educational Principles*:

> He who leaves the plants in a garden to themselves will soon find to his surprise that the garden is overgrown by weeds and that even the basic character of the plants has changed. If therefore the garden is to remain the breeding ground for the plants, if, in other words, it is to lift itself above the harsh rule of natural forces, then the farming will of a gardener is necessary, a gardener who, by providing suitable conditions for growing, or by keeping harmful influences away, or by both together, carefully tends what needs tending, and ruth-lessly eliminates the weeds which would deprive the better plants of nutrition, air, light, and sun ... Thus we are facing the realiza-tion that questions of breeding are not trivial for political thought, but that they have to be at the centre of all considerations, and that their answers must follow from the spiritual, from the ideological attitude of a people. We must even assert that a people can only reach spiritual and moral equilibrium if a well-conceived breeding plan stands at the very *centre* of its culture. (p. 113)

It is certainly unnecessary to emphasize further the metaphorical and ideological affinity between the text of this National Socialist and the last texts of Oriana Fallaci. As for the philo-Semitic effects of this naturalization of political discourse – Sarkozy's 'Kärcher' [high-pressure waterhose] remark being a recent instance, not very poetic, even uncultured – these may well be doubtful, all the more so in that, as far as innocence is concerned, Jews still have more to fear today from *limpieza de sangre* than they have to hope for from the *Reconquista*. But to end on a humorous note, let us return to Alain Finkielkraut's contribution to the sixth number of *Cahiers d'études lévinassiennes*. After his opposition to the philosopher Jürgen Habermas and the sociologist Ulrich Beck on the question of Turkish membership of the European Union, the author mentions Daniel Bensaïd and Alain Badiou, which immediately leads him to explain, by way of advance warning against a possible objection, that 'their philosophy is not the extravagant speculation of certain perverted or deranged minds' (p. 245). He proposes, accordingly, to enlighten the reader as to the real significance of their philosophy and its actuality:

> It is on the contrary completely in phase with the great metaphysical promise of our time: the promise of a humanity finally liberated from the order of filiation, which can substitute, in virtually every domain, the world of choice, of self-service, of fluid, circumstantial, chance and multiform identities for the world of nature and fate. (Ibid., p. 245)

To substitute the world of *capital* for the world of nature and fate is thus the 'metaphysical promise' whose contemporary messengers are Bensaïd and Badiou. It remains for the reader of the *Cahiers d'études lévinassiennes* to decide: Does Alain Finkielkraut propose, by supporting Oriana Fallaci's *The Rage and the Pride*, to reconnect with the world of nature and fate, against the planetary rule of capital? Or is this the last sally of an unlikely, superb genius of provocation?

16. Tying him to a chair in front of a computer, Gabriel demands that he hack a government system, as proof of his talents. The hacker refuses to comply. So with a nod of his head, Gabriel then orders one of his harem to fellate the hacker, as a warning against struggling against the obscene *jouissance* that Gabriel offers as master tempter.

17. Éditions Robert Laffont. The broadcast would therefore have been in late April 2004.

18. The message from the terrorists runs:

We have decided to place in your great city of New York … an atomic bomb. We will explode it in exactly five days at noon New York time if you have not by then forced your Israeli vassals to pledge before the whole world that they will abandon every square meter of the settlements they have built on the land stolen from our Palestinian brothers and sisters since 1967. (p. 63)

But when the al-Qaida terrorists speak of 'settlements built on stolen land', what we should understand, according to the authors, is what their CIA analyst expressed with his comment: 'Can you imagine the firestorm of hate and anger that's going to erupt in this country if a million Americans die for those damn settlements?' (p. 92). In other words, the al-Qaida terrorists did not demand anything more than the withdrawal of the West Bank settlements, and only targeted America for this reason. The reader accordingly learns that, given Israeli intransigence, it is America that is in pawn to a few 'thousand Israeli settlers', and not the other way round, as the terrorists naively believe when they – wrongly – see the Israelis as 'vassals'.

EPILOGUE

1. By way of introducing his claim, Milner spelled this out: 'I have my own thesis on what Bourdieu means by "inheritors": the "inheritors" are the Jews.'

2. Milner finally extricated himself from this false step, in which Finkielkraut had wisely abandoned – if not precipitated – him, by launching a violent diatribe against the sociological text in question, a real somersault. Questioned by *Le Monde* on the meaning of his statement, the linguist spoke of a 'provocation aimed at making people think', going on to justify it as follows:

   If this makes people re-read Bourdieu's texts in a serious and fair way, then I've done my duty. For Bourdieu's book has harmful consequences for all those children of immigrants who succeed, and are forced to ask themselves: 'Does this mean that in the end I didn't fit into a system of domination?' This is the passion that inspired this book, even if I don't ascribe Bourdieu a xenophobic intention. (*Le Monde*, 19 January 2007)

But the question was rather whether Milner ascribed Bourdieu an anti–Semitic intention.

3. *Fragments mécréants. Sur les mythes identitaires et la république imaginaire*, Paris: Lignes–Léo Scheer, 2005, p. 128.

4. Paul Celan used this line from Marine Tsvetaeva as an epigraph for his poem 'And with the book of Taroussa', in his collection *The No-One's-Rose*.

5. Elie Baroukh and David Lemberg, *Cinq mille ans d'humour juive de Deauville à Jérusalem* (Paris: J'ai lu, 1999).

On the Typeface

This book is set in Bembo, a typeface based on the designs of Francesco Griffo for the Venetian printer Aldus Manutius in his 1495 production of Pietro Bembo's *De Aetna*. The *De Aetna* type served as a precursor to the type Griffo later cut for Manutius's most famous printing, the *Hypnerotomachia Poliphili* of 1499.

Under the direction of Stanley Morison, the Monotype Corporation reinterpreted the *De Aetna* type in 1929, pairing it with an italic based on a 1524 print by the writing master Giovantonio Tagliente.

As one of the archetypal 'old-style' designs, Bembo exhibits a classical feel that has made it a popular book face, with its small x-height, delicate stems, and wide capitals. The standard R features a conspicuously long tail. The digitized version of Monotype Bembo produces a much lighter color than the original hot-metal version.